M000315140

Seventeen

Seventeen

JOE GIBSON

GALLERY BOOKS UK

First published in Great Britain by Gallery Books,
an imprint of Simon & Schuster UK Ltd, 2023

Copyright © Joe Gibson, 2023

The right of Joe Gibson to be identified as the author
of this work has been asserted in accordance with the
Copyright, Designs and Patents Act, 1988.

1 3 5 7 9 10 8 6 4 2

Simon & Schuster UK Ltd
1st Floor
222 Gray's Inn Road
London WC1X 8HB

www.simonandschuster.co.uk
www.simonandschuster.com.au
www.simonandschuster.co.in

Simon & Schuster Australia, Sydney
Simon & Schuster India, New Delhi

The author and publishers have made all reasonable efforts
to contact copyright-holders for permission, and apologise
for any omissions or errors in the form of credits given.
Corrections may be made to future printings.

A CIP catalogue record for this book
is available from the British Library

Hardback ISBN: 978-1-3985-2247-3
eBook ISBN: 978-1-3985-2248-0

Typeset in Bembo by M Rules
Printed and Bound in the UK using 100% Renewable
Electricity at CPI Group (UK) Ltd

MIX
Paper | Supporting
responsible forestry
FSC® C171272
FSC
www.fsc.org

THE TRUTH

This is a memoir according to the author's memory of events that occurred thirty years ago. In recollecting details of his life and experiences, he has done his best to make his memory tell a truthful story. Various names and characteristics have been changed; some events have been compressed, others uncondensed; and some dialogue has been recreated.

THE SCIENCE

Research using magnetic resonance imaging has mapped the brain from early childhood into adulthood and found data to prove that the brain continues to develop well into the early twenties, with the frontal lobes, responsible for reasoning and problem-solving, developing last.

In calm situations, teenagers can rationalize almost as well as adults. But stress can hijack what Professor Ronald E. Dahl, MD – Director of the Institute of Human Development, UC Berkeley and Founding Director of the Center for the Developing Adolescent, UCLA – calls 'hot cognition' and decision-making. The frontal lobes help put the brakes on a desire for thrills and taking risks – a building block of adolescence; but they're also one of the last areas of the brain to develop fully.

According to Professor Jay Giedd, MD, Child and Adolescent Psychiatrist at the University of California, San Diego, 'What you do with your brain during that time could have a lot of good and bad implications for the rest of your life.' Teenagers are capable of learning a lot, but the parts of their brains related to emotions and decision-making are still in the works. As their brains undergo rewiring, teenagers are particularly vulnerable to risky behaviour, such as drinking and driving too fast.

From 'The Adolescent Brain – Why Teenagers Think and Act Differently', an article published in EDinformatics.

PROLOGUE:
MARCH 1992

We drive across town. It's late. The closer we get to the house, the more aware I become of each limb, every muscle in my body. My hands are damp as I rub the back of my neck. I try to reason with myself. She's thirty-five. She's my teacher; nothing is going to happen.

I stare at her hands on the wheel, changing gear, wiping condensation from the windscreen. We pass the bridge, a silhouette of suspended light against the dark sky. No people, no cars. I should've been staggering drunkenly across that bridge with the lads. We're almost there now and I have to do something quick, or I'll regret it in the morning. She moves her hand. I lean towards her, take the wheel.

'What are you doing?' she shrieks.

'It's all right. There aren't any other cars. You do the pedals, I'll steer.' My nerves are rattling but I try to sound convincing.

'Okay.' She sighs heavily, checks her mirrors, eases her foot off the brake. 'I must be mad trusting a seventeen-year-old with my car.'

'You're trusting me with your life.'

'Oh, bloody hell! Don't say that.'

'Try not to panic, Miss – you'll get us both killed.'

'Right, that's it – that's enough—'

'No, we're nearly there. Just around the next corner.'

'I'll have to change down.'

'Change down?' I lean in to get a better grip for the bend. Her hair brushes my cheek, I breathe in her perfume.

'The gears. You have to change gear – you do know that, don't you?'

'Right, no, I didn't.' I try to concentrate, bracing myself for the turn.

'But you can drive?'

'Not as such, no. Apart from a tractor, once.'

'But—'

'Corner, Miss. Is this a gear change?'

She threads her arm underneath mine, moves her leg towards me. She changes gear and we're almost touching. I wrestle the wheel sharply for the bend. For a second my hand is cradled in her lap. We drive down the hill in silence.

'Just here,' I nod at the ivy-covered house, bathed in warm orange light from the streetlamp.

'It's nice,' she says, applying the handbrake.

'Yeah, it is,' I say, not taking my hands from the wheel.

'Are you happy here?' She doesn't look at me.

'Sometimes.' I move my arm.

'Goodnight, then.' She looks at me.

'Goodnight, Miss,' I say, and we kiss.

PART ONE

LOWER SIXTH

1

September 1991

I am sixteen and it is the first day of September when I arrive, on my own, on a train 150 miles from home. Three long hours stretching out, momentous from where I'm sitting, staring, blinking out the window, as yellow sandstone turns to red brick turns to rusty ironstone. On my Walkman, The Cure, 'Close To Me', on rewind, repeat. The last song I listened to in my bedroom, while Mum packed my suitcase.

My older sister, Rose, has gone to university and my parents have decided they want a change of scene. They haven't really explained the reason for wanting to move, not to me anyway. All they've said is they will move closer to my new school – an exclusive Top 50 Public School as I am told, repeatedly – when they've found somewhere to live. The housing market is still on its knees after the 1987 financial crash, and in the middle of this mess, my parents have sold our home and are frantically house-hunting, with no luck. For now, I've been sent to live with a family they know, so that I can start term on time. We're not a wealthy, privileged old-money family by any means – my parents work for the county council – and

Mum has managed to convince the school that I deserve a bursary, which, in her conversations with friends, is finessed into a 'scholarship'.

A fresh start is probably just what I need, but my head and heart feel lost. Moving away means leaving my friends and Cat, my girlfriend of one year: a chain-smoking violinist who was always staring out of windows and crying – adorable, in a way.

It's a relief to see the friendly waiting faces of the Andersons – Celia and Ned – outside the station. We load my suitcases into their ageing Saab and set off through the afternoon traffic. Apart from a few words of welcome and a weird comment from Ned about my *new look*, they don't ply me with questions. We've met twice already, first when I visited with Mum when she was having therapy after her cancer, and again when I came for interview at the school. Celia was one of the therapists who helped Mum get better.

I wonder what Ned meant. I don't think I've changed that much this year. Possibly thinner, on account of some parental stress around my GCSE exam results, though I hoped my week by the coast with my uncle Jack and his friends would have added some muscle mass. His invitation to join him was the escape, the freedom I needed. When not on boats I was put on a tractor and told to mow the field, the one sloping down to the sea at a forty-five-degree angle. Or I was chopping logs with power tools and no gloves. Or white-water rafting, the kind that starts with four paddles and ends with none, and no raft.

Or perhaps Ned meant the hair, which I've been growing

since spending a day with long-haired surfers. I let my sister bleach it with Sun-In when I got home, but it doesn't seem to be having the right effect; it's more ginger than blond.

All those days with Uncle Jack ended the same, me red-cheeked, slumped in a chair; Brahms blasting through the house. The evenings were long and liquid, loud with talk. The air was full of ideas and possibilities. I was the new blood, and my future was mapped out around the dining table. Plans were hatched for a world of adventure in two years' time, after A-levels. I would start with a stint in Chile, working in hill villages on sustainable farming projects, making myself useful, getting fit. Then back with Jack for a month of boat skills and preparation, before setting sail across the Atlantic, crewing on a voyage Jack had been planning forever. Grinning, wide-eyed with anticipation, I drank it all in and wished the next two years away.

On the seventh day, the phone rang. I was outside nursing a hangover to the Steve Miller Band, narrowly avoiding feeding my hand into the wood chopper, when the news came through: Mum had got me into some 'toff school' (according to my uncle), and she wanted me home. The bubble burst. Gone was my Huckleberry Finn life by the sea, sailing, driving tractors, exploring creeks and charting the world.

So, here I am in a new city for a fresh start, and on a promise to my parents to work my arse off. Or, as far as I'm concerned, to get it over with as fast as possible, join Uncle Jack, and set sail for a life of adventure. From the Andersons' car window, I spy familiar landmarks from previous trips: the stretch of independent shops, record stores, bars and cinemas, the theatre, the cathedral and its crisp lawns, the leaf-blown avenues of Victorian terraces. My family and friends are hundreds of miles away, but this place has a good feeling to it.

2

September 1991

My new home stands at one end of an elegant curving terrace, both identical and a little bit different to the other houses along the row. In the nothingness, where the next domino piece should be, is a corner garden, walled off from the pavement, overflowing with trees, hedges and plants: a secret garden.

The Andersons are also different, certainly to anyone I've ever met. Celia, floaty and gentle, Ned a stocky ball of energy. He's an artist and works strange hours in his studio on the third floor. His paintings cover every wall in the high-ceilinged rooms and go all the way up the six staircases to the two rooms at the very top. One of these rooms is occupied by their twenty-year-old daughter, Holly, who eyes me suspiciously. A few feet across the landing is my room: a true garret with a bed, a desk and a record player Ned has installed to make me feel at home. He loves music and lets me borrow any of the albums that fill the shelves on the landing outside my room. He's got everything, from 1589 to 1989.

I want more time to explore my exotic new world, sit in my room and write poetry and songs, smoke out of my window, wear clothes made from alpaca wool and colourful hats from the street stalls nearby. But that will have to wait for the week-end because school is starting.

With the Happy Mondays in my ears and my bag slung over the shoulder of my new blazer, I set off for school. Others in the same unfamiliar colours appear as I walk up the hill, deployed like flares to follow at sea. I don't share their confidence or their easy stride.

At a corner they break off into smaller groups, scattering in the direction of grand buildings: plaques on their walls, each one emblazoned with its own crest and colour, matching the ties of the pupils congregating outside. I don't see my house name or colour, so I hang back from the pack, to catch my breath and find my bearings.

I'm at the far end of a manicured cricket ground, sur-rounded by the boarding houses, towers, classroom blocks and a chapel. I amble along the edge of the field and try to picture myself throwing red leather balls from the boundary in summer, getting kneed in the balls in a winter scrum. Neither appeals.

The first few days of school are a whirl of new faces, new places, new ways of doing things. Still, the boys in my house seem friendly and I attach myself to a couple of lads in my year who seem to know what's happening. Nick and Ant are funny, clever, and not obviously hard-working. They don't conceal their lack of interest in team sports either. Together, we perfect countless ways to avoid cold, wet, miserable afternoons on the rugby pitch; a massive relief, because it seems everyone else spends as much time playing sport as they do in lessons.

It's not that I can't be sporty, but the combination of being almost 6ft while weighing a measly 9 stone means I'm dangerously ill-equipped to survive the contact sports this school is obsessed with. Nick is taller and even skinnier than me, while Ant, though stockier, is short, clumsy and sprawls easily. The rugby pitch is not our natural habitat.

We hide out in the Sixth Form study room, doing crosswords and dozing with feet up on ancient radiators that melt the soles of our shoes. We hang around the music block where the teachers turn a blind eye, sharing our disdain for the mud-spattered walls of sweaty changing rooms. My favourite place is Nick's family home, a Victorian town house just beyond the school campus. It is vast; easily big enough to accommodate his siblings and parents, all tall and beautiful. Nick says they have a sort of open-house policy; everyone is welcome.

We congregate on sofas in their large kitchen or spill into the garden. There are hangers-on whenever I am there, mostly boys from the year above. Occasionally, his older brother Jules brings Upper Sixth girls back. It is accepted, even by the boys, that Jules is the best-looking guy in school, and this elevates him a few feet off the ground. The girls he brings back are breath-sappingly gorgeous. When this happens, everyone acts shifty, goes quiet, until Jules ushers the girls off to his room and we can all breathe again. If it gets too crowded, Nick takes me and Ant up to the roof. We can see the sports pitches from here; striped tops and pink legs running around with balls and sticks. With our backs against the chimney stacks we sit, laugh and smoke pot in our uniforms. I might be the new boy, but things aren't looking so bad.

3

OCTOBER 1991

'What do you think you'll do in life? After here, I mean,' I ask them one afternoon. My first month has flown by. There's a slight chill and we're windblown up on Nick's roof, huddled against the red brick. Falling leaves swirl around and overhead from giant plane trees on the avenue.

'Probably something medical, after Oxford,' says Nick.

'Seriously? Oxford?' I ask. It's the first time anyone I know, at least anyone my age, has actually specified which university they're aiming for.

He grins through a long toke. 'That's the plan. Well, Dad's plan, anyway. Cambridge for you, Ant. Music?' He leans forward, hand outstretched, offering Ant the spliff.

'I guess.' He shrugs. 'Everyone else in my family seems to go there. Be rude not to, and I've been playing the fucking clarinet since I was a baby. Had to be for something.'

'Hmm,' says Nick, eyeing me across the slates. 'And you, Joe. What have your parents got in store for you?'

I don't reply for a moment. This wasn't what I meant. I thought we would be talking about life, not more studying. Our dreams, hopes, adventures. Talking about Oxford and

Cambridge makes me anxious. But even through the pot, there's an assumption in their voices, a confidence I don't possess.

'Good question,' I say, still thinking, and decide to sidestep. 'Not Oxford or Cambridge, that's for sure. I haven't got your brains.'

Ant looks up. 'You could sing your way in.'

'And you're good at languages, aren't you?' adds Nick.

'I didn't really mean, what are we going to study or work as.'

They look at me with puzzled expressions.

'What else is there?' asks Nick.

'Adventure. Exploring.'

'What the fuck are you talking about?' Nick reaches for the spliff, plucking it out of my hand. 'Think someone's had a little too much of this good stuff.'

'Yeah, you're probably right.' I shrug, but something inside me sinks. It's not the reaction I thought I'd get. I was all ready to share my plans for sailing across the Atlantic, assuming they'd be on board. I thought they were different.

'Lara or Becky?' asks Ant, changing the subject.

'What do you mean?' I reply, not looking at him, tilting my eyes directly upwards, trying to catch the last shreds of autumn sun. This will probably be our last chance before the rain sets in.

'He means "out of",' explains Nick. 'It's a game. Ant's obsessed with it. Or he's just obsessed with every girl in our year.'

'Random,' I pause. 'Do you mean, out of, as in which of those girls do I like best, Lara or Becky?'

'Sort of,' says Ant. 'But really, I mean who would you rather get off with?'

'Definitely Becky,' grins Nick, sucking hard on the diminishing spliff before handing it to Ant.

'Fair,' agrees Ant. 'So, Joe?'

'Dunno. They're not really my type.'

'Oh my God,' says Nick. 'Don't overthink this. We're not asking you to choose a wife.'

'Okay, Lara, then.'

'How diplomatic,' groans Ant.

We play the game for another ten minutes until we've pretty much exhausted the Sixth Form girls.

'Oh, I've got one for you, lads. Out of . . .' – Nick pauses for dramatic effect – '. . . Miss Sheridan and Miss P.'

'Interesting,' chimes Ant, steepling his fingers thoughtfully. 'Science versus Languages. Nice play. I will say—'

'Miss P,' I cut him off before he can finish.

'Wow.' Nick claps his hands and points at me. 'No hesitation there from young Gibson.'

'I was going to say Miss P, as well,' says Ant.

'Your reasons, please, gentlemen?'

'Wasn't hard,' replies Ant, yawning smoke into the air between us. 'They're the only two female teachers under fifty. Plus, Miss P's well fit. I mean, you just would, wouldn't you?'

'Joe?'

'I agree with my learned, if disrespectful, friend.' I nod across at Ant through narrow eyes. 'But also, I have no idea who Miss Sheridan is.'

'How old do you reckon she is, anyway, Miss P?' asks Ant, passing me the remaining millimetres of spliff.

'Don't know,' I say. 'I'm useless at guessing ages. I guess . . . twenty-five?'

'Thirty-five,' says Nick, confidently.

Ant gasps. 'No way!'

'How do you know that?' I ask.

'From my dad. He's a school governor. They know these things.'

We sit in quiet, stoned contemplation, until Ant can't resist any longer.

'I'd still do her.'

4

NOVEMBER 1991

Autumn is setting in, rainy and grey. The playing fields are churned up from over-use, the grass fading into a brown-green mess. It's too cold for rooftop afternoons. My seventeenth birthday comes and goes with not much more than a couple of cards and a book voucher to mark it. Mum is sorry she can't come down to see me, but she's busy and I guess I am too. There's something quiet in her voice when we speak on the phone. I spend the evening in the company of UB40 until Holly barks something from her room, which isn't 'turn it up'.

For the first time in my life, I find myself working. Dozing in the library turns to reading and before I know it, I'm doing some proper study. It's a surprise, but I have the constant threat of being pulled out at the end of term by my parents if my grades aren't good. Even with my bursary, the fees are a stretch.

I'm beginning to get the hang of school life, including the irregular school days, which are really long, and the Saturday morning lessons as well. I guess it's a boarding school and they want to give the parents their money's worth. I even start going to extra study sessions in the Language Room, organized by Mr Siddel. I actually look forward to them, especially when Miss P takes the sessions. She's the best teacher by miles and doesn't talk down to you; always just really friendly.

By early November, I'm on a roll. I have my routine: lunch, quick smoke behind the chapel, off to the Languages Room for two hours.

On a particularly soggy Tuesday, I get caught in the rain and have to run the long way around the chapel, avoiding the muddy pitches. I'm soaked when I bundle through the classroom door. The room is empty.

'Fuck me,' I exhale, leaning back against the wall, shaking the arms of my sopping blazer.

'Er, language, please!'

There's a scuffling sound coming from the other side of the room. I take a few tentative steps, only to find Miss P on all fours behind her desk.

'Miss, I didn't think—'

'You didn't think you'd find me in my classroom?' She sounds angry, and she's still not getting up or looking at me.

'Sorry, Miss.'

'It's all right,' she sighs, still not moving though, and, since she's facing the wall, I can't see her expression. I'd like to think I'm not staring at her in this position, but I'd be lying.

'Are you okay, Miss?'

'Yep, fine.' She doesn't sound fine. I walk to the other end of the desk and see the problem. She's caught her hair in a drawer handle.

'Don't laugh!' she says, one hand holding the desk, while she pulls at the tangled strands of her copper-coloured hair with the other.

I crouch down beside her, immediately aware of our proximity. I know I should move away, stand up, but I'm stuck in my own way. I'm going to touch her. I can't stop myself.

Just as I reach out, she releases her hair and triumphantly pulls herself up. I snatch my hand back, but not quickly enough. She gets to her feet.

'I was going to help you, Miss,' I say, looking up, my face burning. Her grey woollen dress hugs her slim body, makes her seem so tall standing over me. I stand. Better. She's a few inches shorter and beautiful, like a woman from a perfume advert, with deep green eyes and the sort of face men cup and tilt upwards to kiss. At least, I think she's a woman. I mean, she's definitely not a girl, but I can't believe Nick's right about her being thirty-five. Her skin looks so soft and delicate and clean.

'Miss, can I give you . . .' My hands are trembling at my sides.

'Yes? What?' Am I imagining it or are her lips parting?

'Can I give you . . . a Jelly Bean?'

I bottle it.

5

December 1991

By the end of my first term, I've made a few good friends and passed enough exams well enough to convince Mum I should stay. I've also offered Miss P two or three Jelly Beans.

But that Christmas, everything that can go wrong, does go wrong. In fact, it's gone wrong before I step on the train, but I don't know this. So, when I step out of the station into a bitter wintery air, the red-eyed reception from Mum is not how I'd pictured my homecoming after months of absence, especially since my end-of-term report reads like a dream.

We sit in the car park for what seems like hours, our breath rising in plumes until the heating kicks in. She tells me that Dad isn't well, but she doesn't tell me what he's got. From what I can piece together, his illness has started suddenly and deteriorated rapidly. Cancer? Heart? Stroke? I race through the possibilities while Mum drives in silence.

As we pull into the driveway, I prepare for the worst: Dad lying weak and frail on the sofa, taking my hand, struggling to speak or open cloudy eyes. Mum opens the front door; the backs of my eyes sting. I half expect to find the rest of the family standing round Dad's candle-lit coffin, a vicar

I've never met offering me a kindly pat on the shoulder. But nothing. No one's here, apart from Rose, who's clearly been crying, at the top of the stairs. I know my sister won't accept a hug, but I open my arms wide anyway. To my astonishment, she runs down. I practically have to catch her. She clings to me, and more tears come.

'Where is he?' I ball into her shoulder.

'He's gone!' She shudders.

I can't hold on and collapse onto the bottom stair, my wet face sore from the misery of loss and my guilt at not having been here to hold his hand, say goodbye. I sit there, sobbing and shaking, while my sister and mother take themselves off to the kitchen to make some tea. I go upstairs and lie on my parents' bed, curling my body round my dear dad's pillow.

What must be an hour passes and I wake, drained and headachy. I don't open my eyes, I can't bear to, but I reach out my hand to his bedside table, feeling for the loose change, books, the little white Dinky toy car he'd always kept there. My hand finds the table, but it's empty. I open my eyes, draw my elbow up to support me. They're gone. I sit up and take in the room, my eyes adjusting to the early evening darkness from outside. Everything's gone. All his things. Already. I don't understand. The misery is replaced by a metallic ringing, my heart thumping against the wall of my chest. I try to breathe, calm down and think. My head spins. *Where have they put his things?* I wander out to the landing, outside his study. The door is shut, as it always is when he's working. I want to knock and hear him say, 'Come in.' I want him to call me by one of the embarrassing nicknames he still calls me at seventeen. 'Ah, Sausage. What can I do?'

I turn the handle slowly, half in dread, half in hope at what I might find.

It's empty. Totally empty.

I back out onto the landing. I sit down on the top stair. I don't know what to do. Then I hear the voices from downstairs. My mum and sister sound like they're arguing. I hear Dad's name and shuffle down, one stair at a time, like when I was a kid, so as not to be noticed. I reach the bottom and listen.

'Why did he go? Couldn't he have talked to me about it? All these years, we've always talked . . .' Mum trails off into tears.

'Perhaps he tried,' says Rose, sounding quite fierce, defending a man who can no longer defend himself.

'Oh, rubbish!' barks Mum. 'If he was interested in trying, he'd still be here.'

'He said he was sorry, but he had to go.'

'I was back within the hour, for God's sake! Joe's train was on time; we came straight home. One minute he's here, the next he's gone. He's not well; he's sick. Sick sick sick!'

What's wrong with him? Where on earth is he?

'Where on earth is he?' At last, Mum asks a sensible question.

'London. He said he was going to a friend's in London,' my sister replies, quietly. A dam bursts in my head.

I get to my feet and stand in the kitchen doorway.

'Dad's left us?' They turn their tired, tear-stained eyes to face me. Mum raises a sodden handkerchief to her nose. 'Bastard' is all I can manage through gritted teeth.

Two days later we are still in disarray. Mum is trying to busy herself, but then she'll stumble. I find her sitting on her bed or

21

staring out of windows, furious and sad. My sister is being efficient, independent, determined not to crack. I feel wretched
and confused. Being away at school, I've obviously missed
out on the prologue, the early scenes of our family tragedy. I
spend my time doing what I've always done at home: chores –
tidying, shopping, washing up. There's always something to
do and at least it takes the heat off my anger. That is, until
Dad turns up.

Mum has gone to her parents' and Rose is upstairs studying.
Somehow, I know it's Dad before I answer the door. I expect
us to stand quietly, facing each other in an uncomfortable last-
stand pose. Instead, he gives me a brief heavy-lidded glance
and mutters something about collecting the lawnmower. I
sweep past him towards the garage, trying and failing to be
cool. He follows.

I lift the garage up-and-over door as far as it will go, but
it's broken so only allows enough room for someone ducking
under to get through comfortably. Dad opens his car boot,
then reaches under the overhanging door for the lawnmower.
Still, we don't speak. He can't get enough of a hold, so, despite
my mood, I take the garage door in both hands, bend my
knees, heave it up to my shoulder height. I can't let go because
I'm taking its weight and the door will just spring back down.
Dad grabs the mower – a big, green petrol type – and wheels
it out gently so that he doesn't damage the blades. I know it's
important not to damage the blades, but the care he takes
ignites something inside me which sends a message to my
hands, instructing them to let go of the door. This should be
one of those slow-motion scenes, but it isn't. The door jerks
out of my grasp, onto Dad's head. Fortunately, perhaps, he

has sensed something's not right, and his always-impressive reflexes do enough to force him downwards. The blow from the garage door is more of a glancing thwack than a full, hospitalizing crunch.

'Jesus Christ!' With one hand he grabs the door, pushes it almost through the garage roof and, with the other, pulls out the mower. He catches it by the handle with both hands, lifts it like it weighs nothing, throws it into the boot. It's an extraordinary demonstration which leaves me rooted to the spot when I should, perhaps, be running away.

He slams the boot shut, storms round to his side of the car. He pauses before getting in, looks up at me with a barely concealed snarl. 'I've just about had enough of this family.'

His anger almost lifts me off the ground and for a couple of seconds I can't see or hear anything. When the picture comes back, he's already in his seat, turning the key. With no real plan, I open the passenger door. 'That's right, run away like you always do. God, you're so shallow.'

I don't really know why I said that. For one thing, he hasn't run away before, to the best of my knowledge. As for being shallow, well, that's just nonsense. In short, I've used entirely the wrong words. What's more, Dad's come to the same conclusion and is out of the car, hurtling round in my direction. Now I run, straight for the front door, which I get on the right side of and close just in time.

'Open this door. OPEN the door!' His tone doesn't leave me convinced that opening the door would be a sensible move. I go into the sitting room in the hope he'll calm down and get back in his car. I've forgotten about my sister. Coming downstairs, evidently unaware of developments outside, she's delighted to see Dad's profile through the frosted glass and lets him in. He isn't any calmer and pushes past her.

'Hello, Daddy.' She's nineteen years old, a medical student, but she still calls them Mummy and Daddy, which is both sweet and bizarre.

'Where's Joe?'

'In the living room, I think. Is everything all right?' she wobbles, finally grasping that everything is not all right.

I hear him coming, stand my ground, dig deep for some confidence. He walks in and stops on the other side of the coffee table.

'Look, Joe—' he begins.

'No, you look! Sit down!' I have absolutely no control in my voice or my words. But somehow it does the trick. He sits on the sofa.

'Okay, okay,' he says, patting the air with open palms.

'How dare you leave our mother. How dare you just walk out after all these years. You've destroyed everything. Mum is broken, like cancer wasn't enough. Rose has just started a difficult degree. And I come back from school, and I've got no idea what's going on.'

I'm expecting a comeback from Dad, but he doesn't speak. There's just incredulous silence. Then I become aware of a sharp pain in my legs. I look down, then up, then down again. The coffee table has smacked into my legs and Dad is looking worried. Those fucking reflexes. I didn't even see him move. My legs buckle, more in shock than anything else.

'I didn't mean to—' He doesn't finish his sentence. I see the tears in his eyes. I let him come to where I'm leaning over, supporting my weight with my hands on the coffee table. The pain in my shins, sharper now. He takes me in his arms.

'I'm sorry. I'm so sorry,' he breathes into my hair.

'I'm okay,' I mutter into his arm.

I can't see Rose, but I know she's crying too. It's a gigantic mess.

Shortly afterwards, Dad leaves. He's a wreck. Not much more is said before he goes. No reasons given or explanation offered for why he can't live with us anymore. I'm still angry, but at least we were able to have this fight.

Rose and I sit and smoke in the garden for over an hour. When Mum returns, we hide the cigarettes, tell her what's happened and have a hug. She's shocked but a bit proud, I think. Later, my old school friends come over, take me out, and we get drunk. I feel like a hero.

Over the next two weeks, I find I'm more able to handle the lows of a fracturing home. I try to find some extra strength during the Christmas festivities, especially when I'm comforting Mum or biting my lip in the face of my grandfather's anti-Dad outbursts. I can't blame him, but it's uncomfortable listening. The one occasion I let down my guard is when I meet up with Cat. She's been away for the first week of the holiday and we can't get together until Boxing Day. She drives over. With Mum and Rose out visiting friends, we have a frantic shag in my bed. I'm worried my tension will ruin the moment. I probably do come across as desperate, needy. But she is kind and holds me in the dark until it's time for her to go. I stand in the road with what's left of a shared cigarette, watching her car until it disappears through the fog. She's wearing black leather driving gloves I've never seen before. They leave me feeling a bit excited and a bit cold.

The next night she drives us out to a pub, with the gloves. We have a meal like proper grown-ups, not getting drunk, and over dessert she dumps me.

6

JANUARY 1992

The spring term begins, bitter, wet, with everyone sludgy and stuffed after Christmas. Undeterred, the school chaplain, Rev. Colley, enthuses from his pulpit at assembly on the first day about renewal, hope, working hard, looking forward to lighter days, birds, buds (sniggers from the Fifth Form), new opportunities. His message resonates, and we leave the chapel that morning with brighter faces, more purposeful steps.

After lunch, Nick greets me at the bottom of the dining hall stairs, grabs me in a headlock and drags me over to the Languages noticeboard.

'Have you seen this, new boy?' It's been a whole term, and though it's not meant maliciously, he still likes to remind me that I'm the outsider here. He's right, of course, since most of the students have been walking these corridors for over five years. He reaches up, rips a sheet of paper off the board. *Spring Term Languages Revue – Rehearsals start this week*. Did you know about this?'

'Why would *I* know about this?' I say, wriggling out of his grasp. I elbow him in the ribs and swipe the page as he rebounds theatrically off the wall.

'Because it's Miss P's handwriting, isn't it? She's your teacher.'

'She's your teacher, too,' I say, studying her big, looping letters that fill the page of instructions. Apparently, we are going to put on a show at the end of term – songs, sketches, dances, in French, Spanish and German.

'Yeah, but she's *your* teacher more,' says Nick.

'Er, no she isn't, Nick. That makes literally no sense. Anyway, you recognized her writing.'

This is the kind of game Nick loves to play – shit-stirring to get a reaction.

'*You* recognized her writing, which means you fancy her,' he continues, with inane determination.

'You fancy her, more like.' I push him again. Squealing, he throws his lanky-limbed frame pathetically towards the door that leads to the run of Languages classrooms. A door which flies open, slamming Nick back into me and sending us both sprawling.

Dazed, we look up to find Miss P, hands on hips.

'We were just . . .' But I can't think what to say and stop trying. Miss P walks slowly forward, stands between us. She looks pissed off, bends down, her hand out.

'I'll take that, shall I?' she says, snatching the notice, stepping over me to pin it back on the board.

'Oi, knob-end. What's up with you?' Nick says, catching up with me after last lesson. I'm heading home across the main school quad.

'Nothing,' I say, quickening my pace.

'Oh right, yeah, nothing. Don't be a tit. You're sulking.'

'I'm not sulking. I just don't like being told off,' I snap.

28

'We weren't told off, not really. Anyway, grow up.' He punches my arm, then crouches to retie a shoelace. I carry on walking. I know he's right; it wasn't a monumental bollocking for something major, but still. I was the one caught holding Miss P's notice, so she will think I tore it off the wall. I don't want her getting the wrong impression of me.

7

JANUARY 1992

First thing Monday I have an appointment with the dentist, so I miss assembly and most of first period. I rush back in time for second – Spanish with Miss P, our first lesson of the new term and a chance for me to redeem myself. By the time I reach her classroom the bell has already gone. I knock and enter. Empty, but there's a message on the whiteboard: 'Joseph, we're rehearsing in the Ashton Room, Miss P'.

I read it three times. A message from her to me. I stand back, trace the huge letters in her swirling handwriting with my forefinger. The 'J' is the biggest letter of all.

'Are you thick, Gibson?' I freeze, my finger suspended in mid-air. 'If you've managed to decipher the code, you'll have realized you're in the wrong room.'

I don't know who he is, but this teacher wears ridiculous ties with piano keys or Mickey Mouses on, yet always looks miserable.

'Yes, sir.' I step past him and bolt.

The Ashton Room is the old Masters' common room, wood-panelled, smoke-stained, and no amount of bleach or polish can get rid of its fustiness. I'm surprised Miss P chose this room to rehearse the revue. I open the huge oak doors to a weird scene. My class, standing in two dead-silent rows, rigid, all facing the back wall, boys behind girls. Like zombies. I think about backing out of the room, but from nowhere, music starts.

Para bailar La Bamba
Para bailar La Bamba
Se necesita una poca de gracia . . .

They all jerk into life, some dancing, some nothing like.

'Ah, good.' Miss P holds up a hand from behind the furthest couple, over the wails of Ritchie Valens and stomping feet. 'I can't do this on my own.'

'Do you need a hand with the music, Miss?' I offer, scanning the room. We're an odd number in our class, so there's no one for me to dance with.

'No,' she says, skipping to the end of the girls' row, holding out both hands to me. 'I need a partner.'

I try to be cool, but I can't stop grinning. Most of the boys are looking over, distracted for a moment from swinging girls around the room.

'Loser!' someone coughs.

I get to dance with the most beautiful woman in the room and I'm a loser? What's more, she's a fully grown woman. I throw them an 'oh well' shrug, as my dance partner takes my hands and places them on her hips.

8

FEBRUARY 1992

The following weeks pass in a blur. There are no exams this term for Lower Sixth, so we have at least three rehearsals a week for the revue. I'm not complaining. Any excuse to be in the vicinity of Miss P, especially after school. Anything to delay returning to Celia and Ned's place, where life is a bit lonely. I rarely see or hear them while they're at work in their studios. I read, I smoke out of the window, I play records. A couple of times, I leave my room, step across the no-man's landing, press my ear to Holly's door. There's no movement from within and I don't knock, though she must be in there. Probably holding her breath until she hears my door close.

One Sunday in the middle of February, I break. I should have seen it coming, but still, it hits me like a train. I'm not in the house, having taken myself off for a longer-than-usual walk. I take my new backpack, a New Year's present from my uncle whose gifts are like washed-up messages in bottles, appearing at random, reminding me that adventure awaits and there's a world to explore.

For the first half hour, everything's fine: Massive Attack

on max, pulsing *Blue Lines* through my foam-filled ears; a weak sun lighting my way as I walk through town up onto the Common, 200 acres of green space. The expanse is dotted with families, dog walkers, a few horse riders.

At the summit, I gaze out over the city, sweeping away to the south. On an impulse, I raise my arms out wide for the wind to lift, take me away from here, far from sad Mum, angry Dad, unfriendly Holly.

'Get out of the fucking road, wanker!' a man yells, a car horn slams a wall of noise in my face, drowning out 'Safe From Harm'. Perhaps the wind did pick me up because I've moved from the pavement to the middle of a pedestrian crossing, my arms still raised high.

That's when I break. My arms fall to my sides as I begin a slow descent. Tears collect in two fat pools under my eyelids, balls of water clinging to a tap before their inevitable drop. My chest heaves, throat contracts and the floods come. The steep hill levels, my face stings all over where I've tried to wipe my tears. But it's the sobbing that surprises me and I'm embarrassed. My hands come to my face, pressing and rubbing my eyes. I wander, aimlessly, my compass cracked. I should probably go home, but it's only midday. The prospect of being cooped up in my room all Sunday afternoon doesn't appeal.

I could eat. I should eat. I check my wallet: about five pounds. It should be enough for a beer, a sandwich, maybe some chips. There has to be a pub or café open somewhere nearby. The pavements are empty as I go; it's just unlit shops, office blocks, banks.

A little way up the road, I catch sight of an old man. Thin, straight-backed, wearing a long black coat, gloves and a bowler hat, he couldn't be more out of place. I wonder if he's waiting for a bus or a lift, until he reaches out, grasps the handle of a door in the wall I hadn't seen, and pulls. He stands back and a couple of grown-ups emerge, thank the man, and stroll away. High above the pavement I notice an old-fashioned pub sign. I have to investigate; maybe they do chips.

As I approach, the old man raises his arm and ushers me inside, directing me to a flight of stairs down to a vaulted bar. I do as I'm told, though quickly realize I've made a mistake, and not just because they're playing Terence Trent D'Arby at a socially reasonable volume. It's all a bit parenty and sophisti-cated: dark wood panelling, low lamplight, a smell of sawdust. I look down. There is actually sawdust covering the floor. More like an old ship, or a stable, than a pub. The only differ-ence is the presence of smartly dressed women, solid-looking men, old people probably in their forties, huddled together in booths. Everyone's drinking wine and laughing. Some are smoking long cigarettes; this isn't roll-up country. Fortunately, they're all so engrossed in themselves, they ignore me. I can slip out without attracting attention.

'Table for one, is it?' A waitress with a springy blonde ponytail appears from the shadows, cutting off my escape. She can't be much older than me. 'We have bar snacks and chips and sandwiches and stuff,' she says, with a kind smile. She sits me at a small table by the bar and brings me a menu. I'm so hungry I order everything she suggests, plus chips, and pray it doesn't cost more than five pounds. I'm dying for a beer, but this is definitely the sort of place where even friendly waitresses would ask for ID. She brings a pint of 7Up and a straw, which I discard when she's gone. I'm not twelve, for God's sake.

It takes me no time to finish my food and I feel a bit more normal again. But without the distraction of eating, the events of the morning start to replay in my mind. My eyes sting with the memory and the fear of a repeat performance makes me reach for my backpack to leave.

'Hello? Is that you?' asks a voice I recognize. I turn my head slowly upwards.

'It's not alcohol, Miss, it's 7Up,' is the best thing I can think to say. Or at least, the first thing that comes to mind, automatically when confronted with a teacher, even Miss P. You never know, even with the ones that seem all right.

'What? Oh, don't worry about that,' she laughs. 'Anyway, you're eighteen, aren't you? And it's a Sunday, so you're allowed. I think.'

'Seventeen, actually, Miss.' Why I'm correcting her, putting myself at risk of report, I don't know. Not thinking straight.

'Well, never mind. It's academic, isn't it? You're not drinking alcohol, so it doesn't—' She breaks off. Whether it's the lack of alcohol talking or having to hold a conversation with my teacher, something snaps inside. A tear forces its way to the surface and rolls treacherously down my cheek. I dip my head and wish my fringe was longer.

'Sorry, Miss,' I manage, with as much control in my voice as I can muster, but that fails me too. Before her hand reaches mine on the table, my shoulders are shaking. I'm undone, again.

'Ali, everything okay here?' asks a woman nearby. I don't see her face as I fold inwards.

'Yes,' she replies, quietly. 'A pupil. Give me a minute.' And she turns back to me, squeezes my hand under hers. I wish she would go.

'What is it, what's the matter?'

And out it all pours. Well, almost all. I don't bore her with the details of Cat dumping me, but she gets the rest: Mum, cancer, Dad, our fight, their separation, the dire Christmas, all the sad days. She listens, offers the occasional 'oh dear', 'poor thing', and sits quietly beside me as we both wait for my face to dry out, and something resembling normal to be restored.

'Sorry, Miss,' I say again, 'you didn't need all that.'

'Are you going to be okay?' she asks, after a few more minutes of quiet. Only when someone makes another appalling song selection does she release my hand. I look up. Her face wears an anxious expression, like she really means it, although that might be the effects of Feargal Sharkey. I want to hug her, to bury my head in her neck, be wrapped up in her voluminous hair.

I tell her I'll be fine, that it really helped to talk. She rubs my arm. After we say goodbye, after she's returned to her table and the bemused couple waiting for her, after the doorman has doffed his hat and I'm on my way, I think, I *will* be fine. Thanks to her.

9

MARCH 1992

On the last few days of the spring term, it's curtain up. Having rehearsed for so many weeks, our class has really bonded; there's no question of anyone forgetting lines or moves. We go down like a storm to packed audiences. It's a brilliant feeling.

During the week, I get smirks and comments about my dance partner. I'm sure someone uses the word 'chemistry', but I go around grinning, enjoying the whole thing. I savour every dance. Every hand-hold. Every time I touch her waist. Every time she touches mine. And for the first time ever, school makes me genuinely happy.

After the final performance, it's a quick tidy up, then back to Miss P's classroom for the last-night party. Outside the theatre, everyone's being met by proud parents, but I can see a few of the others already heading down the road in the direction of the Modern Languages rooms. With Mum on the other side of the country and Dad who knows where, I know nobody will be here for me, so I set off after my friends. I need to get to the party before the rest of the cast drink everything.

'Joseph?' Someone calls behind me. I can't tell who it is above the noise of cars and people leaving the theatre, so I pretend I haven't heard. I don't want to be dragged back in for more tidying up. I cross the road and turn a corner before I spin round in the shadows to check they're not following. They are. I run, cut across the quad, throw myself through an open door.

I spot Nick by a table, brandishing plastic cups.

'Joey!' He topples towards me, slurring his words. 'You wanna dreenk?'

'Christ, you work fast. Yes, I do, where is it? I need to catch up.'

'So. You wanna dreenk, *señor*?'

Great. Off his tits and still in character. I take in the rest of the room. They're all pretty far gone, including the two Spanish assistants who are supposed to be in charge. Where's Miss P? I leave Nick by the table to continue blabbering into cups and go in search of alcohol. It doesn't take long to realize there isn't any left and it's a waste of time sticking around. If I go now, I can make The Crown for last orders, which at least is on my way home.

'Oi, Joe,' calls someone heading out the door. It's Chris and a couple of others. 'Coming for a smoke?'

'Read my mind, mate,' I reply. May as well. I step back outside. The others are just ahead, making for the back of the chapel where we won't be caught.

'Hey, wait.' That voice again from the theatre. 'Wait, *please*.'

Miss P comes out of the blackness of the cloisters, carrying boxes.

'Why did you run off?' She is out of breath and not happy as she unloads the boxes by the classroom door.

'Sorry, Miss,' I say, glancing back towards the chapel. They haven't waited.

'I needed your help with these, and you ran off.' She's frowning, shaking her head. I usually like being this close to her, but I'm knackered from the performance, and all I can think about is a pint and a fag. I brace myself for a bollocking, which she'll probably convert into a detention when she sees the state of her classroom. No doubt that will be my fault too. I look around again.

'Are you actually listening to me?'

'Yes, of course, Miss.' I try to nod convincingly. 'Do you want me to help you? Now?' I add quietly, because I expect I should.

'Weren't you going somewhere?'

'Not really, Miss.'

'Okay, well, thank you. If you could put these boxes in—'

'Toilet!'

'What?'

'I was going to the toilet. I forgot, before, when you called me, sort of just forgot really.'

'You're rambling. Go to the toilet, then, but please don't run off again. I want to ask you a question.' She steps into her classroom, and I walk back to the boys' toilets, even though I don't need to go. She wants to ask me a question. I don't like the sound of that, but I'd better go back and find out my fate.

When I return to the classroom, Miss P's shovelling crisp packets, beer cans and plastic cups into a bin bag. From behind, her arched shoulders say it all: she's definitely still angry. I edge a retreat, but she sees me.

'You came back.' She looks surprised.

'Well, you said you wanted to ask me a question.'

'True, but I asked this lot to help me clear up and they vanished.'

She carries on tidying, and I feel a pang of guilt. She's always giving us encouragement and praise, and we repay her by trashing her room and running off. I take another bin bag and start clearing up until the room is back to normal. I glance at the clock above her desk: 11.30 p.m. on a Friday night, sober.

'You wanted to ask me a question, Miss?' I ask, tying the knot on my bin bag.

'Yes. I'm sorry and I know it's late, but would you mind helping me carry these boxes to my car?'

'Yeah, sure.' *Where's the catch?* 'Is that all, Miss?'

'Look, if the others hadn't run off, you could have been out of here ages ago. We *both* could've been. You to the pub and whatever else you get up to on Friday nights, me to—'

Not only has she misinterpreted my question, but she's stopped dead, wearing the strangest expression. It's like she's forgotten something, has gone off in her head to look for it, leaving her face on pause. She's miles away.

'You all right, Miss?'

'What?'

And she's back.

'I just remembered . . . he was coming round . . .' She sounds vacant and that distant look hovers over her face again. Time to go. I pick up two boxes.

'Where's the car, Miss?' I'm out the door. This is getting weird. Maybe she's just tired, but I'm not used to teachers being vague. She follows me out, locks the door. I glance up at the chapel clock. Almost midnight. I hope this isn't going to take long.

We walk out into the teachers' car park, past the staffroom. She turns right at the gate. Dammit. It's the opposite direction to home. Miss P doesn't say a word, but she keeps looking over her shoulder, craning her neck.

'Are they after us, Miss?'

'Who?' She sounds anxious.

'Whoever it is you're looking for?'

'It's my car. I'm sure I parked it down here.' She stops and faces me. 'Sorry, you're being very patient. I do appreciate you helping me.'

'That's okay, Miss. You seem a bit distracted.' Maybe she wants to talk about it. Although obviously not with a seventeen-year-old boy. *Not enough life experience.*

'Not distracted, just a bit ... confused,' she says, her voice drifting.

'Can I help?'

'Can you find my car? Can you remind me whether he said he was coming over after the revue? Did I remember to tidy the flat?' She gives a tired smile.

'I'm not sure where to begin, Miss ... Yes. No. Yes?'

She gives me a quizzical look for a second then laughs and nudges me on the arm with her shoulder.

'You know, Joseph, you're— WAIT! I know where my car is. Come on!'

'What am I, Miss?' I call after her. 'What am I?' I have to know this. She can't leave me in the dark. Am I funny, weird, cool, the man she's been looking for all these years? I catch up as she turns into another road; another avenue of big, identical houses.

'Ta-da!' Miss P skips over to a bright blue Ford Fiesta, which

41

is dwarfed by the surrounding BMWs and Range Rovers, and stretches her arms across the roof like she's giving it a hug.

'My car! Here it is.' She's ecstatic.

'That's ... great, Miss.' She's being weird.

I hope it's not far back to my place. I'm not sure of my bearings.

'Miss, can we go, then? I need the toilet again.' I really do this time, urgently.

'Right, of course.'

But she doesn't open the car door. She walks off.

'Miss, where are you going? Your car's here.'

'I know, but it doesn't have a toilet, whereas my flat does,' she answers, climbing the steps to a huge black door. 'Coming?'

10

MARCH 1992

Miss P's flat is on the ground floor. It's not spread out, so with a couple of turns of the head I absorb the layout: living room at the front, bathroom, kitchen to the side and back, then what must be a study or second bedroom. At the end of a corridor, a door, ajar, a soft light, and I can just make out a mirror, a wardrobe, but even from here it has the sort of stillness you find in someone's private place. It must be her bedroom.

'The bathroom's there,' she points, flitting past me from room to room. She comes out of the kitchen, flashes me a curious half-smile before darting into the room at the front.

'Have you lost something, Miss?'

'No, no,' she calls, wanders back into the hallway, suddenly much calmer. 'I was looking for something, but it's gone.'

I think of the bedroom again. This might be my chance.

'Do you want me to help you find it?' *Please let me look around your flat.* 'I'm good at finding things.'

'No, really, it's nothing. You use the bathroom and then I'll run you home.'

'Oh, go on, Miss, let me help look.'

'I've told you, it's nothing. Leave it.'

43

Damn, overstepped. I feel hot, choked, like I always do when I'm told off. I mumble an apology, dash into the bathroom, lock the door. I stand at the toilet, but I can't go yet, even though I'm desperate. Nerves. It's the same in the changing rooms at school. I can be absolutely bursting but if there's anyone else in there, I can't go.

I'm distracted by some objects on the windowsill. She's got a bizarre collection of shells covered in nail varnish. It looks like a hobby gone wrong. There's a dangly chime mobile, a basket of lavender and a ceramic dolphin watching me from a high shelf over the bath. It gives me a funny feeling: warm and relaxed and yes! Ah. It must be a magic dolphin.

My gaze shifts to the sink. Miss P's toothbrush. It's long and pink. I think about where it's been. Its soft white bristles stroking inside her. Her hand guiding it in, out, her fingers helping it reach the back of her mouth. Her thumb rubbing the head under the tap.

My pulse beats faster. I jerk my head up and spot the dolphin again. He knows exactly what I'm thinking; he's seen it all. And more. I look at the bath where she lies naked. There's a knock.

'Are you all right in there?'

Fine, apart from a massive hard-on.

'I'm sorry I snapped at you ...'

Think boring thoughts: Crafting. Antiques. Volvos. Radio 4 ... . Her voice is so soft and silky.

'Are you coming?'

Christ! Politics. Tarmac. Garden centres. Geometry.

'Joseph?'

'Yep. Sorry, Miss. Be out in a sex. SEC.' My voice comes out strangled, hoarse.

I'm in my teacher's bathroom with an erection. What do I do now?

I steal the dolphin, of course. Perhaps I can harness its powers. I slip it into the pocket of my blazer, rearrange myself, open the door.

I find Miss P on the sofa in the big room at the front. Fully clothed. Shame.

'Have you finished cleaning my bathroom?'

Her eyes narrow. Shit. Am I looking shifty? I fold my arms across the front of my blazer.

'I was joking! Don't look so worried.'

She doesn't seem to be in a hurry, so I search around the room for more delaying tactics. On a coffee table in front of the sofa stand two glasses and a bottle of wine, half full.

'Is there someone else here, Miss?'

She follows my eyes, frowns slightly.

'I don't think so.'

'You don't think so?'

'I mean no. There was someone, earlier, but he's gone.'

'What's his name, this someone?'

'Neil—'

'I hate him.'

'What? You don't even know him.'

'I know enough, Miss.'

She gives a little laugh.

'What do you mean, Joseph, you—'

'Call me Joe.'

'Er ... why?'

'Joseph's too formal.'

'Is it? Well, I'm your teacher, so ...'

'I knew you'd say that.' I walk over to the coffee table, pick up the bottle. 'Drink? I'm afraid I didn't have time to wash the glasses.' I'm busking it.

'That's very generous of you.' She smiles, sitting forward and taking the bottle from my hand. 'But you've got to go now.'

'Oh, go on, Miss – just one glass? We didn't get any at the party.'

'Fine, all right.' She sighs. 'One drink. Then home time.'

'Really?' I can't help grinning from ear to ear. She *must* like me.

She pours two glasses, comes towards me. I love it when we're close because I'm taller by a head. Makes me feel manly. She hands me a glass and our eyes lock. My heart jumps: a fully grown, real-live woman, pouring me a glass of wine. And I don't even like wine.

She turns away to the sofa, leaving me jellified. I don't join her. I might get it wrong. I don't trust myself.

'Can I look at your ...' – I turn to look for something to look at – '... um, records?'

'Yes.' She's so composed.

I flick through the stack propped against the music system on her bookshelves.

'Where do you keep your new stuff, your CDs?' I ask.

'My new stuff?' She laughs. 'That's all I've got.'

James Taylor. Crosby, Stills, Nash & Young. Carly Simon ... who are all these hairy people? I don't recognize any of them.

'Have you finished your drink?' she asks, standing up and, before I can answer, adding, 'It's time to go now.'

'But it's Saturday tomorrow,' I protest.

'Exactly. You still have school, remember? We both do.'

I like *we both*.

'Let's not go.'

'What?'

'Let's skive off. We'll stay here, listen to music.'

'Nice try.' She wags a finger.

'What do you mean, "nice try"?'

'I mean I wasn't born yesterday. Everything I say will be distorted and reported back to your friends. What might seem like harmless fun to you will backfire and make my life a nightmare.'

She's gone all serious. But she is kind of right. Until now, I couldn't wait to get back and tell Nick.

'Miss, I'm not like that. I wouldn't say anything.'

'Maybe,' she says, getting up and leaving the room. 'But I know what rumours can do,' I hear her say from the hallway. 'I work in a school.'

I step from the living room into the hallway where she's waiting. I lean against the doorframe. 'So, no skiving off tomorrow, then?'

'No, sorry.' She reaches for her coat from a hook on the wall.

Reluctantly, I follow her to the front door. How stupid to imagine we could ever be something else. My teacher is taking me home, that's all. She holds open the door for me but as I walk out, I trip, miss two steps and sprawl on the hard ground. I get up quickly, but she's seen.

'Jesus, are you okay?'

'Yep, fine.' I suppress the urge to inspect my leg which stings like fuck, pray she doesn't go back in for plasters and antiseptic.

'What's that?'

'What, Miss?' I stand on the spot, all my weight on one leg.

'Um . . . that dolphin-shaped object by your feet?'

I look down. The dolphin, smiling up at me. Now my face burns as much as my leg.

'Miss, I'm—'

'A dolphin collector?' She answers for me, laughing.

'You're not angry?'

'After this evening, nothing surprises me. Although perhaps I should ask you to turn out your pockets.' She picks up the dolphin. 'Do you want to look after it for a bit?'

'No, thanks. You keep him.' I feel stupid.

We get into her car. The pain in my leg is eased by sitting but, for some reason, I don't have anything to say. Fortunately, awkward silences are averted by Miss P chattering away about the performance – the songs, the dancing, what parents were saying afterwards. I watch, listen, drinking her in. Here, she is all hair, layers of glowing amber waves, caramel ripples, like ice cream from a machine. In profile, I can only see the tilt of her nose, the pout of her lips, her chin peeking out. We pass the bridge and home is ever closer, just a few corners away. And this is when it happens.

I grab the wheel.

She shrieks.

I plead.

Somehow, she lets me steer. On the bend, at the top of the

hill, we have to change gears. I don't know what I'm doing, so she takes over, but doesn't push me away. We're almost touching, and we've stopped speaking, driving downhill and onto the terraced avenue in silence.

'Just here,' I nod at the ivy-covered house, bathed in warm orange light from the streetlamp.

'It's nice,' she says, applying the handbrake.

'Yeah, it is,' I say, not taking my hands from the wheel.

'Are you happy here?' She doesn't look at me.

'Sometimes.' I move my arm.

'Goodnight, then.' She looks at me.

'Goodnight, Miss,' I say, and we kiss.

11

MARCH 1992

It's ages before I see her again. Through Saturday, Sunday, all of Monday, I rehearse what I might say, but the last day of term arrives and I'm still lost for words.

Spanish is the very last lesson before we break up for Easter. The weak March sun is trying its best to warm my back as I cross the quad, but every nerve in my body is on fire as it is. I pause when I see the others waiting outside Miss P's classroom, excitement and apprehension rushing through me. I take my seat beside Nick. I've got this far: no security guards swarmed over me at the door; no headmaster in sight. Just Miss P writing on the board, her back to the room. Do I pretend nothing happened? I suppose that's the right thing to do. Do I act cool, detached? Nick always says that's the sure way to get a girl's attention. This from someone who's never been seen with a girl. Anyway, I've tried this method with a 100 per cent record of failure. What else can I do? *Just be you*. Ridiculous.

Ten minutes into the lesson and still she hasn't looked at me. Everyone's swapping stories about the revue, and she's laughing with the girls on the other side of the room.

Twenty minutes later, she's moved a bit closer. I have to catch her eye. I need a sign. Then she turns, faces my row, and is about to say something when one of the girls cuts in.

'Sorry we left so much mess in here on Friday, Miss.'

She turns. 'Yes, well, apology accepted. It wasn't quite how I wanted to spend the rest of my evening, cleaning up.'

'Yeah, we're really sorry, Miss,' says Nick. 'But at least you weren't all alone.'

'What ... do you mean?' She coughs nervously, her eyes darting towards me for a split second.

'You had Joey to help, didn't you?' he says, clapping me on the back. I freeze.

'Oh, yes.' She looks at me, expressionless. 'I suppose he was here for a bit. I'd completely forgotten.'

Nick wraps his arm around my shoulders.

'Oh, Miss, how could you forget?' He puts on a baby voice. 'Look, you've upset him.' I look down to play along. Nothing else I can do. Thanks to Nick's big mouth she must think I've gossiped. One of the others must have seen me filling bin bags because I haven't even seen Nick until today. She doesn't react but walks back to her desk, starts to write on the board. Her fingers are white as she grips the cylinder of chalk. I hold my breath, anticipating its brittle crack.

'*¡Escuchad todos!*' She calls the class to order, still facing the board. No one seems interested in Nick or me anymore, as her voice cuts the volume. Are her shoulders angry? Is her face set in fury?

'Make a note of these chapters.' Clear and instructional, so no real clues in her voice. 'Easter break reading.'

A slight groan followed by the soft chatter of pens on paper.

She turns. 'We've only a few minutes left, so you can start reading now.'

I want her to look at me. I have what I hope is my reassuring face on, but playful Miss P who just minutes ago was laughing, joking, has been replaced by a marble statue. I keep staring as the others read in silence, but she refuses to notice.

The bell sounds the end of term.

I pack up, follow Nick to the door as he babbles excitedly about his Easter skiing trip. At the door, I look back into the room. She's glaring straight at me, her green eyes shining in anger, accusing. I open my mouth, but nothing comes out and my feet, still heading out the door, stumble over the step into the cloister. The door shuts behind me. I am relieved to be out of there but angry at the same time. Angry with Nick for saying all the wrong things. Angry with her for believing all the wrong things. Angry with myself for being seventeen, wearing school uniform, instead of being thirty-five and just right for Miss P. Angry with myself for being too weak to go back in there and put things right. Angry with myself for not having the guts to tell her how I think I really feel.

'Oi, you coming or what?' shouts Nick across the quad.

'I'll catch you up.' I wave, turn back, and open the door.

'Miss, I need to talk to you.'

'Haven't you done enough talking?' Her cheeks and neck are red.

'Miss, please, I promise. I haven't said anything to anyone.' I can see she doesn't believe me.

In the long silence, she glowers at me. My instinct is to look down, but I force myself to hold her gaze. I have no idea what to say. She wipes her hands over her face, through her hair, looks straight at the back wall. What does this mean? I put my school bag on the floor, perch on the edge of a desk. 'I'm confused, Miss.'

She opens her mouth, but this time it's her turn to find no words. She doesn't move. I've never felt so awkward, but I can't seem to leave.

'I'm confused, too,' she breathes, at last. And we stare at each other even harder. Somewhere inside my head, there's a rush of air, noise like an orchestra tuning up.

'Can I see you? Just to talk, I mean.'

'No, you can't,' she says, more to herself than to me.

I don't know what I'm expecting to talk about, but I'm going to be away for weeks, some of that in Italy with Mum and Rose. She can't just expect me to go and forget what happened, can she?

'It's not fair, Miss. I need to talk. Before I leave for Easter.'

Another long silence.

'It's too dangerous,' she whispers. 'Here, with everyone around. We can't.'

'What about off campus somewhere?'

She gets up, moves to lean against the front of her desk, her hands palm-down on the edge, hair falling over her eyes. She lowers her head.

'Okay.' She nods at the classroom floor. 'One hour only, though. Just to talk.'

'Yes, of course. When?' My heart races.

'When do you leave?' she asks, sounding very matter-of-fact.

'Thursday evening train.'

'Right. I can do Thursday at one o'clock.' She picks up her

bag and coat, walks across the room and opens the door. 'I have to go now. Staff meeting.' She passes me and I walk out with her, our bags brushing together. She locks the door.

'Where shall we meet?' I remember to ask.

She turns her head from side to side, checking the length of the cloister, takes a half step towards me.

'Come to my flat. Don't be late.' She speaks quickly, almost under her breath. 'I'll leave the door on the latch. Just come in.'

12

MARCH 1992

I wake up unnecessarily early on Thursday. I'm so wired, it's like Christmas morning. It's still dark outside and the house is soundless as I pull on a pair of joggers and amble down flights of stairs to the big bathroom. I normally use the tiny cupboard bathroom on the top-floor landing. Although everything is there – toilet, sink, bath with overhead shower – it's like squeezing into a doll's house. When I sit on the loo (don't attempt to stand) and extend my arm, I can place my hand flat against the opposite wall with my elbow still bent. The ceiling, walls and floor have been papered with colourful concert and music festival posters from the 1970s – Reading Rock, Pilton, Isle of Wight, Bickershaw – it's like pooing in a psychedelic dream. But I don't want to wake Holly, risk her wrath at this time of day. The main family bathroom is huge by comparison, with glasshouse-sized plants, views across the city through enormous sash windows. There's even a small sofa.

I take much longer than usual in the shower, mainly washing, but I can't ignore that I'm rock hard this morning, so I deal with that as well. Afterwards, I towel myself dry in front of the floor-to-ceiling mirror. Before dressing, I pause for inspection. The mirror's old, the glass patchy with flaky spots. The reflection is distorted in places, elongating then squishing me as I start to lean and sway. It's a funny effect made weirder by the mirror over the sink behind me. Naked, I bend in and out of shape, into infinity. I stand in profile, then slowly move my hips forward and back. I'm no hunkasaurus like the 1st XV rugby players, but I've always been quite tall. Matured early, Mum says. Had hairy legs by the age of eleven. My shoulders are getting broader, and my waist is narrow. Staying side-on, I shuffle closer to the mirror. My hair's longer now; definitely flickable. But there's no getting away from it: I have Dad's legs – too skinny. Now if I just press my hips forward again – oh yes, that's more like it: thank you very much, ladies and gentlemen, the boy with the massive cock. I raise my arms triumphantly, parade around the bathroom, waving from the windows, acknowledging the imaginary crowds.

'Are you going to be long in there?' sounds a woman's voice from the landing. I jump, tiptoe over to my joggers, gather up my towel. I forgot Celia is an early riser. Outside, she greets me with a smile as I nod, bow apologetically, and take the stairs two at a time.

I spend the rest of the morning in my room. I go through about five changes of clothes, even my double-breasted interview suit that makes me look like an estate agent, before I return to the first look: blue jeans, white T-shirt, denim jacket. I haven't got any interesting clothes, but these are the cleanest. I study a map of the area that I found in the kitchen, trying to memorize routes from here to her, road names, landmarks.

At midday, I can't bear it any longer. I glance one last time in the mirror, hum a few bars of the *A-Team* theme tune. I pause on the top landing and listen. Familiar family noises have been echoing through the house all morning, but no one has bothered to disturb me. They probably don't even know that term is over and think I'm at school, especially with Celia seeing me up so early. I pick up my Doc Martens and go quietly, hardly making a sound on the stairs. Someone's in the kitchen with the radio on, but I slip past, out through the side door and onto the pavement that skirts the crescent. Despite being out of sight of the house, I'm still walking slowly, silently. I feel like a spy. I reach into my jacket pocket for my Walkman and black beanie, pull the hat low over my head, just above my eyes, then the headphones. I press play on my Cure mix tape and instinctively step into beat with 'The Lovecats'.

The most direct route to Miss P's flat would take me right across the school campus. I could be at her door within twenty minutes. I glance at my Swatch. I've got forty-five to play with, but that's fine because I have no intention of going anywhere near school. There are always stray teachers hanging around after the end of term, and I also don't want any local day boys or girls to notice me. I could easily run into Nick or his brother and that would be a disaster. I need to be invisible. I realize I haven't got an answer planned, any reason for what I'm doing if questioned. My head's too fizzing to think about that, so all I can think is to take an even more circuitous route.

At the top of the steep hill that climbs up from the terrace, I turn right, entirely the opposite direction to my destination. At a roundabout I pick the least busy road, avoid the main streets, and then take a series of smaller residential avenues, all mirror images of each other. My Swatch gives me twenty minutes and I think her road must be quite close, so I can slow down. Perhaps I should have brought the map, but I didn't want to attract attention. I wind the lead and headphones round the Walkman, which I bury in my pocket. I come to a road with a line of shops and get my bearings. Her street's around here.

My pulse races. I step off the kerb but stop myself. I haven't got anything to give her. Idiot. I can't just turn up empty-handed, can I? I cross the road and look through the windows of a corner shop, hardware store, hairdresser. It's useless. If I run to the shopping centre, I'll be late – sweating and late. It's no good. I walk back to the corner shop and hope for the best. A radio is playing something very exotic with a sitar and finger drums. The shopkeeper smiles at me across a counter, and I look past him at the shelves of bottles. I take a step forward but, without a word, he takes a chess step to his right, blocking my view with a kind, purchase-denying shrug. He must be used to seeing boys from school in here, even out of uniform. Deflated, I wander further into the shop. If I knew Miss P wanted kitchen roll or Battenberg cake, I'd be on to a winner; there are stacks of them. The music stops, the radio pips one. I stare at my watch, feel my forehead prick with sweat again. Now I'm late. I've got to get out of here; I don't want to waste any of my precious hour. Grabbing a packet of chocolate mini eggs from an Easter display, I notice a bucket of daffodils by the door, and throw them dripping onto the counter. The man chuckles, unhelpfully, and takes his time wrapping, even more unhelpfully.

Looking an idiot with my mini eggs and a pathetic bunch of

daffodils, I stride up the road, and reach the end of her street at last. It's already five minutes past. I don't want to run; she'll think I'm ridiculous if she's looking out for me. I walk as fast as I can. At her gate, I glance up at the window but can't see anything behind net curtains and condensation. I manage to climb the steps leading to the front door without falling. At the top, I remember to breathe. This is it. I push. It doesn't budge. It's a huge door, so I push again. Nothing. Now I'm exposed. I look at the list of names by the buttons on the wall, find hers second from bottom. I press. No sound. Did it work? I press again, longer, but it's quickly cut off with a click, then her voice.

'Hello?'

'Hi. It's me, Miss. It's Jo—'

'You're late.' She sighs through the voice grill. 'Come in, quickly.'

She buzzes me in, and all my careful preparation and detailed planning for this moment seem wasted. Now I'm hot, damp, looking horribly conspicuous with my stupid gifts. Her door opens before I can throw them somewhere. I hold my breath. But she doesn't appear in the doorway. In fact, she's disappeared; there's no sight or sound of her through the now-closing door. I jump forward just before it shuts and edge into her flat. The door clicks behind me. I hear noises in the kitchen; pans, something plastic opening. There's music coming from the living room, Ella Fitzgerald, so I step further inside and take the opportunity to get rid of the flowers, the chocolate eggs, laying them on the dining room table that runs the length of the back wall. On my first visit, it was littered with exercise books, but that's all been cleared and replaced with a simple glass vase. An empty glass vase, I note, satisfyingly.

The room is much as before, but also different somehow. Smaller? Bigger? The sofa along another wall with a small coffee table in front, the bookshelves, records, the big arm-chair in the bay window, I remember. There's a television in the far corner, a vast marble fireplace in the centre of the wall, an enormous mirror above. A kind of chandelier hangs from the ceiling, and there are big, green-leafed pot plants. It's minimal, tidy.

I stand in the middle of the room, wondering what to do. The clock on the mantelpiece above the fire ticks around to 1.15 p.m. I haven't even seen Miss P yet. What am I doing, wasting time studying her living room when we should be talking about what happened? I go towards the kitchen, still self-conscious though less damp, and brace myself for a telling-off about my time-keeping.

'Oh, there you are.' She looks up with a half-smile, half-frown. 'Not been stealing again, have you?' she says, her smile widening as she stands over a pan on the hob, pointing a wooden spoon at me. The light streaming through the floor-to-ceiling window at the end of the narrow kitchen picks out the shining copper tones in her hair. She is stunning; so slim and young-looking in a white shirt, open black waistcoat, a long fern-coloured floaty skirt. How can she really be thirty-five? I can't help noticing her skirt is slightly see-through when she moves in the light, showing her legs through the thin material, going all the way up. I feel warm in my jeans. Her hair is the real difference, tied up at the back so that it sits in a mountainous pile with wispy curly bits hanging down her neck and the side of her face. Her neck is long, smooth and looks far too fragile to support all that hair. I want to run and lift her into my arms. Instead, I stay rooted in the doorway, shifting my hands from my pockets to folded across my chest, failing to think of something, anything, to say. Fortunately, she hasn't finished.

'I should tell you,' she continues, bending down to look in the fridge, muttering to herself, '. . . hmm, not cold enough . . .'

'What, Miss?'

She straightens up. 'I should tell you, I've made a careful inventory of the contents of my flat. And I've locked all high-value items in a safe, including my collection of ceramic dolphins and other sea life.' She grins. I grin back, relieved at her breaking the ice. But when are we going to talk? For that matter, what is there to say? I'm not sure anymore.

I continue to watch my teacher in her natural habitat, going about her home, holding kitchen implements instead of chalk or a whiteboard marker. It's fascinating, even if I do feel out of place. The kitchen surfaces are covered: bags of fresh pasta, tubs of green stuff I don't recognize, salami, French bread, punnets of strawberries, packets of crisps, chocolates. I suppose she must be preparing for a dinner party with her friends. I check my watch, it's already twenty-five past. We need to talk, but it appears I'm going to spend my hour in this kitchen, presumably followed by some rushed dismissive comment as she ushers me out at two o'clock. But, then, I don't know what else I was expecting. I don't know why I'm here. I feel like someone's stuck a pin in my bubble. I should just leave now, but I may as well see the hour through.

'Can I do anything to help, Miss?' Might as well be helpful.

'Ah, yes. Sorry,' she says, a little flustered, 'I'm a bit behind with myself.'

'No, it's fine, I can see you're busy. I could give you a hand if you like, until it's time to go.'

'Go? You've only just got here, and you were late.' She points to a cupboard above the sink. 'But you can make yourself useful if you like. Get a couple of glasses out of there, would you?'

I do as I'm told and take two tumblers from the cupboard. She's at the fridge again, produces a bottle of wine. She looks at me. I look at the glasses then back at her. Without a word, I return them to the cupboard and take two wine glasses instead.

'Better.' She smiles, beckons me and I follow her into the living room. But in the doorway, she halts and exclaims, 'Did you? Are these for me?' She puts down the bottle, holds up the corner shop's finest. I nod. 'That's so sweet of you!' She pauses, looking up at me. I think she's about to kiss me on the cheek, but she just stands there. Now she looks as awkward as I'm feeling. 'Um, let's sit down?'

We move to the sofa and make opening a bottle of wine, pouring two glasses, last forever. But I don't mind. I feel all grown up, drinking wine with my teacher in her flat in the middle of the day. I take a couple of quite large sips and only briefly wish it was beer. Miss P does the same, all the time studying me over her glass.

'So . . .' I say. One of us has to say something. 'That's a lot of food in the kitchen. Are you having a party?'

She looks surprised. 'No, that's lunch. I wasn't sure what you'd like, but I took a guess you probably eat pasta. Is that all right?'

I'm stunned. 'Yes, of course. Oh my God, that would be lovely, Miss.'

'Great,' she says, standing up abruptly, 'I'll bring it in. I'm famished!'

This time I don't offer to help. My head fills with light, the music's suddenly louder, the room brighter. We're having lunch! I down my glass, pour some more. I'm filling hers up as she returns with two big bowls of pasta with dollops of the green stuff and grated cheese.

Despite the huge dining table, we eat on the sofa with the bowls on our laps. And we talk. Not about the other evening. She asks me about my trip to Italy, where I'll be staying, what I'll be doing. It's supposed to be a holiday, but Mum has arranged for me to visit a school in Ventimiglia where a friend of a friend of an acquaintance teaches. She's keen to know who I'll be with, what the plans are.

'I don't really know. It's all been arranged though,' I say between sips of wine and mouthfuls of pasta. 'I think I have to go to a school and follow some of their pupils around for a few days.'

'But it's not even one of your subjects. It sounds ...'

'Yes, I know. Classic Mum.' I shrug.

'You don't seem that bothered.'

'No, well, I'm used to it. A veteran exchange student, me. Most holidays spent staying with families somewhere in Europe, going to school, smiling politely as my opposite numbers play Pink Floyd or Dire Straits songs like they're brand new. Or even worse, something in their own language about motorway crash barriers or underarm hair or ...'

She snorts, almost spilling her drink. I look up from my bowl. She's shaking, giggling, her hand clamped to her mouth.

'I'm not joking, Miss. They're culturally backward.'

She snorts, laughs again and is suddenly on her feet, rushing from the room.

'Miss?' I call after her.

'Mmmm,' comes a muffled reply from the bathroom. Is she choking? I get up, follow her. She's leaning over the sink, spluttering, running the tap, scooping water to her face.

'Miss, are you okay?' I don't know whether to move closer.

'I'm fine.' She lifts her head, beams at me in the mirror, her eyes bright, wet. 'There's a lesson for you – don't eat and laugh at the same time.' She turns to face me. 'Sorry, I guess I didn't expect to be laughing with you.'

'Oh, right. Why not?'

'I suppose . . . after the other day . . . in my classroom, it was all a bit heavy. But this is . . . really nice.' She smiles again. 'Strawberries?'

She's right; it is nice, but it's still confusing. She seems quite in control, though, even if I'm not. In fact, I'd say the more in command she becomes, the less sure of myself I am. Instead of following her into the kitchen, I return to the bathroom, quietly shut the door. I stand in front of the mirror and study myself, half looking for an answer. What am I doing here? What's going to happen next? Do we finish lunch then I go and that's the end of that? The end of what? I run the cold tap, lean over to splash my face. There's a light tap on the door.

'Is everything—?'

'Yep, all fine, thanks,' I say to myself in the mirror. I run my hand through my hair. 'Just . . . looking for stuff to steal.'

I open the door and sense a change in the atmosphere. I

return to the big room where Miss P is sitting on the sofa, sipping from her refilled glass. Everything seems to be moving in slow motion. I don't remember whether we finished our pasta, but that's been replaced by two bowls of strawberries. I sit down, glancing towards the music system. Ella has also left the room, replaced by a Spanish woman singing something about horses, or is it hair?

'She's good, isn't she?' Miss P follows my glance, handing me my wine, also refilled. 'Probably quite hirsute under the arms, but what would you expect?' I catch the mischief in her voice.

'Did I offend you earlier, Miss? I hope not. I'm sure she's a great and famous singer, however hairy.'

'Of course you didn't offend me!' Miss P exclaims, laying a hand on my leg, resting for a moment before returning it to her lap. 'Although I do quite favour the natural look myself.'

I don't know where to look when she says this. My head is full of mixed images. Rude ones of Miss P standing naked in front of me, distracted by slightly gross ones of her covered in bushes of hair. I'm hoping my expression doesn't give me away. I try hard to look normal as my mind leaps around imagining what horrors or delights lie beneath her pastel colours. She stares at me and eats a strawberry. I take her lead, even though I don't like strawberries.

'Have I shown you my flat yet?' she says, biting into another large berry.

I remember standing in her corridor that last time, the door to her bedroom, unable to take my eyes off it.

'No, not all of it.'

'Would you like to see it?'

'Yes,' I say, my voice thickening. I take another glug of wine to stop myself having to clear my throat.

'Have another strawberry first,' she says and, taking one from her bowl, places it slowly against my mouth so I have to open and bite. It's the kind of thing I've seen in a film, but which, it turns out, is a lot harder to execute in real life. Do you take a bite of it or attempt the whole thing in one go? I choose to go for the whole thing. That is not the right choice. Miss P has to snap her hand away. My cheeks are burning.

'I said strawberry, not me!' she laughs, and rises. 'Come on, let me give you the tour.'

As I've seen this room, the kitchen and bathroom already, she takes me straight to the room opposite the front door beside the kitchen. It's a sort of study, quite big, but empty apart from a futon in one corner, a desk with a large computer, a small bookshelf filled with box files.

Out in the corridor she seems to hesitate, then walks the eight or so feet towards her bedroom with deliberate steps. A thumping starts in my neck, my chest, just about everywhere I have a pulse.

She opens the door wide like she's opening a box. A double bed with a big white duvet and matching pillows is flanked by two wooden wardrobes and a small bedside cabinet with a lamp and a clock. On the wall above her bed is a framed print of a Spanish hill village. The wall opposite holds a gold-framed square mirror which makes the room appear larger. Hanging down from the ceiling by a long chain is another chandelier with eight bulbs. I count them and I'm aware of her watching me. I shift my gaze to a long sash window that looks out to gardens, then back to the framed print, study it again for something to do and to avoid looking at her.

I try to think of something erudite and grown-up to say about the picture, but instead clap my hands together, take a stride towards the bed, perch on its edge and say, 'Nice . . . bedr—' But before I can finish, she cuts in.

'We're not staying in here.'

I spring up, embarrassed.

'No, of course not, I didn't mean . . .'

'Well, that's the tour. Perhaps we should finish our strawberries.'

Back on the sofa it's as if the awkward bedroom moment never happened and she's straight into feeding me strawberries again. I play along with this game, though I don't know the rules, but I do know there are only three strawberries left. I wonder if I should just say thank you and leave. We're evidently not going to talk about what happened and, frankly, this whole strawberry affair is not doing much to un-muddy the waters. I should get up now, say goodbye, go to Italy with Mum and Rose.

There is one strawberry remaining. She moves to take it but, instead, stands up, walks over to the bay window. She asks me if I like her pot plants. I snigger, because she said 'pot', then quickly say I do like them, and ask where she got them, whether they're difficult to look after, not that I care. She's clearly not listening because she's not looking at me or the plants but seems to be peering out of the window.

She returns to the sofa. With each move seeming to last a lifetime, she sits, runs fingers through her hair, pushes the table away, shuffles up to me, takes the strawberry, puts it in her mouth, puts her hand behind my head, strokes down my neck, brings our heads closer. I stop breathing. She keeps eating the berry but never swallows and, too late to stop myself, I press my lips against hers.

'Mmgn!' She stifles a cry, swallows quickly. I pull away sharply.

'I'm sorry, Miss, really ... I thought ...' She's looking at me with wide eyes. Mine must be looking at hers with panic in them. I wait to be slapped.

'You could have let me finish eating.' She smiles, then pulls my head towards hers again, opens her mouth.

She tastes sweet and I hope I don't taste of garlic from the green stuff. We kiss and kiss and don't stop, even as she lies back on the cushioned arm of the sofa and I move to lie beside her, my body against the sofa back, my left arm resting by her head. Our knees are bent slightly, hers together but increasingly intertwining mine. Her arms are wrapped around my neck and shoulders now, only my right arm is free. As we kiss, deeply, it finds a place to rest on her waist. She pushes her body into mine. I move my hand slowly but not in any particular direction. It wants to go down but manages to find enough will power not to. My fingers stroke upwards leading my hand until they reach a soft incline. I stop there, fully expecting her hand to come up and pull mine away. That's what should happen now, I think, but instead she runs her hand down across my shoulder, along my back to my waist and pulls me closer from there. She must be aware what's happening further down and responds with a squeeze. Still our mouths don't part, our tongues darting in and out, fast, slow, sealed, swirling in loops to build again. It's like we're replaying the last hour's dance with our kisses. My mind switches as I try to calculate the time. I arrived just after 1 p.m. It must be gone 2 p.m. by now, but the thought vanishes when her hand moves again to rest in the small of my back, her fingers pressing down, sliding just under the top of my jeans. I haven't moved my hand but now I let it climb over the soft bulb of her shirt, press gently from the centre of my palm, shaping my fingers to hold her breast full in my hand. I'm pretty useless when it comes to tits; not that I've held lots, but I never know what I'm supposed to do with them. And this is a fully grown woman's breast. So I massage like this, let my fingers find where her shirt opens. I want to slide my hand in, feel her skin, her soft round shape, but the angle's all wrong. She lifts her hand to unbutton her shirt. Just three buttons, but it's enough. My fingers find their way into her bra. I sense a heat below, a slight dampness. I'd better not come, not now, that would be a disaster, but God, I feel I could any second. I scoop her whole breast out of her bra. They're milky white; a perfect round. I try to think what to do next. I extend my middle finger so it traces around her nipple. I can't stop myself taking it between my thumb and forefinger and squeezing it. I expect a soft sighing noise or a little mewing cry, like in films, not the near scream and jolt.

'Careful – it doesn't come off!'

I want to say something, but I don't want to say sorry because that would break this moment. Perhaps I should say sorry, or she might think I'm a brute or violent or sadistic or something. I say nothing, but close my hand gently over her breast, hold it there, cradling it carefully with just the slightest pressure. It seems to work and our kissing resumes, more delicately now. I've learnt an important lesson. As our kissing finds its rhythm again, I want her to do more with her hand which has been flitting around the top of my waistband through all this. I know I should be patient, but I genuinely don't know how long I can hang on, which is shocking because I've never come without some pretty serious wrist action. Her hand delves further into my jeans, across one buttock. Is this a sign? I start massaging her breast again, wait to see whether she pulls her hand back out. It stays. Slowly, I move mine down along her rib cage to the top of her skirt. She doesn't squeeze or push herself into me like before. It's like she's waiting, so I continue travelling downwards, over her skirt to where a firm mound rises like the edge of a hill or an ocean shelf. My hand is shaking slightly. I rest it again on her hip. I open my eyes, aware only then that they've been closed throughout, find hers shut and realize we haven't looked at each other since she swallowed the strawberry. If she's not looking, I figure she doesn't want me to stop, so I close my eyes again. For a while, I just concentrate on kissing, try to level out my breathing, but as soon as I move my hand the pulses start climbing. Keeping my hand as steady as I can, I take the plunge.

First, I spread my fingers as I would if I were playing piano notes an octave apart, eight keys' width. Second, I try to get the piano image out of my head. This is turning into a military operation but obviously I can't stop now; an article in my sister's *Cosmopolitan* went on and on bemoaning the way men ruin everything for a woman by stopping and starting. I press my thumb into the central folds of my teacher's skirt until her legs part almost imperceptibly and I meet something that isn't material. Something happens to Miss P. She ... ripples. Her body moves in one motion from her feet to her head. As I bring my hand into the gap at the top of her legs and press again with my thumb, her teeth find my lips and bite down. Not too hard, but enough to make me wince. The metallic taste of blood mixes with saliva, hers and mine, and our tongues go into battle. I press again with my fingers, then slide my hand in one movement down her left leg to the end of her skirt, then back up, under it. She arches, her shoulders flattening into the sofa, but I don't stop until I reach another material. We both catch the breath in our mouths when my fingers touch the silk of her knickers. My head spins. Silk! Is this what women wear? I can't believe I'm touching silk knickers – my teacher's silk knickers! Our mouths come together again, harder. My eyes shut tight to block out the world beyond this sofa, and to make sure I don't mess this up. What do I do now? Perhaps she senses indecision or inexperience, takes my hand, guides me slowly. My fingers run up then down, lightly, hardly pressing, just skimming up and down the silk. I slip my fingers round the material; I have to know more. But something is wrong.

'No,' she says.

'No?' I open my eyes.

'No.' She is looking at me. 'No. I'm sorry. I can't.'

My finger is like an enemy to me now. Gently but slightly hurrying, I pull out. What moments before was a journey, an intrepid exploration, takes less than two seconds and my hand is well away, resting on the edge of the sofa.

'I'm sorry,' she says again, but offers no other explanation, turns her head on one side, looking away from me into the room.

I start to move, but she stops me.

'Where are you going?'

'I thought, I should probably—'

'Don't. Please.'

She shifts her body so that I can lie properly along the back of the sofa beside her, and I realize I've been resting on my left arm and it's gone to sleep. I'm not hard anymore, that's clear. Did I do it wrong, then, in the end? I'm swimming with thoughts; perhaps she is too, lying next to me but somehow miles away.

I turn to look at her. 'Are you okay?' I stop just in time before adding 'Miss'. She doesn't answer. I look at the ceiling and retrace. I know I was hard. I couldn't tell how 'natural' she was without looking. There's a bit of me that is scared to look. I suppose it is nature after all; there must be a reason for it, something primal perhaps, for protection I expect. I can hardly object; why would I? It's just that, she did talk about it, so she must be quite into it. I'm not sure how I feel about that, so I try to think about something else. I run the tip of my tongue over my bottom lip, find a tiny crack, hardly anything now. I find the clock on the mantelpiece. It's 3.30 p.m. already. How did that happen?

We lie in silence for ages. Thursday afternoon. Tomorrow I'll be in Italy. I can't bear it. I try not to dwell, but my mind is treading water, unable to empty the ocean of thoughts. Finally, Miss P turns her head, then her whole body ninety degrees to lie on her side so she is facing me. She doesn't say a word, just studies me. I really don't know what to say. I'm scared that if I do say anything it will make her get up and then I'll have to leave.

She opens her mouth as if to speak, but changes her mind, her top teeth biting her lower lip. She keeps looking down the sofa, then back to my face. It's like she's assessing me, evaluating, considering. Regretting? I can't work her out. She clears her throat, begins to rise. So that's that.

But she doesn't stand. She kneels on the sofa beside me, leans over me with her hands firm on my shoulders, kisses me, her hair tumbling over my face. I'm in a den of her, pinned down, there's nothing I can do, except kiss. Is this a 'last kiss'? In her kneeling position I sense she's halfway to getting off the sofa. This is what I expect her to do. What I absolutely do not expect is for her hand to move from my shoulder straight to my belt. She undoes me one-handed and, underneath my jeans, with each pull on my belt, I morph from resigned frustration to uncontrollable excitement. She's still kissing me and I'm trying hard not to grin. Next, the buttons, which can be annoying, awkward, but which she deals with in one swift downward tug. Our mouths part. This time when I open my eyes, she's looking intensely into mine, taking control. I can't believe this is going to happen, whatever's going to happen. She pushes herself up and sits back on her heels. Her hands, head, hair still hiding her face, are hovering over my unbuttoned jeans. She pauses, and for a moment I think she's coming back up, but she's readjusting her legs to bend lower over me. With both hands she pulls my jeans down a few inches. Another pause and I'm harder. It's actually quite painful. Then she pushes up my T-shirt, drops her mouth to my stomach, traces the line of my pants with her lips. I try not to wriggle. It's torture. Her hand strokes across the front of my pants, up and down, and I think I might burst out. She hooks her fingers around the elastic material, slides her other hand inside, taking hold of me, releasing me. I want to shout something, maybe swear a bit.

'Miss P's got my cock in her hand! Miss P's jerking me off! Fuck!' I want to yell, but I keep it in my head as her hand lifts and falls in long flowing movements. Then it happens. Because I can't see through the hair, I don't know it's coming. A wetness, warm on the tip, just resting there, her lips on me. She stays like that for several seconds, occasionally tickling with her tongue, continuing with her hand, up, down, up, down, then in a little further, into her mouth, warmer, wetter each time, still slow, not speeding up like I do in bed, slow so I travel through each rise and fall. At last, she does it, sinks down, her mouth engulfs me. All the way down, all the way up, then out and I am rigid beneath her, poised, my head back, neck arched, waiting for her mouth again, my fingers stretching, tensing.

Then nothing. No mouth, no tongue, just Miss P sitting up, still looking down but her face visible, frowning. Perhaps she's readjusting herself, maybe she wants to take her clothes off, straddle me ... but she doesn't do any of those things. She just sits back. *Oh no, not again, please don't stop, Miss, please!* Her hand releases its grip. I can't believe it. She actually lays my cock down, her other hand pulling my pants up. It's like something died. Then she does the worst thing. She looks down at me, at last, and smiles. Smiles! As if saying, *I hope you enjoyed that, it's enough though, isn't it?* I'm sure my expression is replying, *I think you'll know when it's enough!* Or maybe I'm being unfair and I'm just frustrated and this is normal in these sorts of circumstances, when men and women haven't done this before, together.

I stay lying on my back, confused all over again. I hitch up my jeans, re-button, belt up, while Miss P kneels up, stands, then sits again, and finally drapes across my chest with her head on my shoulder. She looks uncomfortable and I feel like a puppet on strings. I glance over to the clock. I'm shocked to see how long we've been on this sofa. It's clouding over outside, and shadows stretch across the room.

'Would you like something to eat? Or drink?' she whispers. I'm not remotely hungry.

'No, thank you, Miss,' I say, and flinch.

She sits up and looks down at me. 'Did you really just call me Miss?'

'Sorry, I . . . it's habit, I suppose. What should I call you?'

'Not Miss. Not after all that.' She shudders. 'Call me Ali. It is my name.'

'Ali.'

'Good.' She smiles. 'I'm going to the bathroom.'

As soon as she's gone, I sit up, very aware of being out of place now. I climb off the sofa, go to the mirror over the fireplace. I run my hands through my hair, shake my head. It's still me in there, but everything's changed.

It's getting dark quickly now. Miss P – Ali – comes back into the room and heads straight for the windows to close the shutters. I'm leaning against the long table on the other side of the room, sensing an ending. I know it has to come. She's obviously not about to ask me to stay the night. Although I desperately don't want this to end, I don't know where we'd go from here. I expect there's a protocol for what you're supposed to do next, but I'm out of my depth. I wish I'd accepted the offer of food and drink, but I can tell that door has closed. I look around but it's not like last time. I can't just bound around stealing things, we both know that. Equally, I wouldn't know where to begin if we were to have a conversation about this. I laugh involuntarily and she comes over to me.

'What's funny?' she asks, stopping to pick up the strawberry bowls.

'It's nothing, really. Just that ... I was only supposed to be here for an hour.'

'Yes.' She's not laughing but smiles a sort of embarrassed smile, looking down then back up. 'Well, you were late.' Then adds, more deliberately, 'And it's quite late now.'

I take the hint. She heads for the kitchen, and I take one last sweep of the room, the sofa, then wait by the front door. The act of going is making me more anxious than when I arrived. This can't be it, can it? I cast around. I could hide, lock myself in her bathroom. I put my hands to my face.

'Are you all right?' She's reappeared.

I take my hands away; mustn't let her think I'm a nutcase, above all. 'Yes, of course. You?'

'I suppose,' she mutters. 'I wish you didn't have to go.'

Then let me stay!

'I know, I also wish for that,' I say, stumbling over my words, frowning. 'Fucking Italy. Fucking Italians.'

She looks up and laughs quietly, thinking I'm joking when I've never been more serious. She reaches over my shoulder for the latch on the door, walks out with me to the outer main door. We stand facing each other.

'Have a lovely time in Italy.'

'You too,' I reply, automatically.

When can I see you again? I want to ask, but I'm afraid of the answer. What the hell. I start to speak but she beats me to it.

'Don't get seen. Just walk straight out and down the road.

And listen: don't tell anyone.' She grabs my sleeve. 'You won't tell anyone, will you? It has to be a secret.'

'Yes, I mean, no. Of course I won't tell anyone.' Then I'm out on the street, the door to her world closed behind me. I do look back, but it hurts already. I reach the end of the road and I ache all over.

I get home, run upstairs to my room, not wanting to see or talk to anyone. I want to cling to her, the fresh memories. Most of all, I want a wank.

13

MARCH 1992

Ten days on the Ligurian coast, escaping the cold rain of England, sounds like the perfect holiday, but twenty-six degrees is no fun at all when your heart is pounding, stomach churning, and you forgot to pack your sodding Walkman.

Walking around with a secret is made even more oppressive in the heat. Each day I put on a mask of gratitude and happiness, so that Mum doesn't suspect anything, and I don't want to ruin the holiday; I know how much she's been looking forward to our first family holiday without Dad. But she and my sister don't make it easy on me, with the endless questions about school and friends, and I can't help mentioning Miss P a couple of times. If only I could speak to her, but I haven't a clue what her phone number is. I will write.

I go in search of postcards, envelopes and stamps. I buy three and sit on the beach to write them. I tell her about the holiday. I mention Mum but leave out the heavy stuff. I eat an ice cream to celebrate solving my lack of communication.

The next day and every day, I do the same. I start by giving her a quick round-up of the key events. I've met some Italian kids – the ones Mum arranged for me to meet at a local school.

I tell her about the boys and girls I'm hanging out with and that she'd be impressed with my language skills. Mostly, I write about how much I loved Thursday, our afternoon, and how gorgeous I think she is.

The end of the holiday approaches and I'm fidgety. I can see the end and just want to get back. The Italian schools close for Easter so I don't see my new friends much and then not at all. I discover the apartment block has a pool and spend hours hammering up and down. I go to the beach with my sister and decide to run the entire length of it. It's huge, but it uses up time. I swim in the sea. I swim in the pool. I dive. I do lengths underwater. I start packing my case. I want to be out of here and it's annoying everyone, but I can't help it. And at last, we're back in England.

The summer term doesn't start for another four days, but I've prepared for this. On the pretext of play rehearsals for *Hamlet*, which I signed up for in the heat of the moment after the revue, I tell Mum that I have to catch the train back to school. Astonishingly, she doesn't seem to mind. Was I that annoying in Italy? Or perhaps now that we're closer to the summer, when she'll be moving house, her thoughts are less occupied with me. She sees me off from the station, making me promise to keep my grades up, keep washing, don't miss any singing lessons, be a good student and be polite to my teachers.

14

April 1992

Three hours later, my thoughts thrill as the taxi works its way up from the station to Celia and Ned's place. My heart skips beats when the driver's route passes the streets to Miss P's flat, each sight reminding me of that day.

I look around as I unload my bags in the hall. I'm half expecting her to be there, but why would she be? She doesn't even know I'm back. Perhaps there's a letter waiting for me and it's the first question I ask of Ned.

'Um . . . a letter . . .' He's infuriatingly slow.

'Yes. A letter or a postcard maybe?'

'Hmm . . . Nooo, I don't think . . . unless . . . no, I don't think so.'

I sink. After all the cards I sent. I retreat to my room and spend the afternoon in a state of nothingness. I can't believe she hasn't written, at all. And it strikes me that I haven't heard anything from her since that day. What an idiot. What a total twat I am. She's a woman, a grown-up, and I'm just a kid in her eyes. I don't mean anything to her. I'll have to go to school and sit in her lessons and I won't be able to say anything or I'll get into trouble, and it won't be our secret at all. It will just be a load of crap.

I climb onto the parapet outside my window and smoke. I'm scared of heights, but I don't care anymore. It's a balmy April evening. The trees are filling with leaves. Birds are probably singing. I couldn't give a shit.

I'm sitting on my bed listening to Nick Cave and Tom Waits, annoyed at myself that I can't think of anything to do, when there's a shout from downstairs.

'Phone for you, Joe.'

It will be Mum. I head downstairs, the phone is in the hall-way by the kitchen. Ned's standing by it, holding the receiver, smiling. 'It's a girl, sorry, a lady for you. She rang last night as well. Forgot to tell you.'

I take the receiver and wait for him to disappear.

'Hello?'

'Hi, er, Joe. It's me,' comes her voice down the line, quiet, as if holding back.

'Hi. Ned said you called yesterday. I've only just got back.'

'Yes, I rang but, did you get my letter?'

'No.' *For fuck's sake!* 'No, I haven't had anything. Did you get my postcards?'

'Yes, thank you. You definitely didn't get my letter?'

'No, nothing. What did it say?'

'It doesn't matter, not now. Are you busy? Can you come over?'

'Yes, of course.' *Oh my God.* 'When? I can come now, this evening.'

'Yes, how long will you be?'

'Well, about twenty minutes, if I leave now.'

'Hurry.'

*

81

I dart back up to my room, wash, change, then run down all six flights, taking the stairs three at a time, and skid across the hall's shiny wooden floor to the kitchen. I peer in.

'Just going out to see Nick, friend from school, might stay over, bye!'

Ned and Celia barely look up from their enormous dining table. And I'm out the door.

I take the most direct route. Sod being seen. It's exactly fifteen minutes, which leaves me a couple of minutes to lean against the wall a few doors up and get my breath back. I'd had a quick shower, but I'm sweating like a pig now. I flap my shirt to dry my skin, not that it makes much difference.

I ring her bell and I'm buzzed in, no words. She's standing in the doorway, looking flustered. She grabs my hand and pulls me in, kicking the door shut behind me, and before I can say a word or take off my jacket, she's kissing me.

We stand in the hallway for ages, just snogging. Once or twice she holds my head and looks at me intently, then kisses me again. I forget trying to find words to say and let myself soar.

Then, without hesitation or any look or pause, she takes me to her bedroom and undresses me. I undress her. And there we are, naked. Very naked. I want to make excuses for looking ridiculous with swimming trunk tan lines, and not being built like the 1st XV boys.

Perhaps sensing my self-consciousness, she speaks, and her voice is warm and sexy. 'Your hair is lighter.'

'It's the sun, I expect, and my sister dyed it ... it really doesn't matter. You're ...' I want to say something nice in return. I don't care that I'm looking her up and down, I'm probably salivating like a cartoon dog, but I can't believe she's all naked in front of me. I say the first thing, anything, that comes into my head. 'You're completely naked and your skin's all olivey and milky,' because her tits are white and her stomach is darker.

She looks down at herself, perhaps to check, then steps closer and takes hold of me and I'm so hard, so fast. She pulls us towards the bed, throws aside the duvet and we slide in. And we stay there until the sun comes up. We watch it lighten the room and spill across the bed in which we've hardly slept. When we have sex, it is slow and gentle. Probably a good thing, because anything more energetic and it would be all over very quickly, for me. I hadn't even thought about condoms until now, so when I'm about to come I stop, begin to withdraw very carefully. She looks at me with a question, then says, 'You can do it, it's safe,' and, although part of me is full of questions about how this can scientifically be the case, I trust her.

Afterwards, we talk for a bit. She tells me she wrote to me not long after I went to Italy to tell me to forget about her and that nothing could happen between us. But then she says that in one of my postcards I wrote about going to a party with my Italian classmates and she didn't like that, and then she couldn't stop thinking about it. She didn't know when I was returning, but most boarders come back a few days before term so she figured it must be around now for me too. When I wasn't at the house when she rang, she didn't know whether to believe it, and that perhaps her letter had maybe come as a relief to me because I'd met an Italian girl on holiday. By the time I did return, she'd wound herself up into a state and was determined to see me and to apologize for the letter but to explain what she meant. By the time we spoke on the phone, she didn't want to explain anything.

I tell her how I felt being so far away and that I was aching to get back, even though I didn't know what would be waiting for me. We don't say much more. We look at each other a lot. Then we sleep.

When we wake a couple of hours later, we are starving. There can be no question of leaving the flat, in case I'm seen, but there's no need because Miss P has catered for just about every food and drink preference I might have. There's pasta, salad, pizza, strange roll-your-own croissants from a tube (which we agree was a mistake), chocolate, wine, and more strawberries (I still don't tell her).

When at last we venture out of the bedroom, it's already after midday. We fix up a strange feast and transfer the duvet to the sofa. We don't bother dressing. Miss P doesn't open the big shutters, which I find exciting, like we're fugitives. We listen to music, talk about books, eat and drink and fuck, then, as the sky darkens, we return to the bedroom.

We do exactly the same the next day and night and I'm in heaven. By the third morning, I know all about her family; where she went to school and what she did at university; that she had a serious, long-term relationship when she was in her twenties, but it ended badly; how she fell in love with Spain and would love to show me Barcelona.

I suppose I tell her quite a few things as well, but I can't compete; I don't have anything like as much to say about my life. Really, I haven't started living it properly yet, and she's thirty-five after all. So, I tell her mainly about my dreams and ambitions to be a singer or an actor and that, when I was younger, I wanted to be a ballet dancer or racing driver. That I'm excited about trying for an Oxford choral scholarship next year but crapping myself about the entrance exams. I tell her again about my parents' separation and how that came so soon after my mother's illness, but that Mum will be moving house in the summer and that I'll be living with her for my final year of school. That I haven't spoken to Dad since Christmas. I tell her about my uncle and that I want to go sailing with him when I've finished school, perhaps even across the Atlantic.

That evening I put my clothes back on and, this time, when we hold each other by the front door, I am not sad or frustrated. Everything has changed again, but it feels good.

'See you at school,' I grin.

15

May 1992

Every lesson starts with a lecture about how academically crucial this term is. Some offer a few brief words of warning and encouragement. Some take it much further: how the exams coming up are of critical significance for our final year and will determine not only what subjects or places we might be able to secure at university, but have a bearing of great magnitude on our career prospects, which in turn will impact on the house we hope to buy, the car we drive, the clothes we wear, whom we marry, the holidays we take, the lives of our children and children's children, and ultimately the good name of our family. You sit there, knowing it's the 1990s outside, the final decade of the twentieth century, but inside, it may as well be 1890.

The days are warming fast now, and the evenings are long and light. The beech trees lining the playing fields stand fat and full, and the grass on the pitches has recovered well from its winter ravaging under the studs of team sports. When a group of us settles on Nick's roof for the first time since the chill-out afternoons of last autumn, the lads share stories of their Easter breaks: Tom's off-piste skiing in Courchevel;

Chris's driving lessons with a promise of a new car if he gets straight As this term; Ant's National Youth Orchestra tour. I mention Italy but don't get very far. Everyone wants to talk about Glastonbury, who's going, who's got a tent, which bands are playing. I suppose I'm relieved I don't have to face questions about the rest of my holiday. I lie back and stare up at the pale, cloudless sky and let them get on with it. They can jump ahead, but I'm quite happy losing myself in thoughts of last weekend.

After a few minutes I lift my head and look up, snapped out of my dream-state by a change in their voices, their tone lower, hushed, conspiratorial. Nick is speculating about which girls might be going from our year group. I tune in, but a part of me wants to jump up and yell,

Who gives a shit about those girls? I fucked Miss P. What do you think of that? Boom!

The look on their faces would be priceless. Maybe I wouldn't say fucked; it's too harsh. Slept with? Made love to? 'Hey, lads, you won't believe it – I made love to . . .' No, that doesn't work either.

'What are you grinning about, Joe?'

I look up again. They're all staring at me.

'Nothing,' I mumble, then add, 'Girls.'

This seems to satisfy them, and they return to their conversation. The fact is, I can never, will never, tell them about me and Miss P.

The other thing which marks a new term is 'Sign-Up'. Noticeboards announce clubs and sports, teachers trying to get you to join their activity. There's Debating Society,

Duke of Edinburgh, Canoeing, Climbing, Cooking, Dance, Diving, Fencing, Chess, Photography, Computing, Shooting (everything), Physics Club, Backgammon, the list goes on. For the last two terms I've thrown myself into pretty much every activity going, but while my friends run around trying to make sure they get their first choice, I hold back. I'm already doing *Hamlet* and have to prepare for my Grade 8 singing and piano exams, but this isn't why I don't sign up for other activities. What if Miss P wants to do something with me after school and I can't go because I've promised my time to Raft Building Club? I need to be as available as possible. That said, something does come up which I can't turn down.

It doesn't matter that I haven't had a class with Miss P until the very end of that week. In fact, it's probably a good thing that I didn't have to walk straight back into her lessons after just getting out of her bed. It's been exciting, watching her come round a corner, anticipating her standing in the queue for lunch, seeing what clothes she's wearing each day and fantasizing about what's underneath. And I'm careful not to get too close or do anything to make anyone suspect. She's good at it too, almost too good, because it feels like she's hardly aware of me. But then she flashes a quick smile as we pass in a corridor, and I'm jelly again.

On Friday, in Double Spanish, she makes an announcement and it's music to my ears.

'I'm sure you've all signed up for activities, but for anyone who fancies something creative, I wanted to let you know that I'll be running a sketching class on Thursday afternoons. If you want to sign up, there's a form on my desk.'

Sketching classes. Perfect. There's the usual apathy from

the class; most of the boys have cricket or tennis or athletics on Thursdays so that's them out, and some disappointed girls who have already committed to swimming or extra textiles. But one or two put their names down at the end of the lesson as I make my way to her desk.

'What are you doing?' calls Nick from the door. 'You can't draw ... can you?'

'I can now,' I mutter, and sense Miss P's eyes on me as I sign my name and house. We haven't been this close since her flat and I daren't look up. She's inches away but Nick is waiting impatiently at the door. She leans forward to take the form and, lifting it up to mask her face as if to read the names, whispers, 'Come tonight.'

16

MAY 1992

I waste no time hanging around after last lesson. I'm back in my bedroom and showered by 6 p.m. I move around the house as silently as I can, avoiding unwanted conversations and distractions. Not that the Andersons are bothered where I am. They didn't bat an eye when I stayed out for days at the start of term. They'll probably just assume I'm at Nick's if they even check.

With the lighter evenings, I have to take the secret route again, because the school campus and immediate streets will be swarming with staff and pupils. It's risky enough walking up her road, which is still quite close to the school and any teachers who might live in neighbouring streets.

It occurs to me she didn't give me a time and I'm doing all this based on her whispering 'come tonight'. Did she mean now or much later? What if she's out? She could have a staff meeting. I must get her phone number.

Condoms! yells a voice in my head. How did I not think of this before? I think back to us having sex after Italy when she said it was safe. I still don't understand how. I take a quick detour to the petrol station, and my luck is in. I place the bumper pack of forty on the counter with a smug thump. The boy serving behind the till can't be much older than me. He barely looks up. Probably not getting any.

Five minutes later, I'm heading down the street to her flat. A car engine sounds at the top of the road, and I duck behind the tree inside her front gate. I look up at Miss P's windows, but there is no visible life behind the net curtains. I hope no one in the other flats is looking out, or this is going to look very dodgy. Still the car doesn't pass. I can hear its engine, getting nearer, but so slow. Did someone spot me? Perhaps I should have kept walking, but then I don't want to provoke any questions as to why I'm on this side of town. The car brakes just a few yards up the road, but it's not parked. Someone's getting out. I try to make myself smaller. I hear footsteps, hurrying, and a hooded figure runs through the gate into the drive right next to me. They run up the steps and unlock the main door but don't enter. They're hesitating. The figure turns quickly and looks straight at me, crouching at the foot of the tree behind the wall.

'What are you doing?'

'Miss? Is that you?'

'Shhh!' She hurries back down the steps. 'I've only just got back, been shopping, but there's nowhere to park.' She looks furtively around. 'Why are you still crouching?'

'I'm hiding.'

'Yes, well, well done. I think the coast is clear. You're so early. I should've said, it's my fault, it was sort of spur of the moment. I . . .' She's flapping.

'Should give me your phone number, perhaps?'

'Yes, that would've helped. Quick, go in. I'll get the shopping and park. Take this key.'

I dash inside, keeping low, holding her key tight in my hand. I wait for her in the big room at the front. It's showing signs of a school term in progress with papers, exercise books and textbooks piled up on the long table and a stack of essays by the sofa. It feels odd, knowing that some of my work is probably in there somewhere. I turn away as the front door clicks and Miss P comes breathlessly in, school bag over her shoulder and carrying lots of shopping, which I take from her to the kitchen.

I start unpacking, putting things in the fridge. Pasta, pesto (I know what the green stuff is called now), pizza, salad, chocolate, croissants (real this time), cold white wine ... it's looking familiar. I stand and a pair of hands wrap around my middle.

'I don't remember the last time anyone unpacked my shopping.' Miss P is calmer now, her voice warm as she presses into me.

'I like to help. Looks delicious.'

'It's all for us. Wine?' She reaches for the glasses.

'So, you're coming to my sketching classes,' she says.

We're lying in bed. She's on her back and I'm wrapped around her, stroking her breasts. I call them breasts now, not tits; more grown up. We've been in bed for over an hour and it's still not dark. We didn't even finish the first glass of wine.

'Did you get many sign-ups?' I ask, hoping not.

'Actually, only four.'

'Still too many.' I bury my head in her pillow.

'Hey, at least we'll be spending time together.' She slides out of bed and disappears to the bathroom.

I stare at the ceiling and try not to ask myself questions,

but they come. Like, what is this? How did it happen? What's next? I don't have any answers, so I lie back and distract myself with the sounds in her flat, in her road. The toilet flushes. It's weird but sort of sexy.

We stay up late, sitting on the living room floor, with pizza and chocolate and wine. We listen to some of her favourite hairy singers. She threatens me with folk music, but I manage to divert her. She asks me about my hopes of sailing across the Atlantic with my uncle and whether that's a serious possibility. He's keen for me to go, so I hope it will happen.

'Would you like to watch a film?' she asks, and crawls over to a box by the television. I join to inspect her collection. It's mostly European cinema and the odd costume drama. We select *Manon des Sources* and snuggle up on the sofa.

Halfway through the film she asks, 'How are you going to get home?'

'Home? What, tomorrow?'

'You can't stay here tonight, you know that. You've — we've — both got school tomorrow.'

I'm gutted. 'I thought I'd be staying here tonight. Do I have to go?'

'We can't risk you being seen in the morning. Some of the teachers use this road as a cut-through. You could easily be spotted.' She's practical when I want her to be apologetic and as disappointed as me.

'I'll walk, then.' I get up.

'Wait, you don't have to go yet,' she protests. 'There's the rest of the film.'

'No, thanks, it's too late. I'd better go.' If I sound dejected and miserable, it's because I am.

'Look, what did you expect? Think it through. We—'

'I don't want to think it through.' I cut her off. 'I don't know what I expected.'

I feel hurt and stupider by the minute. I take my clothes into the bathroom and dress quickly. She doesn't knock. When I come out, she's standing by the door.

'I'm sorry,' she says and kisses my face. 'We just have to be so careful. You understand, don't you? We mustn't attract attention.'

'I understand,' I repeat robotically. I leave and walk home, straight through the school campus, smoking.

I'm embarrassed by my behaviour, and it's made worse when I have Miss P for Spanish, last lesson on Saturday morning. She has the expressionless statue face down to a tee, giving nothing away, whereas I'm feeling crap about last night. It was so childish of me to strop out, but I'd waited all week to be with her. She could have said something earlier in the evening, then I'd have known what was coming.

She goes around handing back our exercise books and answering a question from across the room when she places my book in front of me. With her body and face turned away from me, she puts the book down and, almost imperceptibly, taps the cover twice with her index finger. Something tells me not to open the book, so I put it in my bag.

Back in the house, no one around, I dig it out. I don't find anything at first but one of the pages catches as I'm leafing through, and out falls a tiny quarter-size envelope with a single 'J' on the front. Inside, a little card:

Sorry. Come back tonight, for a proper night. XX

17

MAY 1992

I don't remember falling asleep, but I wake at 8 a.m. with the sun streaming into her bedroom, birds calling the morning in the trees outside, and Miss P's head resting on my shoulder, her arm draped across my chest. This is that go-to scene in films that signifies *the morning after.* This is the morning after.

Cut to the bathroom thirty seconds later because, try as I might, I can't hold my bladder any longer. I pad to the kitchen, fill the kettle and root around the cupboards in search of coffee. This is definitely what the romantic lead would do next – bring her coffee in bed. I find a tray, mug, milk, sugar, spoon and a jar of Nescafé unhelpfully out of reach on a high shelf. I don't know whether she takes milk or sugar, so I carry those in with the steaming mug.

'What's this?' she says, shuffling her way out from under the duvet.

'Sunday morning coffee in bed, of course.' I beam. 'Just how you like it, I hope.'

I'm on one knee by the bed, holding out the tray. 'Milk, sugar?'

'Ah. Actually neither.'

'Have I made it wrong?' I look around the tray for my mistake. 'I don't drink it myself.'

'No, not at all. Top marks for making a cup of coffee. But I'm more of a tea girl in the morning.'

I stand. 'I'll go and boil another kettle for you.'

'Please don't, it's fine,' she says, sliding out of bed and unhooking a thin dressing gown from the wardrobe door. She puts her arms through the sleeves but doesn't tie it, letting the robe hang open. She steps forward to take the tray, I assume.

'I can manage,' I protest.

'Good, because I don't want the tray and I don't want tea. I want something else,' she says, dropping to her knees. I go rigid, everywhere, and the tray rattles in my hands.

'Careful, I might spill!'

'I won't if you won't,' she says, and takes me in her mouth.

'You owe me one.' She grins a toothpaste smile at me in the bathroom mirror, while I stand in the bath, showering.

'Definitely,' I say, returning her smile. Truthfully, though, I'm not sure what she means. Or, at least, I know *what* she means − I owe her an orgasm − but I need to figure out how she likes it. And by how *she* likes it, I mean how any woman likes it. I don't want to crash and burn, but I have very few reference points for this, and I can't exactly ask someone. I could get a book from the library, but something tells me that's not going to be on today's itinerary. Anyway, it's Sunday, and Monday is the May bank holiday − I'm shit out of luck.

It's not that I'm a complete novice. Cat used to let me fumble around with my fingers, but when I had a go with my tongue, she would twist out of the way. We'd sit up in her single bed, she'd light a cigarette (when her parents were out) and we'd share drags and uncomfortable glances. Invariably she would cry a bit, I would hold her, and that was that. I'd get the bus home; she'd go to Guides.

'So, not a coffee or tea drinker, then?' She looks up from the table, where she's marking homework. It's gone eleven but I'm sitting on the floor with an orange juice and a croissant, browsing through her records, scanning lyrics and sleeve notes.

'Nope.'

'Why's that, then?' she persists.

'Because ... I don't know. Just don't. Mum and Dad have coffee, and my sister likes tea.'

'Right, good to know.' She frowns, clicks her pen and takes another book from the pile.

Half an hour passes and the stack in front of her isn't going down fast. Meanwhile, I've exhausted my trawl through her record collection and wander over to the windows.

'Joe! Get back from the window.'

'Fuck, sorry, sorry. I forgot.'

'I can't afford for you to be seen. How many times do I—'

'Yeah, I get it,' I answer, creeping back to the records and replacing them on the bookcase.

I pull out a chair at the end of the table and sit quietly for a few minutes. On best behaviour.

'You wear glasses,' I observe, out loud. She shifts in her chair but continues to tick and cross and annotate, until she comes to the end of a page.

'Only when I can't be bothered to wear my contact lenses.'

She reaches for another sheet of homework, her lips slightly pursed. 'Sorry, I need to get on.'

'Can I help?' I chirp, serving up my widest smile, and tilting my head to my shoulder. She peers over her glasses, breathes out in mock exasperation, and sits back.

'I give up!' she laughs, throwing her hands in the air.

'Seriously. Want me to do some marking?'

'Give me strength,' she growls under her breath. 'That's really thoughtful. Maybe another time. I've got a better idea. How about we make a plan for the rest of the bank holiday weekend?'

'A plan? Ooh ... That. Sounds. So. Interesting ...' I nod my head and start snoring.

'Or you could go home, and I'll see you in class on Tuesday?' She folds her arms. 'Look, I know this is dull, but if I get all these marked today, we could do something fun together tomorrow.'

'Go somewhere?' I ask, sitting up straight now. 'Like, out of the flat?'

She lowers her head. 'It's too dangerous.' Then, seeing my disappointment, says, 'Unless ...'

'Unless?' I lean forward, wide-eyed.

'I suppose we could drive out, go for a walk in the country. We'd need to drive quite far.'

'Oh my God, that would be wicked! Let's do it,' I shout, propelling myself to my feet and into some impromptu body popping.

18

MAY 1992

With the prospect of a trip to the countryside like a real couple, I get out of Miss P's voluminous hair for the rest of the day. I should do some work as well; I need to finish *Sons and Lovers* and get started on *Great Expectations*.

The plan is to meet the following morning, but not at her flat. She will set off on her own, while I take the train east, where she'll be waiting in a station car park. She suggests I wear a jacket with a hood or a hat, just in case. Good and thorough plan, I have to agree.

I'm buzzing as I steal out of her flat and take a circuitous route of lefts and rights to thread my way back. At her suggestion, I mix things up so it's not my usual way home, but I must have got my bearings wrong. Unwittingly, I've drifted towards school grounds and, before I can change tack, I come face to face with a pack of my year group. There's nowhere to hide.

'Hello, who's this?' cries an unmistakeable voice at the head of the tribe.

'Hi, Nick, hi, lads, girls,' I nod, thrusting my hands in my pockets to look nonchalant and not like I've just come from a night shagging our teacher. Nick seems genuinely pleased to see me, throws an arm around my shoulder, and I'm absorbed into the moving, humming mass.

'Hope you don't have plans, dude,' he says in a conspiratorial tone. 'Because you're coming with us.'

'Where are we going?' I ask, with a quick glance at my watch. 'Because I do have some reading and exam revision.'

'Of course you do – sucking up to Miss P, are you?' he jokes. 'Or Dr Burbidge?' He elbows me in the ribs. 'Either way, it can wait. This is our last weekend of freedom before a shitstorm of mock exams, and we are having drinks, my friend. Right, gang?' he calls out.

A chorus of agreement sounds, and one, 'Stop saying gang, you tit.'

A couple of beers won't hurt. And it will be nice to spend some time with my friends, I figure, as we pile around a long table in The Crown.

It's gone 2 a.m. when I stagger down the hill, fumble my way into the house and crawl up the stairs into the top-floor bathroom. I lean my head against the toilet seat, to draw breath and prepare to puke. I wake, half an hour later, have to peel my face off the plastic and my body off the floor. Eventually, I find my bed and the world goes dark.

19

MAY 1992

'What in God's name happened to you?' Her voice rises. I scrunch my eyes tight as I reach for the seatbelt. I was congratulating myself on even hearing the alarm this morning, let alone remembering how clothes go on and making the train on time.

'You reek of alcohol and cigarettes. Where did you go?' Voice still rising.

'We went out, pub, for a couple of beers . . .' I mumble.

'A couple? And who's "we"?' she snaps, not waiting for my answer to her first question. Probably best not to say anything, as my memory is sketchy. Instead of driving out of the station car park, she sits in angry silence, waiting for a reply. My head thumps as the events of the previous night slide into dim but unforgiving focus.

After The Crown, I did at least try to make a break, but they weren't having any of it. My attendance at The Bell was, apparently, compulsory. Only after falling out of the King's Head (it was dark by now) did it occur to anyone that some food might be required. A round of burgers later, and we were back at The Crown where our numbers were bolstered by more friends from our year. Everything's a bit hazy after that.

'Oh, you know.'

'No. I don't.'

'Well, Nick, obviously. Ant, Tom, Chris . . .'

'And?' She is scowling, and I'm beginning to sweat hot prickly beads on my head and neck. 'It wasn't just boys, was it?'

'Yes, no, I mean, of course there were some girls as well.' And I start relaying their names. 'Lottie, Emmy, other Lottie, Becky, Sophie, Dawn, Lara, Katie. There may have been some others.'

'Oh, well, that's nice, isn't it? Had fun, did you? Had lots of fun with Lottie and Lara and Katie and Becky and SOME OTHERS!' She hammers her fists on the steering wheel.

'It was just a group of us, Miss,' I say, rubbing the damp from the back of my neck.

'Don't. Call. Me. Miss,' she snarls through gritted teeth.

'Sorry. I'm sorry. I didn't do anything,' I plead, knowing how pathetic I sound. What am I supposed to say? I'm completely thrown by her outburst. I know turning up hungover wasn't my best move, but I didn't think she'd react like this and be mad at me for spending time with people in my year group, girls or boys. I opt for saying nothing.

For a long time, we just sit there, side by side and miles apart in the cramped, airless car.

'Promise me.' She turns to me with sad eyes.

'Yes, anything – absolutely anything.'

'Promise me you won't do that again.'

I nod, solemnly, though I'm not clear what it is I'm promising her. She can hardly expect me to avoid everyone at school.

My brain whirrs. Perhaps she just means don't get smashed off your face the night before we go on a lunch date. It must be that. Either way, I'm still nodding as she turns the key in the ignition. Agreeing with her, anything to calm her down, seems like the right thing to do.

She seems less cross twenty minutes later as we drive along a ridge and down another hill, a vertiginous sweep of sharp turns and panoramic views of green. It's breath-taking, but I'm only half concentrating. I'm happy that she's not sad. And that I could make it better by doing what she asked. But a promise is a big thing. I remember my gran saying that. But I don't want to upset her again – she means everything to me. I guess this is one of those times when it's right to make a promise.

'Here we are,' she says, decisively and with a long exhale that leaves the morning behind. We've arrived at midday in a little village, tucked under a hill, a clutch of pretty stone cottages and narrow lanes. It's the middle of nowhere. Miss P pulls into a pub car park, and immediately brightens.

'The Plough.' She reads the sign on the yellow stone wall of the ancient three-storey building. 'God, I haven't been here in years.' She points out some of the pub's architectural features, and I crane my neck to take in the mullioned windows and high gables through the windscreen. I nod along to the history lesson, but she loses me at quoins.

We're going to risk a pub lunch. She's pretty sure we won't be seen so far from school and it's warm enough to sit in the beer garden, which is empty. She insists I stay in the car while she checks the taproom and bar for hazards. A few seconds later, she appears with a beaming thumbs up.

'Now then, it's summer term; I'm having a Pimm's. Shall I get two, or are you still 100 per cent proof?'

Grateful for the improvement in her mood, I answer with an enthusiastic nod.

'I'll be down there.' I point to the tables and umbrellas as she disappears inside.

We wolf down sausage and chips and two more Pimm's before the regulars and bank holiday tourists emerge. It's our cue to slide away, but not back home yet; she wants to show me somewhere. I follow her down the village lanes; *best not hold hands*. We reach a stile at the edge of a wide meadow. We climb over and take a sloping path that cuts a narrow walkers' line between high, unmown grasses and wildflowers. I peel off my jumper and tie it round my waist. The sun, warming our bare arms, sharpens every sense. Miss P, ahead of me, is appropriately dressed in one of her long skirts and a white, frilly off-the-shoulder shirt. I'm probably killing the vibe in my electric blue, Carter *Love* album T-shirt, but hey.

We reach the far side, where the field lifts and lowers us to a meandering brook, sheltered under a stand of mature full-leafed trees. Beech, I recognize, but that's almost the limit of my knowledge. There's a weeping willow (limit reached) further down the bank, and now she takes my hand, looks at me for a moment with a hint of a question (it's the T-shirt I reckon), then leads me to the willow.

Its thin overhanging branches brush the ground surrounding our hiding place, camouflaging our kissing. Still, we can't help peering through the cascading fronds every time a twig snaps or a dog barks upstream. I bet our lovemaking looks natural, sensual and professional, in slow motion. In reality, it's a rushed, self-conscious, grass-stained grope. But who cares – I just had outdoor sex with Miss P while my mates are where? At home with their families, watching TV, not having sex with their teachers. Losers.

20

May 1992

A downside to the school's academic push in the summer term is that the Tuesday afternoon Language Room sessions are now compulsory attendance for all Oxbridge candidates. All except those *elite pupils* who are required for first-team cricket (boys) or tennis (girls). I am neither. The net effect is to reduce the Language Room cohort by zero, proving once and for all that there is no correlation between elite language scholars and sporting prowess. Although, it would be a push to label me an elite language scholar.

Turns out, however, that the school's sole Oxbridge languages candidate this year, is me. And so it is that I stand alone, outside the Language Room waiting for the Head of Oxbridge Entrance while watching my year group run around in the spring sunshine.

'There you are, Gibbon,' balls Dr Burbidge waddling along the cloister. I raise my hand and wait the thirty seconds it takes for him to cover the few metres between us. He places his hands on my shoulders, more for support than anything more meaningful, I suspect.

'Good afternoon, sir. It's Gibson, actually,' I say, cheerily.

He fixes me with what I know are piercing blue eyes, but which in this moment are cloudy dots behind steamed-up spectacles. He chases his breath.

'The school's fortunes,' he exhales, 'indeed, the fortunes and expectations of our esteemed Language faculty, rest on these youthful shoulders,' he says, while massaging and squeezing said shoulders.

I freeze. 'Thank you, sir, I will do my best.'

'I'm afraid that won't be good enough, Gibbs,' he breathes in my face.

'Gibson, sir. My grades aren't bad and I'm reading fairly widely,' I say, defensively, pulling my head out of the way when his spit catches the side of my mouth. I'm desperate to wipe it off, but my arms are pinned to my sides.

'Still,' he grumbles, 'I'm taking no chances. You are our only hope of a place this year, so I have made some … arrangements.' He lifts his hands off and opens the Language Room door, beckoning me to follow. He plumps down heavily in a chair that can barely take his weight. He stares at me again, appalled, it seems.

'Arrangements, sir?' I prompt.

'Shut up and listen, Gibbings. That attitude will never do for Oxford.' He removes his spectacles, shaking his head as he smears the glass with a stained handkerchief. 'I have arranged for you to meet one of my former boys, Ralph Leadsbetter.' He sings the name. 'He's in second year reading French and German at Teddy Hall. He's a good egg and, what's more, he's a Blue. You will learn a lot from Ralph.'

'Gosh, thank you, sir. It's very kind of you to help me.' I muster some feeling.

'I'm not helping you, Gibbon. This is for the school, for reputation.' He coughs and something solid lands on the floor between us. I think I'm going to be sick. 'Ralph will give you a good priming, exam hints, interview technique and so forth. So, make sure to take notes.'

He hauls himself out of the chair which doesn't want to detach, then clatters to the hardwood floor as he straightens up.

'Aren't you coming with me, sir? To the meeting with, um?'

'Leadsbetter, dear Ralph. No, sadly, but one of the other masters will escort you.' We're outside again and he's locking up and shuffling off, when he calls out, 'And it's this Thursday. It's all arranged. Be in Lower Quad car park by First Bell.'

This Thursday. Shit. Thursday is Miss P's first sketching afternoon, and I'll miss it. Worse, I've only got English and German lessons before Thursday, and my evenings are fully booked with *Hamlet* rehearsals. I won't even see her to explain. Fuck Leadsbetter. Fuck Teddy Hall. Fuck Oxford. Fuck.

21

MAY 1992

It's the usual scrum outside chapel on Thursday morning and the main quad outside fills and funnels pupils and teachers through the doors. I'm standing back, avoiding the crush. I can't afford to get my suit ripped today of all days; what would Leadsbetter say? My second motive for waiting is the off-chance Miss P is coming to assembly. I still haven't seen her to explain why I won't be at her sketching activity this afternoon.

'One day, there will be a fire,' muses a voice behind me. 'That should clear some dead wood.'

I turn to find Mr Siddel leaning casually against one of the pillars in the quad.

'Sir!' I exclaim, truly shocked. 'You can't be serious.'

'*Warum nicht?*' He strokes his moustache with thumb and forefinger. Pushing off from the stone, he sidles over to join me. 'Hear you're our man in Oxford today. A New Hope!' He smirks, his moustache stretching across his curled upper lip.

'I suppose so,' I begin, but stop short when I see Miss P emerging into the quad. She shines, resplendent in her academic gown. Moving purposefully in the direction of the chapel, she doesn't see me on the other side of the square courtyard. I want to wave and get her attention.

'Stop salivating, Gibson. Way out of your league, boy,' sneers Mr Siddel. I can feel my cheeks reddening and look down at my newly polished shoes. I open my mouth again, but nothing comes out. '*Urkomisch!*' he laughs. 'Hilarious. Every year, there's always one.'

What do you mean, there's always one? I want to ask, but he's off, chuckling, into the cloister. The chapel bell announces the start of assembly and I have to run before they lock the door. I make it to my house's pew as the organ music reaches its climax, the final chord booming into the vast Gothic crown above. I scan the opposite rows for Miss P's trademark curls. Not that I can do anything from here. Still, if I could even catch her eye, make some reassuring face, then I wouldn't be letting her down. But it's like she's disappeared.

I fetch my satchel after chapel and am being read the rules of what's expected of me by my tutor, Mr Batsford, when First Bell rings out across the school. *Ambassador . . . wear the tie with honour . . . Oxford . . . reputation . . . hope . . .* 'Remember, Leadsbetter is a Blue!' he yells after me, as I make my excuses and run to the car park. What the fuck is a Blue?

There's no one waiting for me by the gate. The hive of activity as everyone makes their way to classrooms subsides. Still no sign of my lift. I'm wondering if I should check in the staffroom when a horn startles the quiet. At the end of a line of parked cars on the road, someone is waving. My lift. I run. A grin expands with every galloping step.

'I can't believe it!' The blue Fiesta's engine is already

running, indicator flashing. I throw my satchel in the back and jump in. 'It's you!'

'Yes, now, wait! Hands in your lap – no touching!' She pushes me off with a mischievous smile, checks her mirrors and pulls out. 'God, you're like a Labrador puppy. Sit still – we're still in full sight of the school. We must look every bit the picture of teacher–pupil professionalism, Gibson,' she adds, to make her point.

I restrain myself, until we're clear of the school campus and accelerating along the edge of the Common. 'Miss – I mean, Ali – can you stop the car, please?'

'Why?'

'I need to kiss you.'

'No,' she fumes in mock exasperation. 'And I think you probably *should* call me Miss today. You know, get into role. We can't afford any slips.'

I sink into my seat with an exaggerated sigh. But she's right, of course, and I'm just thrilled that we have the whole day ahead of us. Legitimately.

She decides not to risk the motorway, though it's the most direct route, anxious that the Fiesta might let us down. On the way, she tells me how she found out about the trip when a note calling for a 'volunteer' was pinned to the noticeboard in the staffroom: 'Take Gibson to Oxford and back'. Clear and succinct, but no takers, until Miss P offered. She wondered whether there might be some objection on the grounds of unmarried female member of staff escorting Lower Sixth boy. She even double-checked with my housemaster, the Head of Department and the Head of Oxbridge Entrance, none of whom raised an eyebrow.

'That only left me needing to cancel the term's first sketching activity, find cover for my lessons and pack that bag,' she says, inclining her head to the footwell in front of me. 'Open it.'

I reach down and unzip the large carpet bag.

'It's exercise books,' I say.

'Yes, I've got some marking to do while you're with golden balls Leadsbetter. But keep digging.' Her smile broadens.

'Aha! Miss, what is it with you and this drink?' I sit back, a large bottle of Pimm's in one hand, lemonade in the other.

'It's good to be prepared,' she says, changing up a gear as the road stretches out ahead.

'Nice plan, Miss. Although I'm not sure how long I'll be with Leadsbetter.' I'm trying not to dampen the mood, but it's true. 'Depends what time we finish, I suppose.'

'Wow. Don't sound *too* keen!'

'Of course I want to. You know I do.'

'Good. Because you never know,' she purrs. 'We might find some time on our own.' She nods at the bag again. 'There's an extra-large punnet of strawberries in there, too!'

'Great.'

22

MAY 1992

Ralph Leadsbetter turns out to be normal. I'm kind of disappointed, having conjured an image of a pompous twit. I was looking forward, sort of, to being greeted by a clown in mustard cords, sports jacket and cravat. Someone I could have a laugh telling Nick and the lads about. In the event, he seems bemused by his old school, to which he's never returned for alumni gatherings and has no intention of doing so.

We spend an hour chatting in his 'rooms'. He shares his experiences of Oxford; he's a choral scholar as well. He gives me a few tips, things to impress the professors with at interview. It's refreshing, and I'm grateful that he doesn't want to hark back to his school days, until it's almost time for me to leave.

'Your teachers – they're all mad,' he says, as if it's a simple matter of fact.

'Agreed,' I say.

'Although, I suspect those teachers we perceive as being eccentric, dodgy even, will in fact turn out to be the most sane and misunderstood. And vice versa.' He looks puzzled for a second, then jumps up to open his study window. 'It's all nonsense, really. My advice, work hard, then get the hell out of there. And if you come up to Oxford, look me up.'

He walks me back to the porter's lodge and shakes my hand. I quite like his life, I think, as I walk away to meet Miss P for lunch.

'How did that go? How's Ralph?' asks Miss P, when I join her in the Vaults café in the centre of town.

'Yeah, interesting. Nice guy.'

'Waste of time if you ask me,' she sniffs. 'Nothing I couldn't have told you.'

'Really?' I ask, reaching for a second bread roll to mop up some salad dressing.

'Of course. I did go to Oxford, you know.' She lifts her hair back from her face with both hands, ties it up in a giant scrunchie.

'Did you?' I'm surprised. 'I thought you went to—'

'As a post-grad, yes. It's hot, aren't you hot in that suit? I'm hot. Let's get out of here.'

The car is parked outside St John's College, a ten-minute walk through the centre of town.

'I've got an idea,' she says, scrabbling in her bag for the car keys.

'Can it involve a cold drink, please?' I say, unknotting my tie and shaking my arms free of my jacket. 'You were right about this suit. I'm baking.'

'It most certainly can, but we'll need ice, and I know where we can get some.'

A few minutes later, we're bumping along a pot-holed lane

in leafy north Oxford, at the end of which is the Cherwell Boathouse.

'We're going punting?' I ask, excitedly. I haven't done this for years.

'Yes! It's a beautiful day, the river will be quiet without weekend tourists and the students still in lectures. We might have it all to ourselves.' She winks.

She blags some ice in a glass from the man in the kiosk while I collect the pole, paddle and seat cushions for the boat. I want to contribute but I only have £5 on me, all that's left of my £20 monthly allowance from Mum. Miss P says that's fine, though I am feeling awkward about not paying for stuff.

'That's *two* things you owe me.' She grins, taking my hand and stepping into the punt. I swallow. Does she expect me to repay my blow-job debt today?

We moor up in some trees hanging over the river. We've been punting for about twenty minutes when she suggests a break and pours two large plastic cups of Pimm's and lemonade over ice. Patterns of leaves form and dissolve on the shallow, dappled water. We're on a top-up, sitting at opposite ends of the low, flat-bottomed boat. She fixes me with her round eyes, placing her feet to the edges of the punt, bends her knees and draws them up towards her chest. I don't want to look away, but I glance quickly, up and down the river, to check we're alone. The punt wobbles for a second, then settles when I return my gaze to Miss P. She's watching me, expressionless, and slowly moves her knees apart to reveal the tops of her legs. The air closes in and the only sound is my breath, heavy with each inhale and exhale. She's wearing the silk knickers from that afternoon, our first time. They are edged with lace, not fitted, kind of loose.

'Do you know what they're called?' she asks.

I shake my head, wishing I was wearing something less constraining.

'French knickers.' She spreads her legs a fraction wider. Not porn wide, more tasteful, like art. Everything is white – skin and silk – although when my eyes adjust, I see the material at the very centre is a shade darker. And that's when I dive, grab the horizontal treading boards under her knees, and bury my face between her thighs. I'm going to push my tongue into her, where I think it's supposed to go, when her hands yank my head up.

'Not here!' she squeals.

I jump back. Her knees snap together and her skirt folds over them.

'Sorry, I thought . . . it's what you wanted.'

'I do, I do!' She leans forward and takes my hand in both of hers, making mine seem smaller. 'Not out here, though. Not like that.' She picks up her cup, takes a sip and licks her lips. 'Later, I'll show you.'

I pick up my Pimm's and down it. 'We should get back, then,' I say, finding my voice, trying to look in control.

But by the time we return from Oxford, after almost three hours on the road, it's too late for anything. She's tired, hot and stressed, she says. Her code, I guess right, for wanting to drop me off. And it's a whole week later before I get to be with her again.

23

June 1992

With mock exams looming, the days unfold with monotonous repetition. The pattern of each lesson is the same in every subject – the teachers setting us hour after hour of class revision, in silence – and it's dull as fuck.

Some are beginning to feel the pressure and showing signs of panic, especially those who don't have an elite sport for distraction. Fortunately, I have two outlets for relieving the tension: the prospect of the rescheduled Thursday afternoon sketching activity, and *Hamlet*. It seems mad to be staging the play in such a busy term, but it's supposed to offer everyone a bit of light relief before the mid-term break and the final push of exams in June. I'm not sure who thought murder, madness and revenge would be light relief, but I throw myself into the role of the raving Prince of Denmark.

'Should we be concerned about this part you're playing?' Miss P asks.

Thursday afternoon has come at last and we're driving out to our first sketching location. The windows are down and Miss P's got the cold fan on full blast. It's another day of high temperatures – apparently the warmest June in a century – but that's not the only reason for the fans. We're not alone. Despite praying that everyone else who signed up would drop out, only one has. The other two – Graham and Anne – are squeezed into what passes as rear seats in the Fiesta. The rear windows are non-opening, and both are pressed as far forward as their leg room will allow, holding the front seat headrests, faces straining to catch the air stream.

'Frankly, yes.' I've been telling them about the production and the weird turn rehearsals have taken. The whole cast is agreed that the director, another boy from our year, is pushing the boundaries a bit far.

'What do you mean?' shouts Anne over the howl of the engine as Miss P urges the overloaded car up a hill.

'It means,' booms Graham, 'that Brad Pitt here – NOT – is going to strip off in the batshit crazy scenes.'

'Oh, my word!' cries Anne. 'Miss, did you hear that, Miss?'

Miss P responds with a crunching gear change and the road levels out.

'We all heard him, Anne,' I say, swivelling round. I glare at Graham. He's a stocky thug destined for a career in the army and there's only one reason he could possibly have for signing up for sketching: to impress Miss P. 'Obviously, that's not going to happen. I'd be expelled, for one thing.'

'Not to mention making everyone physically sick, right, Miss?' he roars, delighted with himself.

'Nudity can be effective and has its place,' she says, thoughtfully, slowing down as we come to a junction. 'But leaving some things to the imagination is more powerful. On stage, I mean. I don't recall Hamlet needing to be naked, so, on balance, I think you should keep your pants on,' she says, emphasizing the last four words, turning her head to face me.

I'm still looking at Graham and Anne. She is staring at the back of Miss P's head, open-mouthed. It's all too much for Graham, whose face is burning red.

'You might want to breathe, Graham,' I say, then to Miss P, 'How far, Miss?'

'Nearly there. Just a couple of miles.'

'Where are we going, Miss?' asks Anne. 'It's very pretty out here.'

The road becomes narrower and familiar. I haven't been following the route, but now I see where we are and clamp my mouth shut.

'I thought you'd like it, Anne. A beautiful spot for sketching nature. We'll park by the pub and walk down the hill. There's a stream we can sit by, and I've brought some strawberries and lemonade.'

'Gosh, Miss, that's so kind. It's the perfect day for strawberries!' enthuses Anne, who I half expect to clasp her hands together, shrilling 'and lashings of cream' at any moment.

'Awesome,' mutters Graham.

'Yay, strawberries,' I lie. The afternoon is going to be a disaster.

From the moment we retrace the steps we took through the meadow and as Miss P starts laying out the sketching materials in the shade of the weeping willow, spells are being broken all around me. Why did she have to bring them here?

'What's the matter?' she asks, when Anne and Graham are out of earshot.

119

'Nothing,' I say, not hiding my disappointment.

'I thought you liked it here.'

'I do, but not with them. This is our place.' My voice rises.

'Sshhh! They'll hear you.'

'Who cares?' I snap.

'Don't be childish,' she swipes. 'Anyway, what makes you think I haven't been here before? Before you.' She shoots a defiant glance, then takes a pad of paper from her bag and holds it out to me. 'Here, draw something.'

I snatch it from her and stumble to my feet. The damp heat rises with me. I want to hurl the pad into the stream and snap the pencils and stamp the fucking strawberries into the earth. On the other side of the bank, I glimpse Anne. She couldn't have heard us, but she definitely senses something. She pauses, her hand gripping the pencil in mid-air, head on one side. My eyes are stinging. I'm suffocating under these trees. *I hate this place*, I want to shout. I take my pad and walk away, with more than one pair of eyes boring into me.

Aimlessly, I wander about, killing time. Eventually, I find Graham lying on his back on a small wooden bridge. He's almost overlapping each end. He's smoking, in broad daylight, his sketching pad and blazer untouched and discarded in the long grass. Even here, at the bottom of the valley, canopied by trees that stretch out of sight in either direction, the grass is dry. There's been no rain for weeks. He shuffles back, lifts his bulk onto his elbows.

'Watch this,' he says, taking a long drag and blowing smoke rings that hover and hold their shape. There's no breeze, not even a wisp. At my end of the bridge is a horizontal metal bar, perhaps to stop sheep crossing. I balance on it, resting my arms on my knees.

'Cool,' I admit. I've never been able to blow rings.

'I bet she's well up for it,' he says, but not in his normal voice. For some reason he adopts a strange hybrid Cockney accent. I don't reply straight away. Obviously, I want to kick him into the water, jump down and hold his fat, jug-eared head under. But as he's the prop for the 2nd XV, it could backfire.

'Who? Anne? I don't think so.' I try a diversion.

'You know who I mean, dickwad.'

My teeth grind in my mouth, but I have to be careful. What is it she says? *Don't attract attention.* I lean down and pick a blade of grass from a high clump beside the bridge, run my finger along its flat edge.

'Oh right, Miss P. No, I think she's got a boyfriend,' I say, keeping calm.

Graham sits up, cross-legged, facing me. The muscles in his legs tighten and stretch the thin material of his school trousers. He takes another drag. He's holding the cigarette between his sausage-sized thumb and forefinger, pointed inward to his palm.

'Don't be a tool, Gibson.' He's sounding like a trader on *EastEnders*. Ridiculous, since I know his parents are lawyers from Godalming.

'Why are you speaking like that? You're not Phil Mitchell.'

He ignores me. 'She shagged an Upper Sixth boy last year on a school trip. Fact.'

I'm on my feet before he's finished. 'Shut the fuck up, you lying fuck!'

'Ooooh! Look who's jealous,' he sneers, but doesn't move.

My nails are digging into my palms. 'What are you going to do about it?' He pushes his tongue into his cheek and mimes blow-jobbing with his hand.

'Boys!' a voice calls, and seconds later Miss P and Anne appear on the far side, downstream. 'There you are. It's gone four; time to go.'

Graham chucks his cigarette butt, which floats in the current beneath us and is gone.

24

JUNE 1992

On the drive back to school, Anne sits up front and barely takes a breath, outlining a painstakingly detailed life map of where and what she is going to study after school. It's exhausting, so I sit back, behind Miss P's seat, and half study the landscape, half replay those minutes on the bridge and the moves I should have made to teach Graham a lesson he wouldn't forget. The troll, meanwhile, is dozing, his tongue lolling at the corner of his ugly mouth, irritatingly close to my shoulder. Every now and then I catch Ali's eyes in the rear-view mirror. I can't tell if she's looking at me or checking the traffic. I try to look kind and sorry.

She drops Graham at his boarding house first, then Anne.

'I'm sorry,' she says in the mirror as soon as Anne's gone. Her cheeks are pink. 'I thought it would work, but it didn't. And I'm sorry for what I said.'

She pulls away from the kerb and indicates to turn left at the junction, back to the staff car park. She drives slowly and I tell her about what happened at the bridge, with Graham.

'Jesus, this place and its wretched rumour mill,' she hisses.

'I know. I could have killed him, the shit.'

Then she laughs and the anger in the car evaporates.

'You defended my honour, sir.' She adjusts her mirror so I can see her smile, and her eyes, sparkling. The car accelerates.

'Ali, you've gone past the gate.' I'm unseated as she speeds up.

'Get down, quick, so you're not seen,' she says.

She drives for two or three minutes, taking a series of fast rights and lefts that leave me completely disorientated, and a bit sick, bouncing around on the back seat.

'Okay, should be clear here. Out you get,' she says, pulling over.

'Where are we?' I peer tentatively out of the rear window. It's a typical street of large Victorian semis, but I can't figure out which. She tells me the name and I recognize it from one of my routes to her flat.

'Meet me at my place in fifteen minutes. No, ten. Just give me time to get in. Hurry, and don't be seen,' she says. 'Oh, and ring the bell three times, quickly.'

'Why?'

'It can be our secret ring.' She winks, and I set off, like a knight, on foot.

I walk the first few streets, enjoying the heady scent of summer flowers from the pretty gardens. Then, checking my watch, I run. It's half past five, the sun is still high and hot. By the time I arrive, I'm dripping. I do the secret ring and the door clicks open. There's no sign of her in the sitting room, kitchen or bathroom. I throw off my blazer, undo my tie, untuck my shirt.

I find her in the bedroom, lying on the bed sheet, the duvet in a heap on the floor.

'You're naked,' I say, from the doorway.

'You're overdressed,' she replies.

'I need a wash. It's boiling out there and I ran the last bit,' I explain, unbuttoning my shirt and dropping it on the carpet.

'No,' she says firmly. 'Take off your shoes and socks.'

I do it, but I feel self-conscious. I had a shower before school, but that's hours ago.

'Now, trousers.'

'Okay, but ...' I shake my head and exhale through my cheeks. I'm standing in my pants. My buttocks are damp with sweat. I'm hard. I adjust myself.

'Come here.' She swings her legs off the bed, planting her feet wide and holding out both arms.

'Look, you are sexy, but I am going to the bathroom, I need—' She doesn't let me finish, grabbing my hips with force and kissing me as she pulls me down on top of her.

25

JUNE 1992

Two days later, the skies burst open in a violent storm. The parched city swells, the exhausted gardens weep for joy, the people take to the streets, greedily soaking up the summer rains. I catch a train home, in a state, not helped by my Walkman running out of battery before The Charlatans have even got through the intro to 'Weirdo'. It's only for the half-term break, but it may as well be the end of days.

In the week that follows, mornings are spent revising for exams, afternoons helping Mum pack up the house. At the end of the week, the removal lorry will come and move us to our new home. Apparently, there are two bedrooms upstairs, for Mum and Rose (although she's at university most of the time), and a bedroom downstairs for me. From the top floor of one house to the bottom of another; but that's not what preoccupies me.

Freedom is over. How will I ever get to see, let alone stay with, Ali?

By the weekend, we're unpacking our old life on the other side of the country. 'A new start for you and me,' proclaims Mum, tearfully. I can't imagine how she's feeling, though losing your home and your husband and leaving your parents, work colleagues and friends – that's got to be tough. Thing is, I've already had 'a new start' and I wasn't looking for another one. I love Mum, obviously, but I'd got used to living without her, having my independence. Now she's going to be breathing down my neck, asking me where I'm going, checking up on me.

But when school returns, Ali's got an idea. On the first Thursday afternoon, she organizes the sketching activity at the cathedral. As it's in town, the others don't have to be accompanied back to school, which means Ali and I can slip away without suspicion.

Everyone's set up with pads and pencils in different parts of the cathedral. Another clever move. Ali walks around, checking on each of us. Anne and another girl, Sophie, take the choir stalls. They are both keen, giggly and annoyingly competent at art. Elsewhere, there's a revelation in progress. Graham, it turns out, really knows which end of the pencil does what. Standing at the head of the nave, he's producing an intricate study of a huge rose window high above the west door. I have a good view of him – and the shower of praise Ali is heaping on him – from my uncomfortable perch in the north transept, where my attempts at drawing a pulpit are not going well.

'That's . . . what's that?' Miss P squints down at my sketch.

'Oh, come on, Miss, I know it's crap, but it's not unrecognizable.'

'It's very . . . is it abstract?' She stifles a laugh. 'Aha, it's the pulpit!'

'Of course it's the bloody pulpit. What did you think it was?'

'I ... it's ... nice.' She pulls up a chair and reaches for a pencil. Leaning over, she offers some practical tips with a few deft strokes across the paper.

'You know you're wasting your time, don't you?' I ask. 'I'm not actually here to sketch.'

'How are you going to get to school and back, every day?' She lowers her voice, changing the subject but continuing the demonstration.

I explain that on some days I can catch a lift with a neighbour who works at the university, but that mostly I'll be getting the train.

She says, 'This is a busy term of exams, and travelling in and out every single day is, frankly, irresponsible. Plus, you've got Chapel Choir on Sundays. I mean, it's too much.'

'Tell me about it,' I sigh and lean back, arms folded, stretching my legs, letting her take over the drawing. 'Have you got any ideas?'

'Well, yes, actually. Why don't you put a case to your mother for staying the odd night, maybe two, every week?'

'Seriously? She's hardly going to agree to that. "Mum, you don't mind if I stay at my teacher's flat, do you? No, it's a she. No, she's not married ..."' I trail off.

'Are you being deliberately thick?' She shakes her head and returns to the pad, her lines harder and darker with each move of her hand. 'I'm trying to do this for *us*, otherwise when will we see each other? I'm suggesting you arrange to stay with a friend near school. What about Nick?'

I stare at the pulpit materializing on the page and don't say anything for a while. It could work. They always have friends staying, Nick and his brothers, and I get on well with his parents. They've got tons of room. Probably wouldn't notice if I was there or not.

'I suppose, sometimes I could actually stay at his house,' I say slowly, working it out. 'And then, most nights I could come to you ... at least once a week?'

'Exactly. It could be a regular thing. You said your mother doesn't know Nick and his family, and she's really busy, so perhaps she wouldn't check up on you – especially if your academic work isn't suffering. You'd have to be a bit vague with Nick – plans change, you have to get home ...'

'The perfect crime,' I say in my best Chicago gangster voice.

'Don't say that,' she says firmly, sitting up and surveying the picture before handing it back to me. 'There, I seem to have done it all for you.'

'Impressive. You really know what you're doing, Miss.'

We put the plan to bed early that evening, over chicken-in-a-basket at a pub far from anywhere and, more importantly, anyone we might know. Another one of her haunts from long ago. Then she drops me off at the train station, as if I'd made the journey from school. I walk home for a second supper with Mum and present the carefully scripted plan.

The next day, I talk to Nick, and by the weekend it's all arranged.

26

JUNE 1992

The days are long, dry, with a heat I've never known for June. It envelops the school. Blazers are discarded, shirt sleeves rolled up, ties loosened. As exams are ticked off and revision books are shelved, the pace of school life slows to the metro-nomic soundtrack of bat on ball, oar on water, and sneezing, thanks to an excessive pollen count. But this is not my life.

Life for me is a list of lies: what I'm doing; who needs to know what; where I need to be next. I have to stick to Miss P's script and strategy. The sex is amazing, thank God. I just wish that what it took to get to her bed wasn't such a hassle.

Keeping all the balls in the air at school is a constant head-fuck, and now Mum's nearby, she's beginning to take more of an interest in my activities, especially outside school. I panic that she's going to want to meet Nick's parents and that both parties – including Nick – are going to discover the truth about where I stay each week when I'm not at home. I can see a car crash up ahead at the end-of-year music scholars' concert, which Nick's dad, as a school governor, is bound to attend. Worse still, Ali has said she will be there too, since she's never heard me sing and I'm supposed to have this voice that's going to get me a scholarship to Oxford. I need to put her off, and Mum, and, ideally, any of Nick's family.

The only person I don't have to worry about is Nick himself, since he'll have finished all his exams by then and has permission to go to Glastonbury. That's another plan messing with my head. There are two of us performing at the end-of-year concert, me and Ant. He's got a car, so the idea is that we'll do the long drive down to Glastonbury together after the concert and hook up with the others for the weekend. We haven't got tickets, but Nick says it's easy to get in; just jump the fence, everyone does it. It means I'll miss Carter and Ozric Tentacles on Friday, but I'll get to see The Shamen, Ned's Atomic Dustbin, PJ Harvey, and Ant says a band called Blur might be good.

By Thursday, everyone is buzzing for the weekend. I loaf about, sweating in the heat and with the stress. If matters couldn't get any worse, there's a loose end I've completely missed, which catches up with me in the afternoon.

'You're going to Glastonbury, and you didn't think to tell me?'

It's true. I'd forgotten to tell Ali. In my defence, we haven't spent a weekend together for a while since our mid-weeknights have become our routine.

'Well, it's a weekend with my mates. I never get to do that,' I reply.

'You never spend a weekend with me either. You're always with your mum.'

'I'm at home – that's where I live,' I explain. 'And this weekend, it's really the last time I'll get to hang out with everyone before the summer. Then it's the holidays, and you and I can work something out, see each other much more, can't we?'

'So, who are you planning to go to Glastonbury with?' she asks, putting me on the spot. But I've been here before, so I say ... nothing. I shrug instead and she storms off to the staffroom, where I can't follow.

When I return home that evening, there's good news. Over dinner, Mum is full of talk about work, which I don't understand and instantly forget. I tune back in when she says she's been invited to a work summer party; it's tomorrow night; it's all very exciting. My heart lifts, but I know I have to remind her that I'm going to be away this weekend ... after the concert on Friday. She goes quiet and busies herself with a pan on the hob. I can see I've thrown a spanner in the works, so I help her out.

'It's fine about tomorrow, Mum. In fact, the concert's not really a thing, to be honest. Small.'

'Oh, are you sure, sweetie?' she says, not putting up much of a fight. 'Okay, I'll definitely be at the next one. You know how I love to hear you sing.'

After dinner, I disappear to my room. I sit on the end of my bed for ages, thinking. I've been selfish. Forgetting to tell Ali about Glastonbury when I could have been planning a weekend with her. A whole weekend, after all. I reach up and unpin the green and yellow Glastonbury flyer from the wall above my bed. There are loads of bands I've never heard of: Bare Naked Ladies (sounds promising), Attila the Stockbroker (less promising), Kitchens of Distinction (is that a band?). At the foot of the poster it reads: 'Probably the most exciting event of its kind anywhere in Europe this summer'. And yet.

I grab my jacket and race down to the phone box on the corner.

'Hello?' she says.

'Hey, it's me.'

There's a pause before she speaks again. 'Oh, hi.' She's still mad at me, but I can change that.

'Guess what? I've got two things to tell you.' I start gabbling. 'Mum's not coming to the concert tomorrow; she's got some party. And . . . ready for this? I'm not going to Glastonbury!'

'What? Why?' She sounds surprised.

'It was selfish of me not to tell you about it. I see that now. I'm really sorry.'

She's quiet again, except for her breathing.

'You don't need to apologize. I overreacted,' she says, her voice softer now. 'Don't not go because of me.'

'Too late!' I yelp. 'I'm not going. It was pretty much spur of the moment anyway. I only really wanted to see Carter.'

'Who?'

'Exactly! Now, can we spend the weekend together? Can we go to bed and not get up? Can we have pasta pesto and even those croissants from the tin and that white wine?'

'Yes!' she laughs. 'All that. And strawberries.'

'Yeah, don't worry if they haven't got any.'

'Do you have to go home after the concert tomorrow, or can you come straight to mine?' she asks.

'I can come straight to yours, and never leave. Until Sunday evening.'

27

JUNE 1992

'I've been thinking, perhaps you should get a girlfriend,' she says on Saturday afternoon.

I don't say anything. I don't need to. My expression says it all.

'I don't mean someone real. A *pretend* girlfriend.'

I don't follow, but she's obviously been playing with the idea in her own time. She slides off the sofa, onto the floor where I'm sitting with my legs out in front of me. She crosses hers and takes my hands.

'If you had a girlfriend, you'd have a more legitimate excuse to go out. It would be more believable for your mum, your friends, the other teachers. And it would take any suspicion away from us. Although I think we're doing pretty well,' she says, going on to explain all the ways in which this fake girl-friend would make life easier.

'Where did I meet her?' I ask, trying to catch up. 'I mean, she can't be a girl from school, and I don't know anyone out-side school.'

She's way ahead of me, got it all worked out. Having a girlfriend no one's ever met makes perfect sense. It answers the question as to why I don't hang out with my friends much. And she could be a girl I met at another school. She should be in the year above, her final year, so she's busy with exams. That would explain why we only meet sporadically. She's even got a name. Tanya.

'Right,' I say. 'Tanya, from the Upper Sixth. Well done me. I wonder what it was she saw in me.'

'Tanya's not real,' she says, punching my shoulder lightly.

I have to put Tanya into action as early as Sunday evening. First, when Mum accosts me making a toasted cheese sandwich in the kitchen, having returned from Miss P's smelling and looking a lot cleaner than I should after forty-eight hours at a music festival. Fortunately, I'm prepared and launch fluently into a story about not going to Glastonbury, having been reminded by my English teacher on Friday evening that I had an S-level mock exam to sit on Saturday. It's not a complete fabrication, but the exam is due the following Saturday. The real lie, or 'white lie' as Miss P calls it, is having met up with Tanya in the afternoon. The question 'who's Tanya?' I can deal with, but I don't have the courage to say I stayed the night with her – that would throw up a load of unwanted questions about where she lives, what her parents do. Instead, I say I stayed over with Charlie (whoever Charlie is). Mum doesn't need to know and doesn't ask, because I get her on to the subject of her summer party and she's off.

Tanya makes another appearance on Monday, and I thank God for the dress rehearsal I had with Mum. I'm doing some last-minute revision for a German oral exam in the house study when the mob arrives. I've got my script and I've been over it a thousand times, but I can feel my forehead beading with sweat as Nick, Ant and a couple of other lads circle the desk. It's an inquisition, and I feel like shit lying to my friends, but I just have to get through it without faltering. They're pissed off and call me pathetic but seem to let it go and have a lot more to say about the festival itself and what I missed. A lot, apparently. Turns out Blur were amazing.

During those final couple of weeks of the summer term, Tanya's profile builds. She's finished her exams and has more time on her hands. Cards start arriving at home, just kisses and hearts, no handwriting. Ali says she had fun choosing them, trying to get herself into the mind of an eighteen-year-old girl. I'm not so sure when I open the envelopes to reveal sepia depictions of *The Lady of Shalott*, *Ophelia* and Rossetti's *Proserpine*. An old-fashioned eighteen-year-old girl, perhaps, though what do I know? I haven't had a girlfriend that age. Cat was seventeen and I was sixteen when we started going out, but these pictures wouldn't have been her style; she was more doodles and tear stains. Ali's thirty-five; it's bound to be different. And Cat dumped me, so, you know, whatever.

Tanya must have sent me at least half a dozen cards when I notice a change in the shape of the hearts and kisses. They're unmistakeably in someone else's hand, and the sight of it is unsettling. Who is this? We haven't told anyone. We don't tell anyone.

My final exam is English Literature, three days before the end of term, and it's not one I'm eager to repeat. I knew I hadn't revised enough; I don't even finish in the time available. But it's more that I can't help but be distracted by the handwriting in Tanya's card. As soon as the exam is over, I'm out of the school gates and taking the direct roads to Ali's flat. I know I shouldn't, but I'm not the one who's changed the rules. At her door, I almost don't bother with the secret ring, but I know it's important. Still, I punch the buzzer.

'What is this?' I'm standing in her hallway, waving the card at her.

'Hello to you too, how was your day, fine thanks, how was your exam?' she says, after letting me in, surprised at me turning up unannounced. Then she sees my face and the card. 'Oh, I see, let me get you a drink. I'll explain.' She heads to the kitchen.

When she returns I'm still flustered and haven't moved. She's holding a glass of water in one hand and wine in the other. 'Water to cool you down – you're overheating. Wine to warm you back up,' she says, sweeping past me into the sitting room.

'You're not taking this seriously,' I say, following her, trying to stay cross. She places the water on the table, turns and, holding the back of my neck, brings the glass of wine to my lips.

'It's only a card,' she whispers. 'I told you, I'll explain, but first ... drink.'

'What are you—?' I manage before she tips the glass and wine pours into my mouth and down my shirt. 'This is weird,' I say, swallowing and coughing. She pulls away, takes a long slug of wine, filling her mouth, staring at me with wide eyes.

'No,' I say, backing out of the room. 'I'm not finished being angry. The handwriting, it's not yours,' I say, weakly, the card limp in my hand. 'This isn't a game, Miss!'

Her mouth full of wine, she starts moving towards me. I

turn and run to the kitchen, but she's got me trapped. She keeps coming and I try to duck around her, but she pins me with her arms against the fridge. I open my mouth to protest, but she pulls my head down and clamps her mouth to mine, and the cold liquid shocks the back of my throat. Her tongue follows, searching for mine, licking my teeth, my lips. Her hand travels up my leg, flattens against my stomach, then slides inside my trousers, kneading my pubic bone as her fingers curl around me. She tugs then she releases and continues downward to wrap my balls. Very slowly, her hand tightens, and I'm held in excruciating, intoxicating suspension.

'You're right,' I say, my voice high and breathless. 'It's only a card.'

She kisses me again, and I can feel her smile widen through her lips as she eases her grip.

Later, while she dozes beside me, I stare at the ceiling and replay what happened, trying to piece together the jigsaw. Was it a game? It was a bloody weird way to answer my question about the handwriting.

Eventually, I learn whose writing it is, and I don't know how I feel about it. She's confided in her friend, Trace. Turns out Trace is the woman who saw me on that bleak day in February, the mess of tears being consoled in the wine bar with the sawdust floor. They used to work together. It feels strange, but Ali says Trace is brilliantly supportive. I suppose that makes it okay. Apparently, Trace's husband, Nigel, knows and he's cool about it too. It feels momentous, bringing other people into our bubble, but I guess if we're going to be a proper couple, people will need to know.

28

JULY 1992

The chapel is packed for the last school assembly of term. The Upper Sixth are going for it, through the well-rehearsed motions of the end-of-year service. The end of their secondary education. Having lived together, most of them, for years, their emotions are barely concealed. Anticipation and the promise of a long summer hang heavy in the air. The fuse of freedom is minutes from being lit. The rest of their lives is waiting.

And I can't bear it. When that bell goes and uniforms are dragged off, when shirts and blouses have all been graffitied, yearbooks signed, when the huddles have fragmented and dispersed and the campus is evacuated, empty, I will be left. Bereft. Lost. There will be no excuse to stay, to see Ali after school, to hide in the back of her car, to sneak down her road and into her building with the secret ring that buzzes me in. Into her world. There will be none of this.

The holiday stretches endlessly ahead. Two months. We speak on the phone every day. But the evenings are when I miss her most, so I make excuses to go for a walk and ring from the phone box on the corner.

The calls make me desperate. I haven't seen Ali since the end of term, not even a proper goodbye – she had a staff meeting and I didn't have an excuse to hang around. In the second week of the holiday, I'm about to tell Mum I'll be meeting up with Tanya when she announces we're going to see Gran and Grandpa, so don't even think of trying to get out of it. And it's like this, one roadblock after another, for almost a month.

Then, at the end of July, there's a welcome escape. The school has signed me up for a week-long residential choir course near London. Ant is going as well, as we're the two hopefuls for Oxbridge music scholarships this year. He's trying for Cambridge and with his brain and all-round musical excellence, he's certain to get in. But then, he's going to be studying music. For me, taking a languages degree with a choral scholarship on the side, it's all a bit marginal. I can sing well enough, but I still don't consider myself Oxford material academically. You've got to be special to make that grade. But I'm determined to give it my best shot, and this course is an important stepping-stone. I must make a good impression.

29

July 1992

'Dawn the Horn or Lottie with the legs?' asks Ant.

We're playing the 'out of' game in the dormitory. The week-long course is nearing the end and, although it's only the afternoon, everyone's pretty tired at this point.

'How have you not run out of girls yet?' I ask, because we've played this game every day after lunch and most nights, after lights out.

'Answer the question,' he insists, through a yawn.

'Well, it's a tough one. You're saving the best till last, I see.' I lean over from the top bunk. He's lying on his back with his long summer holiday hair flopped over his eyes, a thin smile set on his face, his palms together on his chest like he's praying.

'It has to be ... Dawn,' I say, confidently.

'Horn? Wrong answer!' he barks, though on what basis it's wrong I don't find out. Dawn's very nice, not that I've ever really spoken to her. And I don't know why they call her Horn. Or, for that matter, why Lottie is 'with the legs'. She's tiny. Ant pushes himself off the bed, picks up his music folder from the side table, and lopes towards the door. 'Come on, masterclass with James Bowman in ten minutes.'

We might be exhausted after a week of performances, choral evensongs, a trip to Oxford colleges to meet choral scholars and a BBC Radio 3 broadcast, but the training and continuous singing are addictive. I think we're all feeling it. There's a team atmosphere, supportive and encouraging, which I haven't known for years; not since I was eleven or twelve, my cathedral choir days, has singing been such a drug.

'Look around the room,' said the course director on the first morning. 'You are here because you are the finest young singers in the country. The very best.' Cue a lot of nervous glances and shuffling. I'm certain none of us had been bigged up like this before. From our generally scruffy appearance and some peculiar fashion choices – a symptom of forty nerdy teenagers, more used to uniforms, suddenly required to wear their own clothes in public for a whole week – we're not exactly the *in-crowd*. But from the director's team-talk onwards, we were all bonded and pretty much inseparable.

On our last day, we're all seated in the rehearsal room. Shyness has given way to easy laughter. Insecurities replaced with self-confidence, now that we've proved to ourselves and each other that we are, after all, quite good at this singing thing, I reflect, glancing up from the form resting on the folder in my lap. It's the moment we've been preparing for all week, the application form for Oxford and Cambridge. There's a lot of assertive scribbling going on around me, but looking down the list of colleges, I feel like I've missed a session on which ones I'm supposed to pick. I recognize the names, but that's it. I tick New College and Magdalen, because we visited them that week. For the final spot, I hover over St Edmund Hall, recalling my meeting with Ralph Leadsbetter, and I close my eyes. That amazing, strange day with Miss P, and all the others like it. Miss P. Her name sounds in my head, lifts and falls, a silent weight pressing against my brain. I realize I haven't thought much about her all week, but then there hasn't been time to think of anything but singing, really, and mucking about with Ant and new friends. It's been like a holiday, a week off. A week off *what*, though? The hiding, the pretending, the lying, the scheming, perhaps.

I miss her now, though, Miss P.

People are getting to their feet, gathering jackets and bags, handing in their forms. I scratch a final tick in the box beside St Edmund Hall, sign my form and run outside to join the others for a group photograph in the sun.

30

AUGUST 1992

There's a letter waiting for me on my desk when I get home. I double-take the handwriting on the envelope and can't believe my eyes. It's hers, Miss P's own handwriting, not Tanya's. I hear Mum bustling about in the hallway outside my room and, to be on the safe side, lock myself in the downstairs bathroom to read it in privacy. It's not what I'm expecting. For one thing, it's typed.

Dear Joseph,

I hope this letter finds you and your family well, enjoying some well-earned rest.

I have been developing an enhanced programme for Upper Sixth pupils intending to study languages at university. I know you have been thinking about your subject combinations and, given your exemplary results in Spanish this year, I would strongly recommend you include this language in your options planning, alongside French and German.

With this in mind, I am writing to offer you an opportunity that has only arisen since the end of term. A place on our new study programme, organized with a contact

*of mine, a professor at the University of Barcelona. It's for
ten days in the second half of August, staying with a Spanish
family who have a son your age.*

*I appreciate that the timing of this is not ideal – it has to
be after the Olympics! But it would be very worthwhile and
beneficial to your university applications. Please do discuss the
opportunity with your mother and contact me on the telephone
number below. I would be delighted to go through the details
with her, and to reassure her that you won't be completely on
your own, as I will accompany you and will be staying with
the professor and his wife.*

Best wishes,
Miss P

I reread each word, slowly, my mouth hanging open. I can
hardly believe what she's suggesting. It's so . . . clever, brilliant,
organized. I'd never have thought of this. I read it again. It's
pretty bloody credible. But will Mum go for it? Certainly, all
the important words are there: *languages, exemplary, opportunity,
professor, university.*

But she's offering to speak to Mum herself. Christ. A shiver
runs through me, and I wipe my hand across my forehead,
damp with sweat. This is risky.

Contact me on the telephone number below, she writes, and
there, at the foot of the page, is a string of numbers. A phone
number. Nothing special, but I can't take my eyes off it. I
run my index finger over the type. Her precious number, the
digits that connect our voices, our thoughts, all the words we
cannot say in public, the numbers that unlock our secret. And

now she's giving them to Mum. A hole forms in the pit of my stomach and I swallow quick, shallow breaths.

Clever, brilliant, organized. Scary as fuck.

I hide in my room until Mum goes upstairs, then shoot out and down to the phone box. I can't show the letter to Mum yet. I need to speak to Ali first. My mind spins and leaps between the madness of it all to the practicalities and the story we will need to prepare. *It's not a lie, not really*, I say to myself over and over as I run down the hill. I mean, this is definitely going to help me with my Spanish.

'Of course it's not a lie,' she reassures me. 'It's a great opportunity, if you think about it. Your mother would be mad not to let you go.'

We talk it through. Or rather, I listen and try to concentrate, but hearing her say it all out loud is giving me a headache. I'm excited, just a bit flustered, I tell her.

'You do want to come with me to Spain, don't you?' she asks, her voice like liquid. 'I've missed you so much.' It's all I need to hear.

She spends the rest of the call rehearsing what she's going to say to Mum and it's impressively convincing. Helped a lot by her trump card, that 50 per cent of the cost will be covered by a school travel bursary she's managed to negotiate on my behalf.

An hour later, with Mum as enthusiastic as me (for different reasons, obviously) but anxious about the money, I'm sitting at the foot of the stairs listening to one side of the conversation between my mother and my teacher. It does not get more fucking mental than this, but the organizational details they're discussing about the trip are helping to keep me calm. Still, there's a part of me that can't believe Mum's falling for it, and I feel bad about that.

'Well,' says Mum, after she's exhausted herself thanking Miss P for this 'wonderful opportunity' and hung up. 'I'm so proud of you, sweetie. You've clearly made a good impression. She sounds like a very nice, very professional woman. And the professor and his wife sound delightful. Perhaps you'll get to meet them.'

'Yes, she is a really good teacher,' I say, suppressing an urge to laugh like a maniac. *Very professional woman, ha ha.* This is actually happening. We're going to Spain!

In a beat, memories of the choir course evaporate: the dormitory chats with Ant, the new friendships made, the joy of singing every day, the plans for university, for Oxford. Gone.

Two weeks later, Mum is driving me to the coach station.

'Now, have you remembered everything?' she asks. 'I got your passport out of the Important Documents folder, and I put your clothes on the bed. They're all clean and folded. You did pack them, didn't you?'

'Yes, obviously,' I say, turning round to frown at the navy-blue suitcase on the back seat. It's ancient. Mum chose it so I'd recognize it when it comes off the plane in the baggage collection area. You can't miss it, with its *Nuclear Power? NO THANKS!* sticker on the side. I don't see why I can't have a case of my own with wheels, but 'this trip is already costing an arm and a leg', she keeps reminding me. It's true, even with the travel bursary (which I'm beginning to suspect is Miss P's own money), the costs have mounted up, what with the £100

worth of Spanish pesetas and the plane ticket. I think Mum
was relieved when Miss P suggested we take the National
Express coach to Heathrow, instead of the train, which would
have cost a fortune.

'Well, will you?' We're at a red light, and Mum's facing me
with an exasperated expression.

'Sorry, will I what? What was the question?' I haven't been
listening for miles, my thoughts a long way from here, thrilled
at the prospect of Spain, faintly terrified at the imminent
meeting of Mum and Miss P.

'Honestly, you must pay attention. Don't go drifting off into
your little world when Miss P is talking to you,' she says, and
I wince when she says her name.

'I won't.'

'And don't bite your thumb,' she says, pulling my hand away
from my mouth. 'I was saying, I don't have a contact telephone
number for you. Will you call me when you arrive?'

I say I will and mumble something about expensive phone
calls. Fortunately, she leaves it at that when the lights change
and she has to concentrate on getting in the right lane for the
coach station. I see Miss P and my heart skips as I point her
out to Mum. I immediately wish I hadn't. She pulls up right
beside the coach for maximum embarrassment and is out of
the car, shaking hands, before I can stop her. Why can't she
just drop me off?

My heart is beating erratically, and my hands are more damp
than usual. I take my time hauling the case out of the car.

'Have you got everything?' Miss P asks.

'Not you as well,' I say, lugging the case over to the baggage
stand at the rear of the coach.

'Manners!' says Mum in her shocked voice, and, turning to Miss P, 'I'm sorry, I think he's a bit nervous about the flight.'

'No, I'm not,' I whine, annoyed at sounding defensive.

'I hope you've packed for the heat,' says Miss P, pointedly, because I'm wearing what I always wear: jeans, T-shirt, denim jacket and my DMs. 'It will be seriously warm in Barcelona, especially in those boots.'

'You're quite right,' chimes my mother. 'Don't worry, he's got summer clothes and a pair of sandals.'

She needs to go. 'Right, probably time to go, isn't it?'

Mum insists on kissing me on both cheeks and I half expect her to kiss Miss P as well, but she just gushes more thanks. After some excruciating remarks about how good it would be for me to meet the professor and how she hopes I will behave, she's on her way.

We exchange a look of conspiratorial triumph and I want to pick her up and spin her round. Instead, we climb on board and find our seats.

'I hope you don't behave,' she whispers close to my ear as the coach pulls out of the station.

31

AUGUST 1992

We take a shuttle bus from the airport outside Barcelona. The air conditioning isn't working, and by the time we reach our stop near the Gran Teatre del Liceu forty steaming minutes later, we don't so much step as spill onto the tarmac. I neck a bottle of water and stretch my arms over my head, while Miss P plots our route on a giant street map pinned to the bus stop wall.

It's only supposed to be a ten-minute walk to the hotel in the centre of the Gothic Quarter, but the combination of the peak afternoon temperatures and the weight of my wretched suitcase makes it double that. Whenever she looks away, I swap the handle over to my other hand to give my arms a rest. I'm being as nonchalant as possible.

'Do you want to stop for a minute?' she asks, catching me in the act.

'Oh no. I'm good,' I say through my teeth. 'It can't be far now, can it?'

She looks around for a road sign, and points to a junction ahead. 'I think it's just up there and right.'

She's spot on, thank God. The hotel, with its flaking yellow façade and dark green shutters, stands out from the other buildings on the street. We practically fall through the huge wooden door into the cool, marble-floored reception. The man behind the desk is in no hurry, but at last we're shown to our room. The door closes behind us. We're tired, hot and sticky from the journey, but it doesn't stop us grabbing hold of each other.

'I can't believe we're here!' I say, my excitement muffled by her hair, which is tied back and piled on her head. She squeezes me tight, then peels herself off me. Her face and neck are glistening pink.

'Showers?' she suggests, pulling her top up, untying her hair and stripping down to her knickers. She might be thirty-five, but with her skinny waist and flat stomach, she looks so much younger. I follow her lead, anxious to wash the hours away. We stand under the spray, soaping hands, exploring each other slowly after all the time apart. We move cautiously at first, conscious of the distance that's stretched like an elastic band between us. We slip and slither, but I can't wait any longer. I bend her forwards and her hands shoot up and flatten against the tiles. Together again, and the dragging deserted weeks fall away.

Much later, when the heat of the day has passed, we reappear in the street outside. Gone are the jeans and DMs, replaced with lighter, looser summer clothes. And the sandals, which I'm not sure about, but which make complete sense after a hundred metres on the warm medieval stones. Obviously, I wouldn't wear them around the lads, but this is a different me.

We wander, ducking down quiet pedestrian streets, made narrower by the high-sided buildings. No two houses are the same, each a different shade of terracotta red, orange, pink. Just when we think we might be entirely lost, sucked into long, labyrinthine alleyways, we are swept out into vast plazas.

'I'm hungry,' she announces. 'Want to eat?'

'God yeah, I'm starving,' I realize. 'I could kill a pizza.'

'Well, we're not at home, Joe. This is Spain. How about some paella? Patatas bravas? Jamón?'

I barely catch a few words over the city noise, but it sounds exotic. She takes my hand and we set off across a huge square. She seems to know where she's going, but I'm transfixed by this hand, holding mine.

'Stop,' I say, pulling her gently. 'Wait. We've never done this, in public.'

'Done what?' She looks at me, surprised, her eyes shining in the fading light. She follows my gaze. 'Oh, this.' Her voice is quiet. She takes my other hand and a step closer.

'*¡Qué maravilloso!*'

'*¡Qué dulce pareja!*'

A couple are shouting from a table outside one of the restaurants. The man whistles and we laugh and run. I think this is the happiest I will ever be.

32

August 1992

'What was your favourite thing?' she asks, taking a sip from her white wine. It's lunchtime on our final day in Barcelona, we're sitting at a restaurant in the Plaça de la Sagrada Família. Gaudí's magnificent, unfinished church, stands before us. We've checked out of the hotel and returned to the plaza for our last lunch before heading along the coast.

'Apart from the sex?' I ask, formally.

'Apart from the sex,' she clarifies.

'It has to be that, doesn't it?' I nod at the great monument.

The Sagrada Família was as impressive on the inside as it was from the plaza. Vast climbing towers, somehow curving like giant trees, no straight lines. Dream-like. *A controversial masterpiece of geometric purity*, according to our guidebook. Ali reeled off some more amazing facts while I gazed awestruck around the light-filled nave and complex façades, dripping in symbolism.

'What about you? Your favourite thing?' I ask her.

'Hmm, the Gran Teatre del Liceu, definitely.'

We'd been there the evening before. The performance didn't start until 9 p.m., so we had plenty of time for dinner on Las Ramblas, the tree-lined boulevard overflowing with artists, street performers, and those weird human statues. We dressed up, she in a long, floaty skirt and off-the-shoulder top, me in a pair of stone-coloured chinos Mum bought me and my favourite dark blue shirt with white flowers dotted all over it. At the hotel, she presented me with a little wrapped box. Inside, a glass bottle of Chanel Égoïste.

'Is this for me?' I asked. I felt I had to, because it looked more like a woman's perfume, but she reassured me it was for men. The smell was strong and followed me around like a third party all evening. I couldn't tell whether it suited me or not, but she seemed to like it. Apparently, it was sexy and made me smell like a man.

'What did I smell like before?' I wondered, out loud.

'You always smell nice. Now you smell even better,' she said.

The ground level of the opera house was organized with plush red chairs, seating several hundred at least. The tickets for the stalls were too expensive for us, but I was more than happy with our view from high up on one of the many levels. A squat, square-shaped man carrying a large white box on his back went between the rows, calling, '¡Bebidas! ¡Cervezas! ¡Coca! ¡Agua!' I wish I'd stopped him. It didn't occur to us that the late evening would be hot, but two thousand bodies, breathing heavily and applauding every few minutes after each aria, soon melted the opera house and everything in it. I had never sweated so much, and I sweat quite a lot.

'It was baking in there,' I say.

She frowns. 'Romantic, I thought, didn't you?'

'Yeah, sure, but we were drenched by the end. And with all those tourists steaming up the place. That was proper mental.'

I snort with laughter, take a gulp of ice-cold beer from the tall glass in front of me and reach for my cigarettes.

'I think you're missing the point,' she says, like she's my teacher, which only makes me laugh more. Her brow creases. 'What about our photo, before we went in? And when I stood on the balcony outside looking down at you?'

I take a drag of my cigarette, rest it on the ashtray, run a hand through my hair, slightly damp in the airless square. I pretend to give her questions serious contemplation, but the truth is I thought it was all a bit sugary and stage-managed. She made a whole song and dance about it, positioned me on Las Ramblas right in front of the opera house, while she climbed the stairs up to the balcony to pose. Pretty sure it made me look like a tit. She stares intently across the table at me. I don't want to ruin the atmosphere, so I lie.

'What about meeting Carlota and her son — that was nice, wasn't it?' she continues to reminisce.

'Yes, they were friendly,' I agree. 'Bit awkward, though, taking all those photos of me with them.'

Ali had gone to quite a lot of trouble, it turned out, in preparing our cover story. Before we left England, she'd got in touch with all her Spanish friends. So, every day, there was someone else to meet for coffee, drinks, meals, a walking tour of the city. Everyone in Barcelona was lovely. At least, I think so, since I could barely keep up; her conversations with Alejandro, Marcos and Carlota were loud, percussive, largely incomprehensible. I sat patiently, nodding along, waiting in vain for a break in the verbal traffic that would let me try out my schoolboy Spanish and ask the way to the train station or tell them about my hobbies. The opportunity never arose.

Carlota was a friend she'd met years ago. Older than Ali, with short, jet-black hair, a friendly face, but dark, searching eyes and a mouth that crept into the corners of her face when she wasn't talking. She freaked me out a bit. On the one hand, she was friendly, but on the other, she was definitely eyeing me with suspicion. Perhaps she didn't approve of me and Ali, but then why would Ali bring us here and put us in an awkward position? In fact, why would she introduce us to any of her friends if she thought they might disapprove?

If Carlota distracted me, meeting her son, Raúl, was when it really got weird. We were sipping herbal tea on the low-walled balcony of her ground-floor apartment in a noisy suburb, Ali and her friend gabbling and laughing, me nodding, when a Vespa screeched to a halt on the pavement in front of us. In one explosive move, the man, all long limbs and black leather, hopped off the bike, leapt over the wall, helmet still on. I thought I was going to shit myself, like this was the camorra, a hitman for the mob. It wasn't. It was Raúl, Carlota's son. Charming, it turned out, but that wasn't the problem.

On the way over to Carlota's, Ali explained her plan. 'You need to be able to show some proof, evidence that you were staying with a family. It's what I told your mum, remember? Luckily, Carlota's son is about your age, maybe a little older. She's going to get him to come over so we can take some photos of you with the two of them, at home.'

'Maybe a little older?' I ask Ali, out of the corner of my mouth, as the strapping Spaniard, who must be at least twenty, pecks his dear mama affectionately on the cheeks a bunch of times before turning to show Ali the best dental work money can buy, and ignoring me. I try not to show it, but just under my skin a jealous rage is burning, not helped by my clothes selection. Should have gone with my first choice – blue shirt, chinos – but Ali said I'd be too hot, much cooler in the salmon pink T-shirt she bought me in a market and white cotton shorts. I'm really feeling my age and I certainly can't compete with leather man. He's not even sweating.

'It was a little awkward, I agree,' says Ali, tying her hair back. 'But hopefully the photos will come out okay. It was a good idea of Carlota's to have you standing and Raúl sitting at the table . . .' she adds, unconvincingly.

'Know any more game teenagers we can use?' I say mischievously. 'Your other friends got any kids perhaps?'

She throws her napkin at me, but gets the joke, even if I am being half-serious.

'We're seeing Pablo tomorrow. He's driving us to the hotel in Palamós. But he and Sofía have only got little ones, babies really.' She leans back in her chair, snaps a breadstick and dips it in a saucer of fresh picada. I look out across the plaza at the movie-perfect scene of countless couples and take a swig of my beer. Am I one of them now?

'There is something else we could try,' she says, following my gaze. 'Another photo opportunity.'

'Who?' I ask.

'My fiancé.'

I cough, my drink spraying the table and my shirt.

'Not a real fiancé, dummy,' she snorts, as I dab a napkin

at my face. 'Someone we could find, perhaps when we're in Palamós, who we could pretend is my betrothed.'

'You've got to be joking,' I say, hardly believing my ears.

'I'm not joking at all. You have Tanya, or had Tanya, can't remember where we are with her ... I wonder how she did in her A-levels.' Her voice drifts off. 'Anyway, to really throw people off the scent, I need a man with a name, and something more than a summer fling.'

'Yeah, but a fiancé – you're going to tell people you got engaged?'

'Why can't I get engaged?' She folds her arms.

I open and close my mouth and can't find the words for a moment.

'Because, Ali, you're not.'

33

August 1992

That afternoon, a small, round, bespectacled man with a flaw-less tan and a teddy bear-like smile picks us up from outside the hotel. Pablo greets us both with gentle hugs and delicate cheek kisses, before driving like a maniac the hundred-plus kilometres to the picture-postcard fishing village of Palamós.

Its Catalan beauty is lost on me as I stagger from the car, eyes pinned wide, knuckles white, stomach like a washing machine on extreme spin. Pablo, who hasn't stopped talking the entire journey – with a lot of shouting over his shoulder to me in the back of the car – skips into the hotel to check us in. Having satisfied himself that we are in safe hands, he repeats the hug and kiss routine, jumps behind the wheel and screams out of the car park.

'How did we survive that?' I cry, falling onto a sunbed by the pool. Ali, apparently unfazed by the death-ride, slides onto the sunbed next to mine.

'Please tell me we don't have to drive with him again,' I say.

'It wasn't that bad, was it? He's Spanish; that's how they drive.'

'You weren't in the back – there were no seatbelts.'

I close my eyes for a moment, try to regulate my breathing, but I'm not done complaining.

'Do you think we might have a few days on our own now? I mean, your friends are lovely and everything—'

'Yes, they are, and they've been really sweet to you,' she says, like I'm a lucky boy.

I don't say anything.

She turns on her side, reaches out and places her hand on my chest. 'Jesus, your heart's really racing.'

'He drives like he wants us all to die,' I say, not smiling.

'Which is surprising,' says Ali, adding like she's presenting his case, 'since he's one of Barcelona's most renowned psychiatrists with a reputation for showing tremendous empathy and care to his patients.'

'Whatever,' I mutter. 'I just think it would be nice to have some proper time together, having gone to all these lengths, lying to everyone—'

'Hey, shhh! Stop.' She looks around the pool area, but no one's paying attention to us.

'Don't shush me.'

'Don't say that, please, about lying. I did what I had to—'

'It's not much fun, you know,' I say, cutting her off, my voice rising. 'One minute we're walking down a street, hand in hand, and it's like everything is really wonderful, you and me, free. Next thing, *Oh look! It's my old friends, blah blah sickeningly good-looking, smart-suited rich blokes* and you're all speaking Spanish at a million miles an hour.' It's all coming out now. 'It's fucking boring, Ali.'

She sits up, clasps my hands, and I think she's going to kick off. But she pulls me in, our foreheads touching. She sighs.

'I'm sorry.' She strokes the back of my head. 'I didn't realize that's how you were feeling. I'm sorry. Please don't be angry. It will just be you and me now, I promise.'

'Really promise?'

'Promise.'

She kisses me and we hold each other, perched on the edges of our seats, until our clothes start sticking to our skin. The afternoon air humidifies in circles around us and the sun beats down. We are overdressed.

'We're the only people not in swimming costumes,' she says, getting to her feet, pulling me up with her. 'Let's go in and change. Start again, shall we?' She tilts her head, squeezes my hand, smiles slowly. 'Maybe lie down for a bit first?'

Ali has been to Palamós before, with an ex-boyfriend, I'm guessing. She doesn't go into details, but the list she reels off – *things we have to do* – during our week on the coast gives it away.

- Hire a motorboat, find a secluded cove
- Sunbathe naked on boat
- Dive off boat, swim naked in sea
- Picnic on boat, naked

That evening, as the sun burns away, the stone cools on the yellow and ochre plastered buildings, Ali gives me the tour of Palamós. She's brought her camera, and a ten-minute walk into town takes almost an hour. Every few steps we have to stop and snap, but it's not as simple as that. Ali's a stickler.

'I've only brought two rolls of film,' she explains. 'We need to make each photo count. Catch just the right light. It's so romantic at dusk.'

She sets up every shot like an art director on a film set. It's time-consuming. Getting her hair just right takes forever. But I have to admit that the sea and mountains bathed in soft evening light are perfection.

'Are you hungry yet?' I ask, as she fiddles with the self-timer.

'Just one more. Almost done. Isn't this romantic?'

It's not that I don't agree with her, especially the first twenty minutes. But we're closing in on an hour of staged romance. I like to think I'm more spontaneous, more impulsive. But I take my place, as directed, at the end of a boardwalk pier, the water shimmering around me. Ali presses a button and hurries to join me.

'Ten seconds.' She wraps her arms around my neck, lifts her face to meet mine, apparently not at all self-conscious despite the mass of tourists dining at tables a few metres away. 'Kiss me!'

I grab her face and snog it.

Finally, half an hour later (we had to do another take), we're tucked into a corner of a small square behind a church. Taverna S'Alguer is quiet, unpretentious, with tables nestling between olive trees and oleander plants in enormous terracotta pots. Strains of classical guitar music from inside the bar float out and mingle with the hum of contented diners. Our waiter is super friendly, not too handsome, and for the first time in a while I feel my shoulders soften and relax.

Ali looks serene, her face glowing, eyes sparkling across our table of empty dishes. The waiter refills our glasses. When he's gone, Ali leans forward, a conspiratorial look on her face.

'I think we've found him,' she whispers.

'Found who?' I ask.

'My fiancé.' She raps her fingers triumphantly on the tablecloth.

'Oh no, not that again,' I urge, dropping my head back, staring up into the canopy of pink flowers. But she's serious and proceeds to take me through her thinking. It's clear she's spent the last twenty-four hours moving from mulling it over to strategic planning. Not for the first time, I must admit I'm impressed with her attention to detail. She takes a bit of persuading but agrees not to proposition the waiter on our first evening.

34

AUGUST 1992

That night, the hotel's air conditioning gives up and the heat shrinks the room, melts us to the bed. At 2 a.m., after a fitful couple of hours trying to sleep, we've escaped to our tiny balcony, where we sit facing each other on the cool tiles, naked. Ali rolls a bottle of refrigerated water from the minibar across her forehead and chest, while I pour two glasses of Baileys Irish Cream, an impulse – though not a wise – purchase from Duty Free.

The sky is a black sheet. It looks cold, but the outside isn't much cooler than our room. Ali raises her glass to the moon, and I wonder if anyone else is up, watching us from behind the shutters of dark apartment windows facing this side of our hotel. I don't care.

'What shall we talk about?' asks Ali, straightening her legs out in front of her, then drawing up her knees, feet together.

'Can we *not* talk about engagements and fiancés, please?' I plead. 'We've exhausted that one, for now.'

She laughs quietly and her teeth gleam. 'Just trying to make life easier for us, for when we get home.'

'Home.' I exhale the word.

'Hmm. Let's choose a different topic,' she says. 'I know, tell me about when you were a choirboy, at the cathedral.'

'Sexy topic. Why do you want to know about that?'

'Well, I've never understood it, about the voice breaking. When did it happen? Did it mean you couldn't sing anymore?'

'Worst day of my life,' I say.

'That's a bit dramatic, isn't it?'

'Think about it. You invest three years of your time, and I mean all your time, in training and singing. Your voice is a finely tuned machine, like a racing car or jet aeroplane. You do this day in, day out, with fifteen other boys. You're a shit-hot team of professionals at the height of your abilities, even if you are children wearing dresses and frilly ruffs.'

She laughs out loud, forgetting the time, and muffles her mouth with her free hand.

'Now imagine what happens at the end of those three years. One day, you're up there, soaring above the congregation, full throttle around the fan-vaulted heights of your cathedral, volume turned right up.'

Her eyes widen.

'And CRACK! The engine cuts. Breaks. Stops. Dead. Down you fall.'

'Shit, no!' she whispers, at the top of her voice.

'And there's no firing it back up. It's done. Spent. Ceased to be, like a parrot, no more.'

'How can you joke about it?' she asks.

'You get over it. You have no choice. We all know it's going to happen, one day. Still horrible in that moment, though. Mainly because you can't really hang around after your voice breaks. In a way, I was lucky, because it happened near the end of the school year.'

'So how old were you, when—'

'When my balls dropped?' I chuckle. 'I was quite old actually. Thirteen and a half, I reckon.'

'That does seem old.' She sounds surprised. 'I always think of choirboys as being little, angelic, innocent things.'

'We are, to begin with. But we all end up on the pile of fallen angels.'

I slide down the wall, my legs splaying either side of her feet, arms contorted, tongue lolling, playing dead. She doesn't play along, though, not even when my cock twitches, involuntarily hardens and pokes her ankles. I look up hopefully. She's wearing a pensive expression as she swirls the liquid in her glass.

'Right, that's enough about my puberty,' I say to snap her out of it. I shuffle up, transfer my weight onto my elbows, blow some hair out of my eyes. 'Or do you want to know when I got my first erection? Might need another shot of that first.' I hold out my glass.

35

AUGUST 1992

Ali is as good as her word and for the next five days, it's just the two of us. The cloudless August skies blend blue into black, and the nights find us on our balcony, free to talk like we never have, sipping Baileys with scoops of ice from the hotel kitchen. Our browning bodies shine with beads of sweat, and only when our eyelids are heavy do we crawl back to bed.

We wander down sleepily for breakfasts of fresh fruit, yoghurt, strong coffee (for Ali), juice (for me), timing our arrival in the dining area just as the other guests are busy bagging the best sunbeds around the pool.

Ali's itinerary comes into its own. We head off mid-morning, unhurried, a day bag strapped to my shoulders with lunch provisions swiped from the buffet: bread, ham, cheese, chorizo, tomatoes. We stop by a mini supermarket for water, cold beers, and I learn the Spanish for condoms. She makes me ask the woman at the counter.

'*Condones*,' she says, slipping too easily into Miss P. 'You're here to improve your Spanish, remember.' So embarrassing.

We hire a motorboat each day from a man with a gummy smile in the bustling marina, then set out, following the coastline until we find the first deserted cove. The hours pass as we strip, jump, swim, eat, drink and fuck until it's too hot to move. Then we doze, lulled by the silent drift, the soft slopes of the waves below our boat.

Later, when I watch her shower the seawater off, I realize it's the first time since I've known her that she hasn't obsessed about her hair. It's like she's forgotten all about it, until it's time to get ready for dinner in town, which, by her schedule, is two hours before we need to leave the hotel. That's how long her hair takes to de-frizz, and nothing is allowed to interrupt this ritual. A lesson I learnt once and don't reoffend, after an attempt to go down on her mid-blow-dry. I take my notebook to the balcony in these hours, compose poems and love songs I imagine setting to music for her one day. I make a start on the Baileys, sneak the odd cigarette, rest my feet on the rail and bury my head in Bukowski's *Post Office* – a gift from my uncle Jack when I was with him last summer, which I can't believe was a year ago already. Last summer, a world away.

Towards the end of the week, between courses at our familiar table at the Taverna S'Alguer, Ali fishes in her handbag, retrieves the camera and places it on her napkin.

'Okay,' I say, nodding my head, smiling. 'Let's get you engaged.'

'Yes!' She beams. 'I knew you'd come round.'

When the kind, efficient, not-too-handsome waiter swings by to collect the empty plates, the crumbs that remain of our fried calamari and gambas, Ali places a hand on his arm.

'*¿Señor, podemos pedirte un favor?*' she asks, in her slightly exaggerated, almost accent-less Spanish.

The waiter bows towards her, his head following, tilting to one side. '*Pero claro, señorita*,' he says, and it occurs to me I don't think I've heard him speak until now. He's not that old, maybe thirty, but his voice is deep, slow, like in a coffee advert. '*¿Cómo puedo ayudar?*' he says; how can I help?

Ali holds up the camera, which he reaches to take, but she motions to me and beckons him to draw up a chair from another table, placing it next to hers. From the lift of his eyebrows, this isn't what he was expecting. There's an awkward pause. Hastily I stand, move back from the table, prepare to shoot the happy couple. The waiter looks furtively over his shoulder at the bar, his body turning, but with a firm yank, Ali sits him down. She's not going to let him get away.

'*Será rápido, lo prometo*,' she says, promising him that it won't take a moment.

Visibly reddening, he shifts uncomfortably in the chair. I throw him an apologetic shrug. No reaction, so I fix a clown-like smile and count, '*Uno, dos, tres*,' and click three times in quick succession.

'We look like total strangers,' says Ali, through her grinning teeth.

'Enemies, more like,' I say under my breath.

'Quick, take one more,' she trills, turning her face to the distressed waiter. '*¡Una última!*'

Somehow her huge smile forces something similar from him. Seizing the moment, she grabs his arm and, laughing, nuzzles into him. 'NOW!'

I snap, once, twice, but he's on his feet before I can fire off another, speeding back to the safety of the bar.

'Well, that wasn't fun,' I say, dropping into my chair, reaching for the bottle. 'More wine needed.'

We down our glasses, get the bill. Ali pays as usual. Still embarrassed, I find a few coins in my jacket pocket to bulk up the tip. Joining Ali on the street outside the restaurant, I glance over my shoulder. I liked our little taverna, but we can't go there again.

In the early hours, in our usual spot on the balcony, down to the dregs of the Baileys, our nightly conversation turns a corner. We've covered so much historic ground in each other's lives, hers taking longer to recount than mine, obviously, but there's something she's omitted from her timeline. Something she feels it's important I know.

'Sorry if I got a bit weird about the whole fiancé thing,' she says.

I wave a hand, brush it away. I don't want to trawl through it again. We've only got one day left of our holiday, but we're going to be spending most of it with Pablo, his wife Sofía and their kids at their summer house in the hills, before Pablo drives us to the airport. The cost of having Ali to myself for the week, it seems. It's fine; I know I'm lucky to be here with her at all. But I'm desperate to enjoy every hour, every minute we have together before returning to God knows what in England.

'No, please, I want to explain.' She looks earnest. It's unnerving, especially when she goes inside and reappears in her T-shirt and knickers. She sits down next to me, so we're not face to face, and proceeds to recall her university days.

'You see, I was engaged once,' she begins.

'Oh, right.' I'm not sure how to react.

'I was infatuated. But he had a bit of a reputation, you know. I tried to ignore the rumours, but I caught him cheating on me.'

'Really? Why on earth would he do that? He had you; what's wrong with him?' I look at her, take her hand and squeeze it. 'What did you do when you found out?'

'I told him if he was serious about me, he needed to make a commitment. So, he bought me a ring. We were going to get married.'

'But you didn't get married. What happened?'

She looks down, releases my hand, interlocking her fingers, pressing them together.

'He broke it off during my year abroad. Turned out, he was still seeing that bitch.'

We sit in silence. Ali, hugging her knees, breathing heavily, while I feel very underdressed, my mind replaying everything she's just revealed.

'I can't believe anyone would let you go like that.'

'Can't you?' she says, still looking at her feet, her voice small but clear. 'Better not break my heart, then.'

'I would never do that!' I wrap my arms around her; she softens into me.

She lifts her head, looks into my eyes. 'Promise me?'

'God, yeah, of course I promise,' I say. 'I love you, Ali.'

'I love you, too.'

36

AUGUST 1992

Our last day in Spain, I wake after a night of broken sleep, a cramp and a knot of pain at the top of my spine. Ali, on the other hand, is bright, full of energy, presumably something to do with exorcizing her horrible experience. I vow never to treat her like that, to devote myself to making her happy. I do some stretching on the balcony to get the crick out of my neck before we set off for Pablo's summer house.

The tall cypress trees, olive groves and vineyards stretching into the distance on all sides of their converted olive mill provide welcome respite after our week burning up on the coast. I watch Ali across the lunch table, tanned and gorgeous, laughing with her friend, speed-talking with no punctuation. A week ago, this would have pissed me right off, but that sense of alienation seems a thousand years ago. Even Pablo's insane driving on the way over didn't bother me as much, especially when their hospitality – a feast of gazpacho, paella and tortilla, jamón, manchego, washed down with Priorat – is gifted with genuine warmth.

At least, it is from Pablo's side. I'm not so sure Sofía, a robust woman with strong bones and long camorra-black hair, shares her husband's generous spirit. Every time Ali throws back her head in delight at Pablo's latest joke, I swear I see Sofía wince behind massive sunglasses. I wish I could distract her with conversation, but my Spanish isn't up to the job and her withering looks suggest she's not interested in encouraging my GCSE-level efforts, however hard I try. I run out of my stock phrases halfway through lunch, and Sofía takes any opportunity to disappear into the kitchen, where I imagine she's seething her way through another bottle of wine.

Occasionally, Ali looks over to see if I'm all right, but she needn't worry. I'm happy to lean back, stretch my legs out, enjoy these last few hours of our Spanish escape. Reappearing from the house, Sofía carries a huge bowl of creamy dessert in one hand, a six-month-old baby in the other, and what looks very much like a fresh scowl. She thumps the bowl down between Pablo and Ali, although they seem oblivious, and rounds the table in my direction, arms extended, baby dangling in wriggly suspension. I sit up quickly, just in time to catch the thing, as Sofía turns on her heel, heads back to gather up its older brother, toddling in post-nap diagonals across the grass.

Given a job to do, and without anyone really speaking to me, I take to my task enthusiastically. I may not be the guest with the most scintillating conversation, but I can impress by building a rapport with baby Álvaro. That will show Ali's friends that I'm not just a teenage hanger-on. What they don't know is that I've got an ace up my sleeve: I've done babysitting. I run through my set – the knee-bounce game, the tummy raspberry. I'm sure I had more tricks, but we don't get past a minute before it's back to staring at each other and doing the coo-coo-nose-boink with the odd farm animal noise thrown in. Unimpressed, Álvaro removes the dummy from his mouth and pushes it into mine. Laughter erupts on the other side of the table. I look up. Pablo is doubled over, pointing at us, Ali has tears in her eyes, and even Sofía, standing square behind them, might be smiling, or at least smirking.

'*Mira, un padre en ciernes*,' cries Pablo, hand gestures in overdrive.

'What did he say?' I look to Ali. 'All I got was "look" and "padre" . . .'

'He says you're a daddy in the making. A natural.' She smiles when she translates, but looks away, wipes her eyes, and I notice something else in her expression. I can't put my finger on it, but if I had to guess, I'd say . . . pity, with a bit of disappointment. Have I done the wrong thing? Has playing with the baby made me look even younger? I take out the dummy, place it on the table, and hand Álvaro over to his papa.

'Huh, babies,' I mutter, not quite saying 'whatever' but affecting a dismissive, nonchalant tone. I run my hand through my hair, apply my sunglasses and look disinterested. I feel exposed. On the one hand, everyone's reaction to me playing with the baby was funny – I'd made our hosts laugh. But then there was that look on Ali's face, not to mention Sofía's, and was Pablo laughing with me, or at me? I wish I understood, could read grown-ups better. I'd quite like to go now.

'That was a long hug she gave you back there,' says Ali, as we wait for Pablo in the drive by his car. 'Can you still breathe?'

'Yeah, quite odd,' I reply, trying to sound cool, not bothered.

'It looked like she was chewing your ear,' she laughs.

'Actually, she said something. Or hissed something, more like. I couldn't quite catch it.'

'What did she say?'

'It sounded like, "*Erez daymasado coven*" . . .' I try to repeat Sofía's parting shot. 'To be honest, it didn't sound that friendly.'

'The spiky cow,' Ali spits, kicks the gravel and stares back at the house, hands on her hips.

'Wow, harsh,' I say, surprised by her outburst. 'What do you think it means, then?'

She looks at me, neck already flushed, eyes narrow, chin jutting forward. '*Eres demasiado joven* means "you're too . . . young."'

'Why would she—' I begin but check myself. I can hardly defend a fact.

'Greasy fat bitch. She's jealous of me, always has been. God, Pablo will be furious.'

'Fuck's sake, don't tell him, Ali.'

'How dare she!'

'Hey, come on, let's not spoil our last day.'

Pablo is taking his time, but I'm grateful, using every minute to calm Ali down. I take her hand, walk her over to a line of cypresses at the end of the drive. It's more open here, away from the house and garden, and for a moment we just stand there, bare arms touching. I feel her soften, the tension ease, though she doesn't let go of my hand.

'Look.' I can't help pointing at the panorama before us: vineyards tumbling down the hill, the Mediterranean beyond, the endless green falling into blue, separated only by a smudged line of orange, the places in between where the people live, everything slow, still, in the afternoon haze.

Ali takes my other hand, places them both on her waist, then reaches her arms around my neck, and tiptoes to kiss me full on the mouth, her lips parting, tongue finding mine.

'Thank you for a lovely holiday,' she whispers, her heels returning to earth. 'Beautiful boy.'

'Not too young?' I ask, pulling her closer.

She gasps, looks down. 'Mmm, definitely not,' she murmurs, feeling the hard pulse in my shorts. She presses against me, rubs up and down. 'Wish I could do something about that.'

I'm about to suggest she does when a voice calls out.

'¡Vamos! ¡Vamos!'

We turn to see Pablo trotting down the drive, waving his keys, a wine-shaped package in his hand – a leaving gift.

'Damn,' I say, with a theatrical sigh. 'There's always the aeroplane. If we survive the motorway.'

'Come on,' she says, waving back, breaking into a run. 'Last one to the car sits in the front.'

37

AUGUST 1992

It's pathetic, I know, but I'm in tears on the coach from the airport. It doesn't help that it's grey, wet, the sun nowhere to be seen; it's August, for God's sake. I stare hopelessly out of the window at the sad English evening rolling by, knowing that all too soon we're going to be wrenched apart. I don't want this time together to end. I want to go back to Spain, live it all again, even the excruciating photoshoots with Carlota's son, the awkward waiter, buying condoms from the little old shopkeeper. Most of all, our middle-of-the-night talks on the balcony, naked swimming, sex on the boat. I don't want reality. I don't want school, exams, uniform and rules. I don't want to see anyone – Mum, teachers, my friends with their predictable summer holiday stories. I'm beyond all that now; I've grown. All I want is Ali, to myself, forever.

She's weepy too, until she falls asleep, her head on my chest, my arm numb around her shoulders. I wish I had my Walkman; I could really do with Robert Smith right now. When the bus pulls into the station, I'm drained, cried out, thankful that Mum isn't picking me up. That was another of

Ali's brainwaves, to say we were travelling back a day later. We fall into her flat, into bed and a long, heavy sleep.

Next morning, I wake to an empty bed and noises off. Not breakfast noises – more like books or boxes being moved. I get up, pad down the corridor, into the sitting room where the lights are on. Ali's on the floor, head down, surrounded by textbooks, exercise books, handwritten essays she's organizing into neat stacks.

'Morning, sleepy boy,' she says, then looks up. 'Oh. Naked sleepy boy.'

'What are you doing?' I yawn, stretch, raise my arms above my head, interlacing my fingers. She studies me for a second, then returns to her piles of paper.

'Boring school stuff. It filled my dreams all night, so I had to get up, get things in order, you know? No, of course you don't know. There's some orange juice in the fridge. I think it's still in date.'

'This light's a bit grim. Want me to open the shutters?' I offer, picking my way across the carpet to the windows.

'No, leave them,' she says curtly.

'Oh yes, sorry, I forgot. My head's still in Spain,' I say, stepping back.

'How can you forget?' She sighs, sits back on her heels. 'This isn't holiday, Joe. We have to get back to normal. We have to be extra careful.'

'I know, I know.' I crouch on the floor beside her, and she lets me kiss her neck. An idea comes into my head as my lips brush her skin. 'Imagine if I gave you a love bite.'

'What is wrong with you this morning?' She pushes me off.

'Jesus, I don't know, playing. I wasn't actually going to do it,' I say, getting to my feet, keeping the suggestion of going back to bed in my head. 'So . . . plans for today?'

'Well, you can see what I'm doing. Term starts in a few days. I've got staff meetings, lesson prep, calendar planning.' She pushes her hair up, ties it back with the scrunchie from her wrist. 'Sorry,' she says, putting a hand on my leg, rubbing my calf. 'Look, give me fifteen minutes. Have a shower or something. Get dressed. We'll have breakfast, but then—'

'It's all right, Ali. I was just trying to keep the holiday going. I've never been so happy.'

She smiles up at me. 'That's sweet. Me too. Uh-oh,' she adds, noticing the effect of her hand on my leg.

'Last chance,' I say. 'For a while, I guess.'

'Get in that shower!'

After my shower, we sit at the big table, her school stuff pushed to one end. She eats muesli, which I don't understand, while I have toast and honey. She drinks coffee, I drink milk (the juice was off). She looks appalled, but I explain that I always have this toast-honey-milk combination when I stay at my gran's. When I say it out loud, I immediately regret it, and change the topic.

'So, when are we going to see each other?' I ask hopefully.

'It's going to be hell for the next few weeks. A new school year; it's always crazy.' She rests her elbow on the table, chin in her hand. With her other hand, she reaches for mine. 'Busy term for you, too. Upper Sixth.'

'Yes, you're right,' I agree, and for the first time my school brain kicks in. I run my thumb along her fingers in turn as the prospect of what's to come this term fills my head. 'I suppose we can't run away?'

'Not really. But you'll still come over, right?' She brightens, pushes her fingers against mine, pressing our palms together. 'Thursday nights – you're still going to "stay" at Nick's, aren't you? And weekends, I'll be free, apart from marking.'

'Yeah, I hope so,' I say, sounding vague.

'What do you mean, "hope so"?' She takes my other hand. 'What else are you going to be doing?'

I breathe in. 'Well, I just know Mum's going to be on the case this term. Especially in the build-up to the Oxford exams, the choral scholarship trials.'

'Oh, *Oxford*, your *mother*.' She pulls her hands away. I don't know how to respond, but I can feel my cheeks colouring.

'Yeah – mums, huh.' I look down at my hands. 'She just wants me to do my best.'

'Is this because I was doing schoolwork this morning? Are you punishing me?'

'No, of course not, Ali. Obviously not.'

'And Nick – staying there – is that going to change as well?'

'No, well, I don't think so. It's not really up to me.' I stop before the words *'it's up to Mum'* spill out, but she's already there.

'Don't tell me: your mum again. Christ. You need to stand up to her.'

'I will. I promise. Don't worry, I'll definitely stay on Thursdays. And weekends, when I've got Chapel Choir. I'll make some excuse to stay on after, get the train home.'

This seems to reassure her. At least, she's stopped pouting.

'Hey,' I say, 'it will be nice to see the holiday photos. Are you going to get them developed this week?'

'Maybe.' She smiles but fixes me with narrow eyes. 'I'll have to ask my mum.'

PART TWO

UPPER SIXTH

38

SEPTEMBER 1992

The first week of the new school term hits the whole year group like a train. Teachers, housemasters, form tutors are all on the warpath before we've barely got out of the starting blocks. Every assignment in every subject is *your highest priority*. Homework increases, deadlines tighten and detentions hover like Damoclean swords for anyone thinking of slacking.

The scene is set, and to my horror most of my peers are dashing onto the stage, slotting into character. It's like they've been prepared for this final performance their whole lives, whereas I'm reeling, still fumbling around backstage, struggling with my costume. I realize that my friends – Nick, Ant, Chris, Tom, all of them – spent their summer holidays with one thing in common: predictable continuity. Nothing exciting happened to any of them, while I cling to my memories of Spain and Ali, the forbidden freedom, the intoxicating taste of a life that could be waiting for us. But those memories slip out of focus with each passing day.

Then there's home. Mum, surprisingly incurious about the Spanish trip. At first, I think she's on to me, holding back, waiting for just the right moment to confront me, tell me she knows everything. But she's indifferent to my stories of Barcelona, life with a real Spanish family, which is bloody annoying given the lengths I've gone to, an entire ten days of fabrication.

She seems distracted. She sits me down in the kitchen *for a talk* and I tense, brace myself for the big reveal, the shouting, the grounding.

'While you were away,' she begins, kneading the tablecloth, 'I "met" someone.'

I fiddle with my bit of tablecloth.

'Right. What's his name?' I ask, like I don't really want to know.

'His name is "Gordon",' she says, pinching the air as if not fully accepting this name. 'He's very kind. High up in . . .' – she stalls, looks out of the window for an answer – '. . . a large company, manufacturing or engineering.'

Well, the main thing is he's high up in wherever it is, I think, but don't voice. Then something takes hold of me. An image. It's Dad, looking sad, depressed. My lips swell, my eyes sting, but I don't know why. I should be happy for Mum. It feels strange, though, like everything's different, uncertain. I smile with my mouth closed, swallow, then make some excuse about homework, go back to my bedroom, fill my ears with Blur, and pretend to work. I'm quite into Blur, actually.

My gut tells me to catch the next train back to see Ali, but I know that's not an option. For one thing, I haven't seen her properly all week. There was a brief brush outside chapel after start-of-term assembly; other than that, all I've been granted are stolen glances across the classroom.

*

By week two, the outlook for extracurricular activities with Miss P is dire. I can hardly breathe under the weight of assignments, when I'm called into a tutorial organized by the Head of Oxbridge Entrance with a guest appearance from the headmaster himself. According to Nick this meeting is billed as a 'motivational reckoning'. I don't know what that means, but motivating it is not: a stark warning to *each and every boy here* (half the candidates are girls) to *not fail the school, our teachers, our families*. Open-mouthed, I look around the room to see if I am the only one who was expecting a rousing message of hope, encouragement and good wishes to send us, in a united, mutually supportive way, on the path to a world of academic prosperity. Dispiritingly, I think I probably am.

The message hits home, though, establishing a routine of long days filled with hours of reading, revision, surprise tests (*Surprise!*) and mock exams. The phrase 'free period' is banned, replaced with timetabled 'study periods', and most of these have to be supervised in designated classrooms. Sadly, none of mine are supervised by Miss P, so I don't even get to see her under exam conditions.

As if the workload wasn't enough, extra singing and piano lessons are added to my groaning schedule. It turns out that the Head of Music forgot to mention, when putting me up for a choral scholarship, that I would need to pass Grade 8 in both disciplines to stand a chance at Oxford, *with distinction in singing, Gibson, if not piano as well*. I'm drowning in Debussy, mired in Mozart, buried in Beethoven, and that's before I even turn a page on Schubert's relentlessly melancholic song cycles.

'If only the stress ended there,' I complain to Mum on the weekend. She's going out with "Gordon" but pauses in my bedroom doorway. She listens, though doesn't venture any further into my room.

'Then there's the commute,' I continue. 'It's an hour from when I leave home before I even get to school. Same at the end of the day.'

'But you're doing ever so well and just think, if you get into Oxford,' she says *Oxford* like *Heaven*. 'All my friends are *terribly* impressed,' she adds. I throw my head into my hands.

'Oh God, don't tell everyone, Mum. What if I don't get in?'

She answers with silence. I sink lower, my palms covering my eyes. I haven't told her everything yet, either, but I already know what her reaction will be.

'Well, I'd better—' she says, edging away.

'Hang on, Mum, there's something else.'

'Oh dear.'

'Try not to make a thing about it, because I haven't accepted yet. My housemaster wants to make me a prefect, but I really don't think I've got the—'

'Do it!' She claps her hands together. 'You absolutely must, darling. It's an honour, a tremendous privilege, and it will look marvellous on your CV.' And with that, she ruffles out of my room, no doubt anxious to share the 'marvellous' news with "Gordon".

39

OCTOBER 1992

Masturbating to Guns N' Roses is my activity of choice and necessity by the third week of term. My Thursday night encounters with Ali have dried up before they even started, and I've been excused Chapel Choir most Sundays to rest my voice, so we can't see each other at weekends either. I'm pretty sure I'm not a sex addict, but after Spain's diet of several times a day, I'm getting withdrawal symptoms. It doesn't help that I haven't had much time for phoning either, and when we do speak on snatched, rushed, faceless calls, I feel like I'm saying all the wrong things. Hiding in the bathroom or late at night in bed has become a full-scale, heavy-metal wank fest. I have to buy more batteries for my Walkman. It's getting me through the monotony of school hell, and as I don't really have any other hobbies, it's almost something to look forward to. Until a new obsession replaces *Mr. Brownstone*.

On my daily train journeys, I read. At first, it's not for pleasure; falling behind is probably a flogging offence. The Upper Sixth year reading list looks like a library's worth, stuffed with the usual suspects: Dickens, Brontë, Austen, Eliot,

Hardy, Lawrence, Forster, the inescapable Shakespeare. But once I've waded through as many of them as I can find in the school library, I start to explore the novelists further down the list, a far more interesting crowd: Hemingway, Woolf, Carter, Lorca, Pagnol, Stoker, Stendhal, Kerouac, Roché, McEwan. I bury my mother in *The Cement Garden*, criss-cross the States in ecstatic delirium in *On the Road* then drive off another road at the hands of a mad woman in *Jules et Jim*. I'm travelling dangerously with Hemingway, living as a free spirit in Woolf's bohemia, falling hopelessly in love with Manon in Pagnol's Provence.

The hours become days, then weeks. With everyone furiously head-down in study, I lose myself in those pages and wonder whether it's too late to change my university subject to English. After the stink they've kicked up about me being this year's *only hope at Oxbridge* for the Languages department, I hold my tongue.

Then it's all change again, a month or so into term, when our German teachers launch an oral offensive. In September, lessons were dedicated to preparing two topics for the final written exams: in my case, the recent reunification of East and West Germany in 1990 and, because I'm learning his song cycles for my singing exams, the life of Franz Schubert.

Come October, they put us into pairs to practise our conversation skills. It's quite nice to be teamed up with a classmate, especially as I don't have any other subjects with this group. In fact, despite a year of studying together, I hardly know any of them outside class. Or in it, for that matter, and certainly not the girl they put me with, the exceptionally shy Gulika Sharma. The only thing we have in common is that we both started school here on the same day.

The hum of voices swirls around the room, fragmented phrases piecing together into sentences, breaking into stifled giggles, repairing, building again, while Gulika sits in some kind of fugue state as I attempt to ask about her chosen topic. It's at best interrogation, at worst a form of torture. I'm actually sweating. After ten minutes, I give up, look at the clock, appalled there's still twenty minutes of this to go.

'What's the matter?' I say, retreating to English, in my most calm voice.

'. . .' she replies, unhelpfully.

'Look, this is something we have to do, you know? It's for the exam.' I try to catch her eye, but she's staring at the table.

'Okay, I'll go first, shall I?' I offer. No response. I begin, '*Franz Schubert ist am 31 Januar 1797 im Himmelpfortgrund, Österreich, geboren . . .*'

Three minutes later, I've prattled through my summary of his life. I've even thrown my comedy German accent at some of the words, like his ludicrous-sounding birthplace, to raise a smile or even just an eyebrow. Nothing. May as well have been speaking to the wall. I finish with a weary sigh, turn back to my desk.

'I can't,' says the tiniest voice I've ever heard; it's almost inaudible. I have to face her to check it really came out of her. She's looking straight at me through two thick-framed lenses, her eyes a drowsy dark brown. Careful not to draw any attention to us, I speak in a low voice.

'What do you mean, you can't?'

'I make too many mistakes,' she replies, still holding my gaze.

'Oh, come on, Gulika, your marks are always at the top of the class,' I say, trying to reassure her.

'In writing, yes; not speaking. The boys make fun of me, and I make mistakes. My accent is wrong.'

'Really?' I ask. I hadn't noticed, but then in this place, I wouldn't be surprised. Gulika can only be one of a small handful of non-white pupils in the school. I feel my cheeks warming, a mix of anger, shame, embarrassment. I hear how stupid and ignorant saying 'really?' must sound. I angle my body towards her, shield her with my back to the others.

'Listen, for starters, the boys are all twats. In fact, anyone who says your accent is "wrong" ...' – now I'm doing the air quotes – '... is a ...' – I look for a word that is appropriately strong enough but that won't offend her – '... a massive—'

'Twat?' she says, quickly dipping her head, but I know she's smiling from the two dimples that lift her cheekbones.

'Gulika!' I whisper in theatrical shock.

She looks up again, brighter, less agitated, and we share a smile.

'*Fünf minuten!*' barks Mr Grice from behind his newspaper, feet up on the desk at the front of the room. Not a care in the world, as usual.

'Can you help me?' Gulika now asks.

I nod. 'Of course. How?'

'Not here. Could we practise for the oral exam in the library? Maybe in a study period?'

'Okay,' I agree, since she's not going to speak in class, which means I won't get to practise properly either. 'We're supposed to be supervised, in here, but I'll explain to Mr Grice, if that's all right with you?'

It is, and after class I get permission for us to spend the rest of the week's study periods in the library.

40

OCTOBER 1992

Furnished entirely of wood, accessible only through an enormous oak door and housing over 15,000 books, the school library is the 'architectural jewel in the school's crown'. That it's a hazardous death trap with no fire escape doesn't appear in the school prospectus. In winter, the librarian, who has been in post since the 1860s, installs a portable gas heater, which he trundles up and down the aisles. Not so much a house of learning as a perilous tinder box; all it would take is just one spark.

But it looks nice when showing new parents around, so that's the main thing. And they love all the old colonial shit. A line of mahogany cabinets under glass cases separates the narrow aisles, displaying Old Boy medals, trophies of war, weaponry, etc. Either side, spaced out at wide intervals, are eight floor-to-ceiling bookcases, at right angles to the room, creating bays of tables and chairs for silent study. Or snogging, when the librarian isn't around.

I'm late arriving and think I may have missed Gulika, but I find her, ensconced in a corner about halfway down the room. She's tiny, like a bird, but even smaller in here, dwarfed by the mountainous shelves. Her head buried in a book, her face obscured by long, black hair, she's almost invisible to the naked eye. She's a neat worker, with no other textbooks or exercise pads on the table. Wary of making her jump, I pause at the edge of the bay, rap tentatively on the side of a bookcase.

'Oh hi,' she says, peering up, eyes blinking behind her thick round glasses. Lit by a huge stained-glass window, she looks different – brighter, happier, more relaxed for sure. I take the chair opposite.

'Sorry I'm late, Gulika,' I say, dropping my bag noisily, pulling my books out. 'Have you been here long?'

She looks around, stiffens.

'Oops, sorry, again,' I say in an exaggerated whisper. 'Library rules, of course, no shouting, no speaking, no breathing, ha ha.'

'It's fine. I just love the peace in here,' she says, her voice lilting, her face serene and exotic. I bet she does meditation and headstands in her free time. 'By the way, you can call me Lika, if you like?'

'I do lika – I mean like – sorry!'

She laughs softly. 'Stop saying sorry all the time. Shall we have a go at our German oral?'

Two words that don't fit easily together. I decide now isn't the time or place to share that thought.

'Yes. Do you want to start?'

Lika's command of German grammar – sentence structure, cases, rules – is immaculate. I'm supposed to be good at this, but her precision makes me sound sloppy. She's super brainy, that's obvious. What she isn't, is audible. As her mini-presentation on early twentieth-century German politics proceeds, her voice recedes. I'm having to lean across the table, straining, catching only the bare fragments of her speech when she takes breaths, regrouping at the start of sentences. She looks up.

'Yeah, it's good, Lika. Keep going, I'm listening,' I say, not wanting to put her off now she's come this far.

'But I've finished,' she says, with a shrug. 'That's why I said, "*Und das ist das Ende meiner Präsentation.*"'

'Right, yes, of course.' I lift my hunched forearms off the table and sit back.

'So, what did you think? Be truthful with me.' She looks earnest, anxious, not for approval I suspect, more for accuracy. I shuffle around in my chair, trying to form a coherent sentence that won't betray how little of her presentation I heard.

'Your grammar is spot on,' I say weakly. 'And it's an interesting topic, really well-researched.'

She narrows her eyes at me. 'What did you think of the comparison I made with the British political system at that time? Did it work?'

'Definitely. That was a good . . . comparison.'

She nods her head slowly, looks out of the window.

'Hmm. Thing is, I didn't mention that in my talk.' She side-glances me.

Busted.

'Why are you lying?' she asks.

'I'm not! I mean, I am,' I falter. 'Okay, you got me. I didn't hear a word, Lika.'

'What? Why on earth did you let me continue, then?' She places her hands flat on the table, where another person might have slammed them. I doubt she's ever slammed a door or raised her voice at anything or anyone.

'I didn't want to stop your flow—' But she cuts me off.

'The flow of the river to the empty boat is meaningless without its sail, its sailor.'

I stare at her magnified eyes, my jaw open.

'Bloody hell, Lika. That's deep. Where did that come from?'

'It's something my *nani*, my grandmother, told me,' she says mysteriously. Well, probably not mysteriously, but I'm entranced nonetheless.

'Say something else like that.' I lean forward again. 'What else do you know?'

'You can be a clown in the crowd, but I'm not your performing monkey.'

'Wow! That's brilliant!'

'No, you don't get it,' she says flatly. 'That wasn't a saying, silly. I'm telling you off.'

And the way she says it, the image she conjures, the thought of Gulika Sharma telling anyone off, sends me into a fit of laughter that sets her off as well, despite her best attempts to hold it in behind the hands she clamps over her mouth.

'Lika, you're funny—' Instinctively, I reach my arms across the table, palms open, about to clap.

'What's going on here?' A spat whisper, making us jump in our seats. 'Joseph Gibson!'

'Miss!' I freeze, my arms still stretched out, my teeth involuntarily biting my lower lip, heat rising fast to my cheeks.

'We were just—' I begin, choking my words, folding my arms over my chest.

'And who are you?' she fires at Lika, ignoring me.

'Miss, Gulika Sharma, Miss,' says Lika, shrinking. I wince. Her answer sounds like a terrified child. I want to protect her, but as I glance from one to the other, Miss P to Gulika, Ali to Lika, I'm torn. No one speaks for a moment. Lika looks like she's about to cry. Ali, eyes glued to my classmate, is breathing hard, her neck and the top of her chest, where the blouse exposes her skin, flaring. I try to think. There must be something I can say to cool this down. 'Ali, you're massively overreacting,' I can hardly say.

'Miss, we're studying for our German or— ... speaking exam.' I find my voice at last. 'Mr Grice knows; he gave us permission to work in here.'

Slowly, Ali drags her gaze back to me, but it's as if she doesn't want to see me. I will her to calm down, implore her with my eyes, but when our eyes meet, I'm forced to look down.

'This. Is. A. Library,' she says, puncturing each word. 'And you are final-year students. You should be setting an example, to the lower years ...' Her voice wavers, trailing off. Raising my head, I catch her swallow. There is wet around her eyes.

'We know, Miss, we're really sorry,' I say, emphasizing my words. 'It won't happen again.' Her eyes are shining. I can tell she wants to blink or wipe them, but she fights the impulse. My heart is hurting now I can see how upset she is behind her anger, finding me here with a girl.

'It's nothing, Miss. It's not what you think,' I want to say, but I can't in front of Lika. And I can hardly tell her how much I miss her. Because suddenly, in this moment, as it occurs to me how little I've seen her, how we haven't been together, alone, for over a month, I miss her so much. I want to get up, take her hand, hold her tight.

'I promise you, Miss,' I say, with all feeling. 'It absolutely won't happen again.'

'Good. Make sure it doesn't.' The harsh edge has gone, but her tone remains cool, or perhaps just spent. She frowns again in the direction of Lika and clears her throat, says in a softer voice, 'It's almost the end of the study period. You should think about packing up.'

Then, without another glance, she's gone.

When I hear the library door close, I stand, peer around the bookcase to make sure.

'Oh God, oh God.' Lika is already on her feet, stuffing the book into her bag. 'Will she tell on us? My housemistress is a fierce woman; she will punish me severely.'

'No, of course she won't tell,' I say, though I'm not completely confident. No, surely Ali wouldn't do that; it was nothing. Unless, out of spite at me. 'It's not as if we were doing anything terrible, is it?'

But Lika hurries past me. As the door shuts again, I turn to gather my books.

'Christ, that's all I need,' I mutter into my bag, grateful at least that the library is empty and no one else has witnessed this drama.

'It's your own fault.'

I brace, swing round. I step back, almost tripping over my chair. It's Ali, standing in the same spot as before.

'How? But . . . I thought you'd gone. You went.'

'You hoped I'd gone, more like.' She takes a step forward. I can see she's been crying. Her eyes are dry now, but red around the rims.

'Eh? Why do you say that?'

'Do you think I'm blind? You and little miss—'

'Whoa, Ali! I mean, Miss. You've got this completely wrong. We were studying.'

'Oh really? You were holding hands!'

'What? No, we weren't. She . . . I . . . were just . . . laughing about something.'

'Laughing at what? At me?'

'Oh my God! Obviously not.'

'This is why you haven't come to see me, isn't it?' she says, jabbing a finger at me.

'For fuck's sake.' I throw my arms up, unable to find the words I need. I am burning all over now. I can't take this. I want to get out of here, but she is blocking the way.

'Well? It is, isn't it? *She's* the reason.' She points at the door, her arm arrow straight.

I want to scream, but hold it in. I take a deep breath. 'I promise,' I say quietly, as though respecting library etiquette, but in fact I'm just drained. Ali doesn't look convinced.

'I'm sorry. I don't believe you,' she sighs, lips thin and pursed when I desperately want them to soften, refill.

'Do you really think *she* is a match for *you*?' Now I'm pointing, although I feel guilty for chucking Lika in front of the bus.

'I don't know what to think,' says Ali, bending forward, her hands gripping the edge of the table. Lowering her head, she murmurs something.

'What did you say?' I ask. 'I couldn't hear you.'

Her shoulders drop. 'I said, perhaps we should just . . . call it off. Stop all this.'

'No, no, no,' I say urgently. 'Please. Don't say that.'

'It's too hard,' she sighs. 'You're going to hurt me, I know it.'

I step towards her. She doesn't move.

'I'm not. I would never hurt you.'

'You will. You'll make me jealous.'

'No way. You don't have to be jealous. Look – you've got me. I'm here. I'm yours.'

She straightens up, runs both hands through her hair, pulling it back off her face. I want to put my hand on her neck but, just as that thought comes, the bell for end of lessons goes. Within seconds the sounds of hurrying feet, of voices released, echo around the quad outside. I can hear them on the stone steps of the tower and will them to pass the library. I speak quickly, repeating myself, because I can't think of what words I should be saying. I just know we can't leave this here.

'Ali, please, give me a chance. Let me make it up to you.'

She opens her mouth to speak, but whatever she was going to say is silenced by a loud bang. A small troop of excitable girls giggles into the room. They see us, or rather they see Miss P, and clam up, shushing each other exaggeratedly.

'Sorry, Miss,' they chime, in unison. As they pass, I recognize a couple of them from Chapel Choir, and they acknowledge me with raised eyebrows, put-on pouts, more giggles.

Meanwhile, Ali, deliberately changing her stance, moving slightly away from me, turns to me and says in her measured classroom voice: 'So, if you can finish the Gómez essay and get it to me by the end of the week, I'll mark it over the weekend.'

'Yes, Miss,' is all I can summon, although the girls have already planted themselves in a bay at the far end of the library.

'Or maybe, we can mark it together.' And this time when

she looks at me, the daggers have gone from her eyes, her voice is a little warmer, though her expression is inscrutable so that I have to check I've heard correctly.

'Do you mean, sorry, I ... when?' I stutter.

There are more feet in the tower, threatening another invasion.

'Well,' she says, not blinking, 'if you are serious about me, like you say you are, come this weekend, after Saturday lessons.'

I hitch my bag onto my shoulder, make a thing about getting both arms through the straps, which I never do, but I'm trying to think.

'Or does Mummy want you to stay home?' she says, with absolutely no hint of a smile. I try not to flinch or let her see how her words sting. Truth is, she's hit the sodding nail on the head. It's not so much that Mum is on my back to be at home all the time. It's more that I've got into a routine now that is just about keeping me on top of my workload. Not that I'm not gagging to see Ali, to go to bed with her, wake up beside her, eat croissants and pasta and drink wine like we used to. I find it hard to juggle both worlds, is all. But that's not what she wants to hear. Definitely, unequivocally, life-threateningly, hideous-scene-inducingly, not.

'I'll come.'

41

OCTOBER 1992

After Saturday morning lessons, I run back to my house study
to change out of my uniform; it's a room of my own, the only
privilege I can make out for being house prefect. I need to
move fast, under cover of the lunch rush, and get off campus
before I'm spotted. I'm in luck – the other boys are sprinting
the other way to the dining hall. There's a chance my tutor,
Batsford, will be in his office, in which case I'm screwed, as
he's bound to call me in for a chat to discuss house matters, but
I keep my head down, use some straggling Fourth Formers to
shield my passage past the office, then dart along the corridor
to my room. It's a tiny space and doesn't have a lock – *can't
have you getting up to no good in there* – so I'm quickly out of
my school trousers and into jeans. I'm pulling my school shirt
over my head when – shitting hell – Batsford calls down
the corridor.

'Ah, Gibson, splendid.' How did he know? 'Two minutes,
when you're ready.'

'Yes, sir,' I call from behind my door, dragging the shirt
back on. 'I'll be there in—'

'Now, thank you.'

It's not worth annoying him, so I make my way to his office, half in, half out of uniform.

'What's this – has the weekend come early?' he says, peering over his spectacles as I enter, tucking in my shirt. 'Lessons may be over, but school isn't. I'll need you on the touchline this afternoon. It's the house rugby semi-finals, as well you know, and our chaps need all the support they can get.'

Ours is not the 'sporty' house. We're not the most academic either. More music, drama, art. I want to argue that, prefect or not, my presence pitch-side isn't going to make an ounce of difference to the result. We're fucked out there. My expression must be giving this away.

'Yes, we'll be like lambs to the slaughter, again,' he says, not exaggerating. 'But the boys need you. Your house needs you. We must all play our part.'

'Thing is, sir.' I have to get out of this. 'I've got a mountain of reading to do.'

'You're always reading, Gibson.'

'Well, yes, for Oxford, the exams ...'

'Oh, yes, of course,' he sighs. Of all the teachers, Batsford seems the least interested in academic achievement. Or perhaps he thinks I'm wasting my time. He might be right. 'How about you come for the first half, then toddle off to the library or home after that?'

'Um.'

'Excellent. That's settled.' He waves me away. 'And back into uniform, there's a good chap. Dismissed.'

I retreat to my study, close the door and slump to the floor. Of all the Saturdays he could have chosen, why this one? The house rugby team is always getting shat on, week in, week out; this will be no different. My mind whirrs. Unless. Does he know what I'm actually doing? Surely he'd confront me if he suspected I was skipping school to go to Ali's. But how would he know?

I change back into uniform. I need to get a message to Ali, to say I'll be late. Not a good start to a weekend of bridge-building. I look at my watch. The lunch hour is well underway, it's unlikely she'll still be in her classroom, but it's worth a try. I make a point of treading heavily down the corridor and raise a hand at Batsford as I leave the house in the direction of the dining hall.

Instead of taking a right, I go left until I reach her classroom. I knock. No reply. I try the handle. Locked. Fuck. But there is something, a hint of her in the air, her perfume; it's unmistakeable. I'm guessing she's in the staffroom, so, as inconspicuously as possible, I make my way to the door.

'Ah, young Gibson.' I'm greeted with a bulb-eyed smile and I'm relieved that it's one of my favourite teachers. Dr Goodwin, Music. 'What an unexpected, indeed, jocund delight.'

'Thank you, Miss,' I say, unfazed by her eccentricity, because this is how she speaks all the time. 'I'm looking for Miss P?'

'*Quelle coincidence.*' She flicks a strand of hair from her eyes. 'A popular lady. For have not five minutes elapsed since last she was sought?'

'Oh right. Yes, she's a popular teacher.'

'Hmm.' She fixes me with a pitying gaze. 'I regret, you are too late,' she says leisurely. 'I know she was here, but I couldn't find her then, and I'll wager I won't find her now.'

'So, she's not here, miss?'

'Correct. Would you like to leave a note in her pigeon-hole?' She gestures to a notepad and pencil on a shelf by the door.

'Maybe, um . . . yes,' I stutter. 'Just say, the essay you wanted handed in today is going to be a little later than planned, if that's okay.'

She raises her wispy eyebrows, presenting me with the pad and pencil. 'I haven't, to my knowledge, been appointed pupil secretary by our auspicious governors, Gibson.'

Apologizing, I take the pad, scribble the note and hand it back. Dr Goodwin edges backwards, her owl eyes still on me as the door closes, slowly, between us.

After two hours I'll never get back, stamping up and down the touchline shouting futile words of encouragement at a team intent on winning the prize for heaviest defeat, I manage to slide away. I'm running hopelessly late, have no idea whether Ali picked up my note, but out of habit take a route which twists and winds. What's more, I'm still in uniform, so I'm extra watchful. With my run of luck, our relationship dangling by a thread, not to mention the elaborate story I sold Mum, now would be when I get caught.

I tread carefully, pausing only outside the corner shop. Memories of that first encounter, way back in March, a whole two terms past. I should buy a bottle, I think, but he wouldn't serve me alcohol last time. I don't have the energy for more humiliation. Still, I can't turn up empty-handed. I choose the least offensive bunch of flowers from a bucket on the pavement and walk the final few hundred yards.

With my bag heavy on one arm, the other pushed inside

my blazer to conceal the damp flowers, now soaking my shirt and skin through the thin fabric, I reach the end of her road. I can see the big sash windows of her sitting room, halfway up the street.

What's waiting behind the glass? Am I coming here to be forgiven for what happened in the library, for my absence all term? Or is she going to dump me?

I take a few deep breaths, feel my nerves, sharp like pins all over my body. I glance over my shoulder. What if I just . . . went home? Got the train. Read my book. Listened to my music. Hid in my room. *Don't be a coward*, says a voice in my head. *You're too far in. You can't do that to her. You can't stop now.*

The voice is right. Standing her up now would be mean, pathetic. The sort of immature thing some of the lads at school might do. Well, I'm not them. I start walking. I look around, make sure the street is clear before ducking into her drive and quickly up the steps to her building. I do the secret ring; she buzzes me in. The inner door to her flat is ajar, familiar and inviting. She's probably in the kitchen, I guess, or the sitting room with her marking. But she's not. She's here, standing in front of me, a white bath towel pulled across her body, another wrapped around her head.

'You're late.' She looks cross, like I've turned up unannounced. 'What's that?' She points at my chest. 'Something else you're hiding from me?'

I wince at the stab of her words but open my blazer to reveal the flowers. Some of the petals, crushed, drop to the floor.

'I'm sorry I'm late,' I say, adding quickly, 'and about what happened in the library, and about these rubbish flowers.' I hold them out, losing more petals. I bite my lip hard. I can't even get this right. 'Great,' I sigh, looking down. 'Failed again. I'm really sorry. Perhaps I should just go.'

'No, you're not going anywhere,' she says firmly. 'These,' she adds, taking the useless flowers from my hand, letting them fall, 'we probably can't revive. But you and me,' she says, pushing me back against the door, meeting me with bright, searching eyes. 'Well, let's find out, shall we?'

She stands back. Still holding my gaze, she moves a hand across the towel, following the shape of her breasts, then untucks the corner. She steps out of the white bundle of cotton at her feet and presses against me again. I can feel her nipples through my shirt, the pressure of her thighs, her pubic bone, my body responding, hardening. Her hands work the clasp of my belt free, unzip and her fingers hook round my underpants, sliding them down as she sinks to her knees. We haven't even kissed yet, but her lips are on me, nipping the base of my cock, running up its length, back down. I hold onto the towel still covering her hair. I hastily calculate the hours since I showered. Too late to worry about that, as she grasps my erection and buries her head. Am I imagining it, or is her hand tightening? I tense. She's taken one of my balls in her mouth. Why? Now the other one. I'm paralyzed, completely at her mercy. I feel a sensation like all my blood is rushing to the danger zone, but then she lets go.

'Have you stopped breathing?' I hear her say and instinctively breathe out. She's right; I don't know how long I've been holding my breath.

'It's . . . been a while,' I croak.

'Mmm, too long,' she says, tracing her tongue to the tip,

circling slowly, then swallowing me whole, her hand stroking in rhythm with her mouth. My body jumps, I think I'm going to come, my hands wrench the towel on her head.

'Ouch!' she squeaks, muffled by my cock in her mouth, then pulls me out. 'Hair!'

She gets to her feet, hands now around the towel, easing it off, untangling strands of hair that are still attached. She discards the towel and grins at me, her face glowing with exertion, her lips slightly swollen.

'Ha ha,' she sniggers, looking down. 'You were lucky – narrow escape.'

'Oh my God!' I cry, both hands shielding my genitals. 'You wouldn't, would you? You wouldn't ... bite me?'

She snorts then, folding at her waist, laughs from somewhere deep in her gut.

'Yeah, just to check, is that a no?' I ask, taking her elbows to stand her up.

'Of course I wouldn't. Probably wouldn't.' She's still laughing but reaches for my hand. 'Come on, before I get carpet burns. Bed.'

The giggling has stopped, but Ali's raw urgency remains. It's like being in bed with an animal that's been caged, starved, every move greedy and unpredictable. Her arms flail, her hands grab, slap, fingers claw. I move away to avoid being scratched, torn, keeping my hands clamped to her breasts.

It's not exactly comfortable, having my arms stretched in one direction, while the rest of me is planted between her legs. It's when she lets go of my hands and I have to do both moves that I lose control. An image of standing in the playground at primary school, patting my head while rubbing my stomach, flashes unhelpfully before me.

The wild animal has calmed down and I seize the moment to withdraw. Then, without warning, her hands are in my armpits, forcing me upwards. I scramble, place my hands either side of her to support my weight so as not to flatten her.

Our bodies become one fused mass. I rut for all I'm worth, my hips slamming against hers. My breathing is fast, in sync with each thrust. I can hear a beat getting louder in my head.

Dada-Dada-Dada Dada Dada Dada-Dada-Dada Dada Dada.

Wait, that's ... a theme tune? Is that ... *Knight Rider?*

Da-dada-daa Da-dada-daa!

I can't hang on much longer, not like this. I look for her eyes, but they're closed tight.

'Ali,' I whisper urgently, 'I don't have a condom.'

She replies, but I can't hear the words.

'Ali,' I say, louder, still pumping. I glance to her bedside cabinet. I don't want to break the spell, so in my sexiest manly voice, I say, 'They're in the drawer.'

'No,' she says, eyes still closed.

'Really?'

'It's okay. It's safe.' Her words jar with short breaths. 'You can come.'

'Oh my God!' I can't believe it. She's letting me come inside her.

A memory of our condom-less first time flashes past me, but I still don't know why sometimes it's safe and other times not. Is she on the pill? How does that work? Why now? Everything about this shag is so different somehow.

These are not the thoughts, the questions, that I ask myself in that moment.

I just come.

We lie, side by side on the bed, both of us staring at the ceiling, only our little fingers touching. I can't stop grinning, then I start to replay and I'm full of questions. But I don't know how to frame what I want to ask. I turn my head on the pillow, open my mouth.

'So—' I begin.

'Shh.'

There's a blank, statuesque look to her face, not sad, but not happy either. She isn't blinking. She looks a thousand miles away.

'Shall we get up?' I whisper.

'Not yet,' she says.

I stay there, motionless, for another minute or so. Ali's eyes have closed again, perhaps she's asleep. I close mine too, but under the duvet, I inspect myself. It's strange not to feel the synthetic shrink-wrap I'm used to after normal sex. What I get is a spent, gluey, lolling form. I've never felt so naked. It's as if I've just had sex for the first time. Exciting, daring, naughty, rude. All those words drop from the ceiling like flakes of plaster. But other words come crashing down behind – *filthy, disgusting, wrong, humiliating, failed, expelled* – falling in heavy slabs of masonry, exposing the flat upstairs, people peering from above, arms folded, heads shaking. Mum, Dad, my sister, Cat, Mr Grice, Mr Batsford, Dr Goodwin, Nick, Ant, Lika – oh no, my grandparents!

'Argh!' My eyes snap open. My body jumps. The bedroom is spinning and I'm gulping for air.

'Hey,' says Ali, sitting up, a hand on my chest. 'What's wrong?'

The room slows, round and round, like a fairground ride, coming to a halt.

'What happened?' I ask, recovering my breath.

'You were asleep. You must have been dreaming. Hope it wasn't about me.'

'I saw . . .' I check what I'm about to say, try to act normal. 'No. Ha, it's nothing.'

'Right, well, I'm starving.' She kisses my nose, slides out of bed into knickers and a baggy T-shirt she picks off the floor, and pads off to the bathroom.

Hot and clammy, I throw back the duvet. Everything's still in place, yet everything's changed, somehow.

'Stop overreacting, you idiot,' I say out loud. 'She let you come inside her. That's real sex you just had.'

The rest of the weekend, well, that night and Sunday morning before I have to get to school for chapel and choir, is perfect. Like our long weekends in the summer term. Lazy, lounging, laughing. We eat all our favourites, drink ourselves into a sweet haze and listen to records.

In the night, we find each other in the half-light and have more unprotected sex. I'm too sleepy or too drunk to go down on her. It's no-bells shagging, no whistles blowing, but no falling bricks and mortar either. In the morning, we wake early to a thick mist in the garden outside her bedroom window. I peek through the shutters in the sitting room when Ali's in the shower. Her road is almost invisible beyond the front gate, the fog slithering over the garden wall. I retreat to the kitchen to help with breakfast.

We don't get dressed, but drag the duvet through, huddle together and watch hours of TV, hardly moving from the sofa. Ali says she has a surprise for me: our photos from Spain. We pore over them, remembering, but I can't help feeling it's a lifetime away. She holds up the picture of her and the waiter from the restaurant in Palamós.

'At least you got one where he's not looking shifty,' she laughs.

'That's the last one I took. You'd just thrown yourself at him. Poor man,' I say.

'I've got plans for you, *señor*,' she says, putting him to one side of the pile. She picks up two others. 'Here, you can take these for your mum.'

I study the faces of Carlota and her son, Raúl, my supposed exchange partner, in his black leathers. 'Jesus, you can see his stubble. She's never going to believe me.'

'She probably won't even look. Doesn't sound like she was that curious,' says Ali. A bit catty, I think, but I don't say anything. Don't want to ruin the atmosphere, and we've established that any talk that involves Mum often gets frosty.

When it's time to go and I'm standing by the door, back in my uniform, I ask, 'Can I have something, borrow something, of yours?'

'What do you mean?'

'I don't know.' I shrug. 'Something to make you feel closer.'

'I'm not sure,' she says, looking around. 'It can't be anything too obvious.'

On the hook behind the door, I leaf through her coats and scarves. At the very back is a grey woolly hat, but baggier.

'What's this?'

'Oh, I haven't worn that for a while. It's a snood,' she says, reaching for it.

'A what?'

'A snood. It's a kind of scarf, a sort of hood, but you wear it on its own. Look.'

She wraps and folds it around her neck, then pulls one side up at the back to cover her head.

'You look like a gypsy.'

'That's why I rarely wear it.'

'I like it. Can I borrow it, just for a bit?'

She thinks for a moment, taking it off, running it through her hands. She lifts it to her face, inhales through her nose.

'I suppose you could. I don't think I've worn it at school since last autumn. It smells a bit musty.' She hands it over.

'It smells of you,' I say. 'What's your perfume called?'

'Samsara.'

I stuff the snood into my bag. Before she can object, I've opened the door and I'm in the hall.

'Hey. No goodbye?'

I turn. 'You know I hate this bit.'

She presses the latch, runs over, kisses me, then holds me by the shoulders, her arms extended out in front of her, like she's studying an unidentified object.

'See you in school, then,' I say.

'Hmm,' she murmurs, not taking her eyes off me. 'Call me, won't you?'

Retracing my way on yesterday's pavements, back to school, I'm filled with a sense of unease. *How is it I'm fully clothed, but still feel naked?* During the chapel service, my attention to the music veers off, I even stop singing in the middle of a psalm.

They're passing notes on paper up and down the choir stall, each person adding to it on its way through. I hear the sniggers, but I don't get involved. When the note is handed to me, I let it drop to the floor. I can't be doing with this childish shit.

We didn't make a plan to meet up. *Why didn't we make a plan?* She let me borrow her snood. I thought everything was cool. *Why was she looking at me with that weird expression, like I was a stranger?* After chapel, Nick invites me for Sunday lunch with his family, but I tell him I need to get home, to work. On the train, I have no concentration for reading or music, and the journey passes like the blurred view through the window. My spirits start to lift as I walk home. For once, I'm glad to be there. I can't wait to shut the door of my bedroom. I don't even mind performing for Mum's friends, if she doesn't turn it into a full-length recital.

I pause at the front door, my hand in my trouser pocket, forefinger outlining the hard, jagged contours of the key. Not quite ready to come home, it seems. Not quite able to open this door. I remove my hand, hold the key to the lock, like a question mark in mid-air. Maybe it's nothing, but I can't shake the feeling that I've left a question unanswered, somewhere in Ali's flat.

42

NOVEMBER 1992

A few weeks later I get my answer, but by then, I've kind of forgotten all about it.

November sets in with its usual joylessness. The fun bits of autumn, like carved pumpkins, toffee apples and trick or treat, disappear in the foul mush of leaves clogging the roadside. As colder rains fall, the pavements between school and train station become perilously slippery. The clocks fall back an hour, which makes my journey to and from school darker, more threatening. Even cars, trucks and buses seem set against me, bunching up in belching lines through the city centre, their suffocating stench slowing my passage.

But worse than all this, I don't see much of Ali and never out of school. We speak less on the phone because she's often out in the evenings. *Interminable staff meetings*, she tells me. I can see the pressure of it on her face, in her behaviour, in class. She looks exhausted. I feel sorry for her, being a teacher, working so hard. It can't be easy. We talk about getting together, but she's not as pushy as she has been, and although I desperately want to escape to the flat, I'm not pushing it either.

School is pitched at the loudest volume yet as I get closer to what I'm calling The Horror. There's no other way to describe it. A week-long nightmare, looming like a Kraken from the deep, submerged but poised, chomping at the bit (if sea monsters have bits) to consume me whole, then spit me out on the streets of Oxford. New College, my first choice, has given me a green light and confirmed the date for my choral scholarship trial. I have to go up and stay in college for a few nights, because in the same week, I'll sit exams and be interviewed by the Modern Languages department. I am shitting myself.

'What are we doing after our Oxford exams?' shouts Nick from across the lunch table in the raucous dining hall. Nick's not up for a music scholarship, so the lucky sod gets to sit his papers here in school.

'I don't know,' I shout back, skewering a cube of mystery meat on my plate. 'What is this stuff?'

'Well, you better think of something,' he says, leaning across the table, ignoring my question, 'because this lunch, right here, marks the end of anything remotely resembling fun for us, for weeks.'

'Great, thanks for that.' I push my plate away.

'Seriously, come on, mate, let's plan something for end of November. Stay at mine, we'll borrow my brother's bong, get wankered with the lads. I'll see if I can convince Lottie and her friends to join us. We've got to mark it.'

He's beaming at me from under his riot of curly hair, but I can't summon the energy to return his smile. Still, I agree we should plan something. We get up to leave, clear the congealed contents off our plates into the waste bin and stack our trays. The dining hall is on the top floor of a grand Victorian building and, opening the doors, we see the stairs are empty. We glance at each other.

'I suppose, I could be tempted to—' I begin, trying to snap out of my mood.

'Race you!' Nick shouts.

We bound down the four flights, taking eight steps in single leaps, Nick whooping.

'Walk, gentlemen!' barks a voice, as we spin the corner for the last stairway. It's too late. Nick clatters to a halt, but I'm still mid-air when I connect with his back, and we hit the wall, a hot mess of limbs and cries of pain.

'Boys!' I recognize the voice of Mr Finch, a boarding housemaster and rugby coach.

'Sorry, sir,' we say in unison, picking ourselves up.

'What is it with you two? Always throwing yourselves around,' says another voice behind Finch.

'Oh, hi, Miss P,' says Nick, looking past Finch.

Crap. I hastily separate from Nick, but too late to look composed.

'Tuck your shirt in,' says Finch, pointing at me, then, spotting my prefect's tie, 'You should be setting an example.' My face burns.

'Yes, sir, sorry.'

Finch mutters something to Ali, then, placing a hand on her lower back, continues up the stairs. I hate him for making me feel small. I hate his ruddy complexion, his bulging muscles. Most of all I hate him touching her.

I think she feels for me too. She glances at me briefly. I think I see a sympathetic tilt of her head before she's guided away.

'What a dick,' says Nick when we're outside.

'Who does he think he is?'

'He's a rugby coach. They're all dicks.'

'Manhandling Miss P like that,' I growl. I can't help myself, the bile of humiliation rising inside me. 'How dare he?'

'Easy tiger,' says Nick, patting my shoulder.

I shrug him off, my temper made worse by the blast of cold air as we walk across the main quad towards the house. I'm grateful for the snood, wrapping it tighter round my neck. Reaching the cloister, I stop. Nick isn't beside me. I turn. He's standing in the middle of the courtyard, staring straight at me.

'Nick?' I say, raising my arms. 'Come on. It's cold.' He doesn't move. 'What are you doing?'

His brow is knitted, his mouth open as if he's about to speak, but he doesn't.

'Mate, have you frozen?' I rub my hands together. 'Wait, are you hurt from the fall? Sorry, dude.'

Nick puts his head on one side, his hands in his pockets, and starts walking towards me.

'Good, can we go now?' I say, taking a couple of steps into the cloister.

Before I register him, he's there, at my shoulder. He reaches out, scrunches a handful of the snood. Not violently, but enough for me to feel it taut on my throat.

'Oi!' I choke, turning, but with his other hand he pushes me. 'Hey! What are you doing?'

He presses his face to my ear. 'What are *you* doing?'

'Eh?'

'This isn't yours.' He pulls at the grey wool, loosening it, so that it unravels. I watch, speechless, as he loops it over my head and holds it in both hands, interrogating the fabric. He glares at me, an expression of astonishment. I can't speak. In horrible slow motion, he lifts the sagging material to his nose and sniffs.

'That smell,' he says in a low voice. 'I knew there was something different about you today. Come to think of it, you've been wearing this all week. Fuck me. I knew I recognized this weird scarf thing from somewhere.'

'Nick, shut up!' I push him off me, grab the snood out of his hands.

'Joe, this isn't yours and you know it. It's Miss—'

'Not here. My study.'

I march across the staff car park, into the house, along the corridor. Nick is right behind me. We dive into my study, close the door. I lean against it. Nick sits on my desk, but immediately stands, shaking his head.

'Nick. Nick, listen to me.' I throw the snood on the floor, hold up my hands to calm him down.

'Jesus fucking Christ,' he says, flapping his hands in the tiny space.

'Shh! Keep it down, mate, please.'

'Mate? *Mate?*' His arms fly up. 'How are we mates? I ... I don't know who you are.'

'Please, I know how it looks. Let me explain,' I say, having no idea how or what to explain. 'Come on, sit down.'

After more hand-waving, head-slapping, hair-scraping, and a fist-punch into the desk at which we both grimace, Nick slumps into the chair. For a few minutes, neither of us says anything. Nick rubs his knuckles in silence while my mind races, trying to figure out what to say, how much to tell him. I'm all lied out, so some far-fetched story is out of the question.

The thing is, I'm almost relieved. I want to tell him. He's my best friend, after all.

'Oh my God,' he says quietly, looking up as if finding an answer to an elusive test question, but not quite believing he's right. 'You're shagging Miss P?'

I know he deserves more than a shrug, but it's all I can think to do in the moment.

'How the fuck? *Miss P?* Shit, are you fucking mental? How did you pull her?'

'Hey, whoa.' I stop him. 'I didn't pull her. I mean, it's not – I'm not the . . .' I can't find the words to say what I mean, to say it's not like that.

'You need to tell me what's going on,' he says.

'Okay, but first, you've got to promise me something,' I say.

'Yeah, yeah, I know what you're going to say. *Don't tell anyone.*'

'Nick,' I say firmly. 'I'm serious. No one, absolutely no one, can know. This gets out, I'm fucked. Expelled. My mum will disown me.'

'Fine, I promise,' he says. 'Fucking hell, man, what have you done?'

For the next hour, Nick sits patiently and listens, at least to begin with. I pick my way tentatively through the maze of eight months, taking care to stick to the main path and not stray into the margins. Despite this, I can see he's gagging to hear about the sex. I stand my ground, tell him it's none of his business. He seems happy enough with the morsels I throw from the trail, gaping at me wide-eyed and groaning when all I'm really doing is describing any woman's naked body.

Where he goes quieter, looking away, out of the study window or down at his knees, is when I tell him about the summer holiday and Spain. But to my surprise, it's not the trip itself that bothers him.

'So, your mum was okay with you going to Spain with Miss P?' he asks. 'Does she know about you and her, then?'

'No, of course not. Al— Miss P sort of arranged it all,' I say, 'with Mum, on the phone.'

'That's weird,' says Nick.

'How is it weird? How else were we supposed to—' I can't find the next words, but Nick can.

'Deceive your mum?'

I glare at Nick, angry because he's right, but his face doesn't show any sign of satisfaction or triumph.

'They get on well,' I say feebly. 'Mum really likes Miss P.'

Nick snorts, shakes his head. 'Mate, that's so fucked up.'

I choose to ignore whatever point he's trying to make. I know lying to Mum was bad, but I truly don't know what else we were supposed to do.

'Oh God,' says Nick abruptly, holding his head in his hands. 'Hang on a minute.'

'What?'

'I've just realized something.'

My stomach turns. I wish I hadn't even started this. I should have just said I'd pinched Miss P's snood from her classroom or something. Nick looks like he's counting on his fingers.

'All those times last year, in the summer term, when you were going to stay with me in the week but said you had to go home instead. Were you with her?' He doesn't wait for me to reply. 'And Glastonbury! Don't tell me you didn't come because of her. Oh! The sketching activity – all those after-noons – you told me yourself, you're crap at drawing. What else? That trip to Oxford?' On and on he goes, unpicking events, laying bare my lies with forensic dexterity. I feel sick.

'Yeah, all right, Nick, enough,' I say, speaking over him. 'I'm sorry, okay?'

The small room sits in stunned silence, the two of us sus-pended, both, it seems, in dismay after this unravelling. Nick hearing it all for the first time. Me, breathlessly reliving it. I pinch my lips with my forefinger and thumb, unsure what to say next. Nick sighs.

'It's . . . impressive,' he says, not unkindly. 'So, what about now? I mean, is it still going on?'

'Well, it hasn't been that easy to see each other this term. Too much work.'

He nods. 'Yeah, I can see that. You have been working quite hard. Listen,' he says.

'Are you about to give me some wise advice?' I interrupt him.

'No.' He shakes his head again. I think he's going to laugh. 'Mate, I wouldn't have the first clue where to start. I can hardly take it all in, to be honest.'

'I know. Sorry. Probably shouldn't have told you. In fact, I definitely shouldn't – it's supposed to be a secret.'

'Er, yes, I get that. What I was going to say is, I'm not going to tell anyone.'

'Ah, fuck. Thank you.' I exhale sharply, my shoulders drop.

'You'd be screwed if this came out,' he says flatly. 'I know you don't want to hear this, but I'm your friend and I care about you.'

'Sounds serious.'

'It is. You've got to end this, before it gets even more out of control. Before a teacher finds out, your mum, before you get expelled. Before you get so distracted, you fail your exams or something.'

'Hang on,' I say, indignant. 'I can have a girlfriend and study at the same time, you know. There's loads of people in our year going out together.'

'Christ, mate, you can't compare this to ... anyone or anything. The guys in our year, it's not serious, it's just a bit of a laugh. And, Joe, are you really calling Miss P your "girlfriend"?'

'Of course I am,' I say unconvincingly. 'What else is she?'

'She's your teacher. She's *our* teacher. She's a grown-up!'

He can see me tense at this.

'All right, all right, I'm not going there. But can't you, somehow, ease it off? You said you've hardly seen her this term, anyway. Can you keep it that way?'

I can see he's trying to help, and maybe he's right. I don't know what to think. Part of me, a big part, wants to tell him to *piss off, you don't understand, she loves me, it's amazing.* But another part of me is sitting on the train, reading a book, detached, free. Or gazing out at the fields flying past, dreaming of sailing, adventures with my uncle. It's like a jigsaw and no matter how hard I try I can't make the two pieces fit. I want both, I think.

'I'll try,' I answer. 'It's hard. She's amazing. But you're right, it has been out of control. And I need to focus on my work.'

'And you need to stop lying to your mum. Or at least, no more lies about this.'

'Yes. I'll try.'

Nick stands, takes me by the shoulders and sits me in the chair. The energy drains out of me, my eyes sting, my throat stiffens, my body shakes. But I feel better.

The next day, at the end of Double Spanish, I try to be cool, act on my promise to Nick. Miss P is handing out books from a stack on her desk. She's been clearing the shelves of old copies of novels. If we don't want them, they'll just be binned.

'Anne, you might like the Álvarez,' she says. 'And you should read this one ...' she says, walking towards me across the room. Her voice sounds distant, breathy, even though she's standing directly in front of me, '... if you're still thinking of choosing Márquez as one of your essay topics.'

'Thanks, Miss, I am,' I say.

She places it in front of me but doesn't let go immediately. Some of the others are crowding around her desk on the other side of the room.

'*Cien años de soledad*.' I read the title, moving my hand to take it from her.

She still has two fingers on the cover as she turns to address the class, something about revision and a grammar test for next lesson. Her hand is shaking, like it's cold. While she speaks, she taps the book with her index finger, before returning to her desk. My pulse jumps. She's done this before. I pick up the book, flick through the pages quickly. There's a small, loose sheet of paper tucked inside. Something like a stone drops to the pit of my stomach, rattles my nerves, then shoots back up to my chest. With Nick's words still echoing, I drop the book into my bag. Whatever I agreed, I can't help the excitement,

the fluttering inside me. In my study between lessons, I read
the note. It's brief, urgent.

I need to see you.

Come after school, please

X

43

November 1992

I stand in her sitting room, in my blazer and tie, my school bag still hooked over my shoulder. Ali's by the windows, closing the shutters. To keep us from being seen. Despite her efforts, they don't close fully; there are always gaps. But today, she seems more determined than usual to shut out the light. She gives up, drops her arms by her sides, and looks at me, at last.

'I'm pregnant.'

'How?' is all I can ask, my bag slipping.

'You tell me how. Obviously, you weren't telling the truth.'

'What? What does that mean?' I can hear my voice rising already.

'You said your balls didn't drop until you were in your teens,' she says, adding, 'or something,' sounding equally defensive and on the attack. 'And that means, because I read about it, I assumed—'

'You assumed ... what?' I cut her off, my words thick in my throat, slow with disbelief, my neck burning, my bag strap slipping through damp hands.

'That you couldn't have children,' she says, in a tone only fractionally less certain than before.

I stare at the floor, don't answer for a whole minute.

I want to scream, *Is this a FUCKING joke? Are you FUCKING thick? What FUCKING planet are you actually on?* Instead, I just stand there, my head ringing in alarm. I dare not open my mouth until the voice in my head has stopped swearing.

'It's a phrase. A thing you say, that's all.' I'm struggling to find the right words, made harder by the realization that this grown-up – someone twice my age – a teacher for God's sake, doesn't know this. My eyes fixed to a spot on the carpet, I say, 'It's basic biology, Ali. How don't . . . I mean . . . didn't you study puberty? Or go into the science block at school?'

'Yes, but . . .'

I glance up. Now she's staring at the carpet, possibly at the same spot. I haven't seen this look on her face before. I don't know what to say or do. I really don't want to get into a debate about scrotums and testicles, but I also have no idea how to deal with the grenade she's hurled at me. Should I try and hug her? What do I do?

'Shit,' she groans, then sweeps past me into the bathroom, leaving me alone with the distinct impression I'm still on the wrong side of an argument I didn't start.

'Is this my fault?' I ask out loud, to an empty room.

44

NOVEMBER 1992

We don't kiss goodbye.

I watch her hurry away from me, hooded, head-bowed, into the clinic. She has to dodge a crowd of women, hovering near the entrance. They'd warned her about them when she'd made the appointment.

Just ignore them.

As instructed, I don't hang around either.

Don't attract attention.

I set off into town, on pavements I don't know.

We didn't kiss goodbye. That's all I'm thinking as I clasp the straps of my backpack, quicken my pace.

'Don't hang around,' she said, on the train down here.

'What should I do, then?'

'Explore? There's a pier, I think.' She shrugged. 'Have a coffee or something.'

'You know I don't like coffee. Or tea,' I said, catching her eye. Puffy, red. 'I'll be fine,' I added, attempting a smile. I started drumming a beat on the seat rest.

'Don't do that,' she snapped, then returned to the letter

she'd been holding, reading, folding and rereading ever since I joined her. Instructions from the clinic. There was no heating in the carriage; it got colder and colder. I rubbed my hands together in my lap, blew air into my cheeks a few times, fought the urge to fidget. Must have been nerves.

The train squealed and shuddered into the station.

'I'll be done by three,' she said, as we made our way through the concourse and sheltered outside under a high, glass canopy. 'Please, don't be late.'

We left the station and walked through the rain to the clinic.

'Is there anything I can do?' I asked, catching up as she set the pace. 'Anything I can get for you?' She didn't reply.

She slowed and came to a stop under the signpost at the driveway entrance to the clinic. She turned to me with a look I couldn't quite read and didn't know how to return. Anguish? Anger? Pity?

We didn't kiss goodbye.

There's a bar on the pier. It's only eleven, but my anorak has failed spectacularly and I'm drenched, shivering in the November rain. I need a beer.

'I'll need some ID, son.' The barman's voice echoes in the cavernous room. I wince and slide my Young Person's Railcard across the counter. He doesn't pick it up, just stares. I look down at my sodden shoes, raise my hand to remove the card from his gaze. I turn and face the sea of vacant tables, the stained beige carpets, full-height windows patchy with condensation, the menacing, grey waves beyond.

Don't attract attention, she said. But I have nowhere to go.

'Brrr, second thoughts,' I lie. 'Can I have a hot chocolate, please?'

I sit in the window, numb hands wrapping the sticky mug. I lean over the steam to inhale the sweet smell, but all I get is the tang of sweat, nicotine, stale air. I take a sip but jerk my head back as it scalds my lips and tongue. I spill half on the table and the rest on my jeans. I gasp, my mouth wide open, bubbles of heat burning my throat. I put the mug down and fold my head to my chest, biting my lip as the hot liquid seeps through the cheap cotton and onto my legs. I told Mum I wanted Levi's for my seventeenth. 501s. I was really specific, but I know she bought the first pair she saw in the first clothes store she went to. They are thin and useless. I may as well be naked.

I hear a cough behind me. I turn. The barman is shaking a bar towel at me from across the empty room. Busted. I fetch the cloth and try to act normal; retreat to the window, wipe the table, the chair, dab the floor. When the barman disappears through a door at the back, I have a go at the stain on my jeans. I stand in the window, close to the glass, and pat the faded red Budweiser towel against my legs. My underpants are damp. They're sticking to my skin. I need to find a toilet but, for now, I take another seat at the round table and reach for my bag. A pack of cigarettes pokes out of the top and I'm tempted. I wasn't going to smoke today, she doesn't like it, but then I didn't know how this day was going to play. With my luck, I'd end up burning the pier down.

I push the packet to one side and pull out some books instead. I only threw them in at the last minute, not knowing how much time I'd have to kill. *Jules et Jim* and *Manon des Sources*, my A-level texts, *Deutsch Heute* German grammar, and my exercise pad. I open the page with the intimidating To Do list I wrote in class and shudder at the sight of everything I should be ticking off this weekend. It's all piling up now. How am I ever going to get through it? I've already had an extension for my English and German homework.

To Do:

- French essay, *Manon des Sources*, Monday
- English essay, *Jules et Jim*, Monday
- German grammar test revision, genitive case, Monday
- German essay, *Wiedervereinigung*, Monday
- Spanish verbs, Monday
- Oxford entrance exam – revise!

Might have been an idea *to do* this homework when it was set, weeks ago. But since Miss P broke the news, it's been impossible to concentrate. I've fallen behind. How can I expect to pass the exams for Oxford, let alone impress in the choral scholarship trials? I flatten my hand over the list and look out to sea. It's still grey; low cloud is building, closing fast, filling the horizon.

How has it come to this? How is it that I find myself in an empty pub, on a freezing November morning, miles from my friends, miles from home? No one knows I'm here, except my teacher. And she's in the clinic.

I can't think straight. I have to get out of here. I pack up, take the still-sopping towel to the bar, and leave. An icy wind catches and holds my breath in the doorway, the force of it tugging my backpack and pricking the skin under my sodden jeans. I forgot to go to the toilet and dry them, which was a mistake, but I'm not going back in there now. Battling through a swirling gust that threatens to lift me off the pier and drop me over the rail, I half run, half stumble to the road.

A department store is probably the best bet for a bathroom, but a familiar sign catches my eye. Our Price. I can't walk past and not go in. Music is supposed to be my life (or at least one of my top three favourite things), but I haven't been to a record shop for ages, and I've missed a whole bunch of new releases. The last single I bought was what? I want to say Blur, but I know it's probably more like The Shamen, 'Ebeneezer Goode'. Christ. Surely I can do better than that.

I duck out of the high street and fall into the sickly-sweet embrace of 'A Million Love Songs' playing over the shop's sound system. Take That. No, I won't be taking that. I go straight to the back of the shop and flick through the tapes and CDs in the rack with my middle fingers and thumbs. God, there's so much I've missed. Where have I been? Not in town, that's for sure. Not anywhere we might be spotted. Far away from school, prying eyes and *people who wouldn't understand*, she says.

I keep flicking. There's the latest R.E.M., but I don't really want to buy the whole album. I've listened to 'Everybody Hurts' so many times, I think it's damaging my health. I make my way to the door, but at the end of an aisle there's a stand promoting the new Bob Marley box set, *Songs of Freedom*, which looks amazing, and a CD collection by someone called Nick Drake. I've never heard of him, but his song titles seem to fit my mood: 'Day Is Done', 'Things Behind the Sun', 'Black Eyed Dog', 'Poor Boy'. I find my wallet to check how much money I've got. Fifteen pounds, and that includes the £10 that Mum left for me on the hall table beside her note: *Have fun, sweetie, see you tomorrow, M xx* (wish she wouldn't call me that). She expected me to spend the money on food. Then again, she expected me to be hanging out with the lads today and staying over with Nick, after *The Last of the Mohicans* at the Odeon. Our last moment of freedom before uni exams, was how I think I spun it to her. *Sorry, Mum.*

'Are you going to buy that?' says a sharp voice behind me. The shop assistant. I look down at the four-disc set in my hands. It's so tempting, but it would clean me out. I won't need the money for food, there's usually plenty at Ali's, but it doesn't feel right.

'No, I think I'll leave it,' I say.

'Right, can you stop stroking it and put it back on the shelf, then?'

I return to the rain and my search for somewhere I can dry off. Five minutes later, just as I feel like giving up and going back to wait out the hours in the train station, I round a corner and find myself at the entrance of Debenhams department store. By now, I'm soaked to the bone, dripping, leaving little puddles wherever I stand. I pace around the shop, desperately looking for the toilets, trying not to look desperate. *Don't attract attention.* Every time a shop assistant appears, I veer off in another direction, like Pac-Man pursued by ghosts until, at last, salvation. The gents.

Thanks to the position of the hand-dryer on the wall, I am able to get up close to the warm airflow without having to pull my jeans completely down. I emerge, twenty minutes later, renewed, refreshed and only slightly stained. I wander around, wondering how long I can stay. It's getting busy with Saturday shoppers and there's probably a limit to how many trips I can take up and down the escalators before someone stops me.

I get to a restaurant on the fifth floor and peer in. The place is wall-to-wall grannies, but I can't face the outside world again and I'm starving. I order fish fingers, chips and beans, a bread roll, Twix and a can of 7Up. I eat as inconspicuously as I can, then take a book from my backpack and open the pages, immersing myself in the arid, Provençal landscape of *Manon des Sources*. The restaurant is warm, the hum of the oldies hypnotic, and I only manage a few paragraphs before I start to yawn.

The crash of cutlery on a tray jolts me awake. I panic, my eyes darting round the room, until the clock on the wall reassures me it's 2.15 p.m. and I'm not in trouble, yet. I have forty-five minutes until I need to be at the clinic. I'm not looking forward to it, but I said I'd come. I just want to do the right thing.

I take the escalator down, passing floor after floor of stuff. Big signs direct hungry shoppers to Homewares, Electricals, Beauty, Fashion. I take a detour to see what counts as fashion around here, but it doesn't take me long to rule out literally everything they're selling for my age group. It's all a bit . . . dadish. I have to walk through Womenswear to get to the next escalator. There's a photograph promoting the 'Autumn Collection', blown up to fill an entire wall space: a woman walking down a country lane, kicking up the dry leaves. She is laughing; she is happy. She gives me an idea.

I arrive at the clinic in good time. The crowd outside has grown. It stirs and rustles with intent when I appear in the drive. I wouldn't call it a mob, but some are carrying placards, and others are handing out leaflets. I make my way to the door, try to get the receptionist's attention by ringing the bell and knocking on the glass, but she won't let me in. I want to reassure her that I'm not one of them, but that would mean shouting to be heard, and there's a lot of aggression building behind me. So, I wait.

The receptionist stands and comes to the door. Behind her, a dark figure is moving slowly. Another woman, a nurse, is guiding her. The door opens. When the receptionist tries to hold me back, the nurse says, 'It's okay, he's a friend, apparently,' and beckons me in. I ignore the look of surprise on the receptionist's face and reach out with a smile, but no one else is smiling.

'Why did you come to the door?' she says, when we reach the station after a painfully slow, wordless walk. 'What were you thinking?'

I'd taken her silence as tiredness after the anaesthetic, or whatever, but she sounds and looks exasperated.

'I'm sorry, I just thought, with all those people outside . . .'

'You didn't think,' she says, opening her bag, taking out her purse as we approach the ticket barrier. 'I felt so stupid, having to make an excuse for you. It was the last thing I needed.'

The uniformed man waves her onto the platform while I'm still rummaging through my pockets for my own ticket. I join her as she's stepping onto the train, and I offer my arm again. This time, she takes it and lets me steer her to a pair of empty seats. She sinks heavily against the window, with a sigh. Part of me wants to ask her how it went, but the other part knows when to shut my mouth. I look past her through the carriage window.

It's already getting dark. As the train gathers speed, dots of light appear in a string on the horizon, stretching out to sea. I can just make out the silhouette of the pier, and the wretched bar.

'What did you do with your day?' she asks, moving only her head, the rest of her still pointing away.

'Oh, I did what you suggested. Explored town. Found somewhere to revise.' I figure she doesn't need to know the detail. Also, I think now could be a good moment to give her my present, to cheer her up. 'Actually, I got you something,' I say, reaching for my backpack and pulling out a Debenhams bag.

'You really shouldn't have,' she says, like I really shouldn't have. She leans on the table and pushes herself up, lips pursed with the effort.

'Sorry it's not wrapped or anything. But I saw it and thought of you.'

She opens the bag and lifts out a shawl, reds and oranges fading to greens and browns as it unfurls. I don't know why, but I'm holding my breath as she studies it.

'It's cashmere, I think,' I say, recovering my breath.

'It's mainly polyester,' she replies, fingering the label. 'But thank you, anyway.' She passes it back to me.

'Don't you want to wear it?' I feel deflated. 'It'll keep you warm.'

'Maybe later. I'm tired. Might close my eyes for a while.'

'How was it?' I ask, before I can stop myself. 'Sorry, I mean, did it go . . . okay?'

'What, the abortion?' She gives me that look again, the same expression she wore at the gate this morning, her eyes piercing and raw, before they close. I try not to swallow, but I can't help myself. I still can't help feeling guilty. Like this is all my fault.

I stay with Ali that night. She isn't hungry so we don't eat. I run her a bath and listen at the door in case she needs anything. I expect to hear her crying, releasing her emotions now she's home, on her own. But there's no sound from the bathroom, except for the occasional splash.

In bed, we don't touch, but she accepts a kiss before turning over to lie on her back. Despite the exhaustion, I can't sleep for ages. Then, when I do, I'm awoken by Ali moving about, restless.

We say goodbye in the morning, both of us with red-rimmed, sleep-deprived eyes.

'I could stay a bit longer if you like?' I say, although if I'm being honest, I would quite like to go home.

'It's fine. I probably need some time on my own today.'

We hold each other in the corridor by her front door.

'I'm sorry,' we say, at the same time, which is awkward. It's strange how both saying sorry makes it sound less meaningful, but she manages a fragile laugh. She strokes the side of my head.

'Please, don't ever leave me, will you?' she says, her eyes searching mine for an answer. 'And don't ever tell anyone.'

'Of course not,' I say. What else can I say?

45

December 1992

The weeks that follow are probably the most important of my school life so far. Oxford entrance exams, choral scholarship trials, A-level mocks, and a call for interview at the local university, which comes like a prophetic omen, I reckon, cruelly predicting the outcome of my shot at Oxford.

I put one foot in front of the other, hope my steps are credible enough, even though I feel like I'm wading through time. To the invested onlookers at school and home, every day signals a major event, with every action I take, every word I speak, every note I sing, of *critical significance* to the rest of my life.

The Head of Oxbridge Entrance waves me on my way, with a *don't let us all down* shaking fist. Dad sends me a good-luck postcard with a picture of Nigel Mansell. Mum delivers a long-haul lecture before dropping me off in Oxford with a wide, hopeful smile, betrayed by her forehead, wrinkled like a stave of music.

'I'll do my best,' I say, but I have no idea what that means anymore.

The thing is, to all of them, what they see is what I still

was when term started, three months ago: focused; ambitious; getting good marks; singing at my best. Maybe I don't look so different, on the outside, and when the mask slips, it's *just nerves, that's all, only to be expected, you'll be fine.*

No, I don't think so. Why can't you see I'm breaking?

It's around this time, as the heat of expectation rises, that I first feel the itch. Is it waiting outside the audition room in Oxford? Or, a week later, when I put down my pen at the end of one of my mocks? I can't remember because it's nothing, really. An unremarkable tingling in the crease of my left elbow. I rub my thumb over the skin, then forget about it. Until a few days later, I'm pinching at my other elbow through the fabric of my school shirt. I become aware of its raw roughness, fold back my sleeve to reveal a patch of red. Within days, it's crept up my arm. During an exam, I finish a question and sit up in my chair. I've been writing with my right hand, my left supporting my head. I hadn't noticed my fingers, but they must have been scratching my scalp. There are flakes of dried skin all over the desk. I sweep them away before anyone sees, but I'm mortified and dare not touch my head again in case more of it falls off. Afterwards, I run to the toilet to confront my distress, shaking quantities of white powdery skin from my hair, furiously brushing my shoulders and arms.

Over the coming days, I retreat even further into myself. I go to class, but I'm not present. The only thing I'm grateful for is that most of our language lessons are being covered by random staff, while our usual teachers – including Miss P – are occupied with pupils taking other exams. Outside of lessons, I keep to my study in the house, even though the university entrance interviews are mercifully behind me, the exams are over and the end of this wretched term is in sight. I avoid my friends, disappear to the toilets as soon as the bell goes, picking at my head, my arms, removing every speck but always finding more. I don't make any sudden moves, try to be still, convinced that the slightest turn of my head will result in a shower of dandruff.

I use the excuse of the December chill to wear my beanie. But when I take it off, the inside is coated in a layer of skin. Finally, Mum agrees it's odd and makes an appointment with the doctor, who, after a cursory inspection, pronounces 'atopic dermatitis – typical in a boy your age' – and promptly prescribes steroid cream. Mum, who's gone a bit homeopathic, insists I use it sparingly and stocks up on organic bio-yoghurt. I pass on the yoghurt, spread the cream all over, seal my skin in its pungent glue, and hide monastically in my bedroom for an entire weekend. By Monday morning, there's some improvement. At least, I can move freely without parts of me visibly peeling away.

46

DECEMBER 1992

Just before the holidays, when I've pretty much given up thinking I'll see her this side of Christmas, Ali calls me into her classroom one day after school.

'Hello, stranger,' she says. 'Do you miss me?'

I say yes because it's true. I miss her, but I don't tell her about the battle with my skin (just about under control now thanks to a repeat prescription) and that it's been a relief not to have to take my clothes off in front of her. She tells me how busy she's been these past weeks, apologizes for being so quiet, hopes my interview for the university in town went well, doesn't ask about Oxford.

'I'm going to my parents' for Christmas. But can you come and see me, at my place, before term ends?' she asks.

'Do you mean, to stay the night?' I reply with a question, perhaps subconsciously remembering the last time she summoned me. I know she's not going to tell me she's pregnant again, but I can't help being on my guard.

'Yes. And I want to give you your Christmas present.' She smiles, and, realizing I haven't seen that smile for so long, part of me melts. The other part of me thinks, *Shit, I haven't got her anything!*

Mum's diary is full of social events with "Gordon" (she's still air-quoting his name, which is unnecessary since I have now met him, briefly), so it's easy for me to escape for a night on the pretext – well, lie – that I'm going to an end-of-term party at Nick's. As far as I know, he probably is having one, but I stopped listening at lunch, preferring to zone out when both he and Ant were congratulating each other. They'd found out that morning that they'd got offers to Oxford and Cambridge respectively. My letter must have arrived at home, so I wouldn't receive it until tomorrow.

After the final assembly, I emerge from the chapel into a cold afternoon. It's not even five o'clock, but the shadows are long in the moonless dark. Grateful for the cover, I lose myself in the crowd of departing bodies, keeping my head low, until I'm through the cloisters and into the staff car park. I shut my ears to any sound that might resemble my name being called, fetch my bag from the house, and slide through the school gate and out. I could play it safe, take the usual detours to Ali's, but I can't be bothered. Or, rather, I find myself at the end of her road before it occurs to me. I don't know why I'm feeling careless. Is it because I'm trying to be cool about not knowing the contents of the potentially life-changing letter waiting for me at home? Is it because I've been so preoccupied with my horrid eczema, and I'm suddenly terrified it's going to flare up the second I undress and stop me from getting an erection? Is it because I haven't seen Ali properly since the abortion and that memory is rapidly breaking the surface of my consciousness? Is it because I can't get rid of the image of a dead baby, and that if I wasn't my stupid age, Ali could have kept the baby? I raise my hand and, before I know it, I've smacked the side of my head. I probably deserve it, and it does seem to do the trick of pulling me back to the moment.

I stand at her door, waiting for the unlock buzzer, inhaling lungfuls of cold air which catch in my throat. I'm tense, braced for a heavy night's debrief. But thirty seconds later, Ali wraps me in a tight hug before I've had a chance to remove my blazer and bag. When she lets go, I see she's changed out of her usual school outfit into a skirt and top. In fact, everything about her and the flat is out of kilter with the winter outside. She looks like she's back in Spain, a smell of pistou is coming from the kitchen, but the real give-away is the music she's playing – 'La Bamba'. This is not what I was expecting.

'Um … Merry Christmas?' I shrug, returning her beaming smile.

'I know, I know,' she says. 'I thought it would be nice for us to, you know, try and go back to a happier time. Wine?'

Then she leaps at me again, presses her mouth against mine. I kiss her back and estimate she must be at least two glasses down already. Fast work.

'Yeah, fuck it, why not?' I remember what's in my bag. 'Wait, let me give you my present,' I say, producing a bottle of red wine, presenting it to her with both hands as though it were a precious vase.

'Great!' she says. 'I think that's the first time you've brought me wine.'

Yeah, but I bet they'd refuse me if I tried to buy it myself, so this

I nicked from Mum's kitchen cupboard. I don't even know what type it is, ha ha, is what I don't say. Nonetheless, Ali seems thrilled, and whirls off to the kitchen.

I hang my things on the front door hook and take stock. I'm relieved Ali's so upbeat, albeit pissed, but she's gone to quite a lot of trouble with her scene-setting. I stick my head around the sitting room door. There is nothing remotely Christmassy here, no tree, no decorations, but, then, perhaps people don't go to much effort when they live on their own. Still, I'm surprised there are no cards.

Ali appears with two enormous glasses of red wine. I take a sip, while she puts her glass to her lips and necks half of it before coming up for air. Trying not to show my shock, I gesture over her shoulder.

'That smells delicious.'

'Shall we go to bed?'

'What, now?'

'Yes, now. Don't you want to have sex with me?'

'Of course.'

'Come on then,' she says, in a louder than necessary voice, grabbing my hand.

She's not slurring her words, but she's erratic, out of character, behaving like she's drunk. Her eyes are shining, her cheeks are pink. All I know is that I daren't question her; that feels like it would be a mistake. So, I let her lead me to the unlit bedroom, remove my clothes, push me onto the bed. In seconds, I'm going down on her.

Half an hour later I collapse on my back. I gaze up at the ceiling, trace the cornicing around the room a few times, and wait. Under the duvet, I'm stirring with anticipation, but in the dark room, it's eerily quiet. I'm aware that I'm holding my breath, waiting for something.

With a sigh, Ali pulls up the covers, rolls away. And in an instant, my cock is dead soft, unstirring, in my hand.

'Merry Christmas,' she murmurs.

47

December 1992

The following morning, we have a proper catch-up. I decide to take my lead from Ali about the abortion. If she wants to talk things through, I'm ready for it, though it's still messing with my head, and I don't really know what I can or should say. It's been six weeks since that day and she never brings it up. Instead, she talks for ages about her year groups (which is boring), about some of the other teachers (which is quite funny, but also worrying; they're even more weird than I thought), and what she thinks about the pupils in my Spanish class (mainly about the stack of exams she must mark over the holiday).

'Including yours,' she says pointedly. Finally, she asks, 'So, do you think you've got a place at Oxford, then?'

I'm pleased she's taken an interest, at last, although her tone gives her away. She's obviously not interested.

'Dunno.' I shrug. 'I wasn't very focused.'

'Huh,' she mutters, lifting her coffee cup to her mouth, looking away as she sips. 'Why not?'

I stare at her across the breakfast table.

'Well, because of what happened, just before.'

'What do you mean?' A slight frown appears, and it hits me that her question is genuine. I shift uncomfortably, feeling too big for my chair.

'You know . . . the baby?'

'Sorry, what?' Ali's eyebrows shoot up. Her voice remains controlled, low, but the atmosphere in the room cools several degrees. 'Are you . . . please tell me you're not going to make that all about you. Because—'

'No, no, of course not,' I cut in.

'Because, just to be clear, that would be inappropriate.' She looks down at the table, like she's thinking hard about her next words, like she might be giving me difficult feedback on a homework assignment. She lifts her head. I feel so small under her glare.

'It was my body, and you don't see me whinging, do you?'

I guess it's not a real question, so I keep my mouth shut, but I do move my head from side to side.

'So, I don't want to hear you ever use that as an excuse if you don't get into Oxford, or anywhere else. Or if your grades slip.' She emphasizes these last words.

'Obviously, I won't. Sorry, I didn't mean . . .' I don't finish my sentence. Instead, I stand, pick up my juice glass and walk around the table. 'I'm sorry . . . Would you like some more coffee?'

'Yes.' She hands me her cup, and adds, 'I'm glad you understand.'

Later, we make up, in bed, in our usual way.

'Thank you for asking about Oxford, anyway,' I say, when I think it's safe enough to do so. 'I know you're not that interested.'

'You do understand why, don't you?' Her hand patters across the faint hairs on my chest.

'No, I don't, actually.'

'Seriously?' Her hand pauses. 'Isn't it obvious?'

'Erm . . .'

'If you go to Oxford, what happens to me? What will I do? Had you thought about that?'

The fact is, she's probably right, I haven't had the energy to think about what happens to me and her – us – if I get into Oxford. I can barely see beyond the next week let alone that far into the future. Does it have to be the end just because I'm not nearby? I figure now is not the moment to repeat my plans for deferring my university place and taking a gap year sailing across the Atlantic.

When I leave the flat that afternoon, my mind is spinning. One minute, I'm on a complete high, fuelled with adrenalin from twenty-four hours with Ali. Next minute, the roller-coaster is plummeting, usually it seems because I've opened my stupid mouth, rammed my foot in it, made a dreadful mess, wasted our precious time with my immaturity. When will I grow up?

Arriving home, as if I couldn't feel more crap about myself, Mum is waiting for me in the kitchen, with an odd expression on her face. Sort of pity and disappointment rolled into one tilt of the head. In front of her, on the dining table, is an envelope.

'I'm sorry,' she says, tilting even further over, her eyes following my gaze to the letter. 'You didn't get into Oxford.'

'What? How do you know?'

'I opened it completely by mistake, sweetie,' she says, very quickly on the defensive.

'Jesus, Mum.' I drop my bag, snatch up the envelope, and read. It's brief. Didn't pass the academic exams. I sigh and sink into the chair opposite Mum. It's not totally unexpected, and on the plus side Ali will be delighted, but I can't hold back the waves of disappointment flooding through me.

'All that work,' says Mum, stealing my exact same thoughts, trying to sound soothing. 'The school will be disappointed, of course.'

School. Fucking hell. You have no idea. I open my mouth. I desperately want to say something.

I don't want to hear you ever use that as an excuse if you don't get into Oxford.

48

DECEMBER 1992

The days leading up to Christmas are quiet. Time enough to regroup with myself, get over the hump of academic rejection, take a break from study, and dive headlong into books and bands.

Mum has some party or other every day. I agree to be dragged along, but it soon becomes apparent I'm only there to sing. I don't mind joining in with the odd carol, but when I refuse Mum's pleas to perform my Grade 8 pieces, using a sore throat as an excuse to hide my embarrassment in front of her friends, she loses her incentive for inviting me. It's a relief. Her parties are deathly, full of people eating hummus and droning on endlessly about the new European single market, Bill Clinton's imminent inauguration, and the recent separation of Prince Charles and Princess Diana.

Ali and I have a few calls. She has to call me now that Mum's started receiving itemized phone bills, meaning I can't risk her grilling me over unfamiliar numbers. When we do talk, Ali tells me about catching up with old school friends where she grew up, and in return, I try to speak knowledgeably about the changing political landscape in Europe and

America, *according to a report I heard on Radio 4,* and about the books I'm reading. I tell her I've started buying the *Guardian.* I'm determined to appear more grown up for her. She replies that she's impressed, but perhaps a few days' revision before term starts would be an idea.

On Christmas Eve, my sister returns from university, my grandparents arrive, and we trot through the usual rituals. It's nice to be together, but I hate the way family gatherings force everyone into playing a set role. How they automatically cast me as the youngest, treat me like I'm a child at a difficult age. Two days is my limit. Thankfully, it's Mum's too, and her social merry-go-round cranks back up, so she's out most of the time. Rose, too, has had enough and makes a hasty retreat to party through to New Year with her housemates. My grandparents don't leave straight away, but they're not a problem. They provide a gentle, background drone, bumbling around the house, Gran knitting or cooking, Grandpa finding little jobs to do.

I haven't spoken to Ali since before Christmas Eve and I'm getting restless. So, on Boxing Day afternoon, I walk down to the corner and take a risk with a call to her parents' house from the phone box. I'm in luck. Ali answers and isn't mad at me. Apparently, unless they're expecting someone to call, her parents will usually let the phone ring out. It's the same with the doorbell, she adds. If they're not expecting anyone, they simply won't answer it. I don't speak for a moment, struggling to comprehend the weirdness of this.

We share Christmas stories, which doesn't take long. Ali's parents don't drink, don't go out. Christmas dinner is served at 12 p.m., table cleared by 1 p.m. I make disbelieving sounds, but Ali says she's used to it and that it's a relief to have a few quiet days to recover from the long term. I see her point, but still, sounds bizarre. Meanwhile, I rattle through the Gibson family Christmas playlist, culminating in the *annual review*, which I explain is a Christmas Day custom where, traditionally, my parents would reel off the highs (theirs) and lows (usually mine) of the past twelve months. This year, I tell her, when it came to me, Mum took the opportunity to not so much look back, as to cast forward. That the summer would present an ideal period for reflection. The A-level results wouldn't be announced until well into August, at which point, all being well (for which her definition is straight As), "we" might consider reapplying to Oxford.

'Seriously?' asks Ali.

'Oh, yes. Mum won't give up until we've exhausted every avenue.'

'But what if you get into the university here? You can't just withdraw a few weeks before you're supposed to start.' Ali's voice rises down the line. I can feel the heat of her words through the clammy plastic receiver against my ear.

'That wouldn't bother Mum,' I say. 'But I was planning on taking a year out anyway, wasn't I? You know, sailing with my uncle and everything.'

There's a long, breathless silence from the other end.

'Ali – you still there?'

'I assumed,' she says at last, her voice quiet, stuttering, 'that, with you and me, you'd changed your mind. With everything we've been through. That if you get into university here, you'd start this year.'

I don't know what to say and I'm searching for some reasonable words when the phone pips in our ears, signalling that we're about to be cut off.

'Ali, listen—'

Before I can get the words out, she says hurriedly:

'I'm coming to town. Tomorrow. Meet me at eleven at the café by the square. I want to talk ab—' But the phone goes dead.

49

December 1992

I wasn't expecting to see Ali for at least two more weeks, not until the start of term, so despite her reaction on the phone, I'm buzzing as I hurry to meet her. I've replayed our conversation and I'm sure it was made overcomplicated by having to talk about this stuff on a phone, detached, so many miles apart. I'm sure we'll be able to resolve everything face to face.

I plug in my Walkman and head into town with Nick Drake's 'Northern Sky', from the *Bryter Layter* album Uncle Jack got me for Christmas. As I quicken my pace down the bare streets, I feel more confident that Ali will understand.

At the chime of a city clock, I step into a tunnel of icy wind and pull Ali's grey woollen snood around my throat. Lifting my collar to hold it in place I press stop when I reach the square and stand in the middle in silence, frozen to the spot. And it begins to rain.

Out of the corner of my eye, a small movement. A dark figure is standing in front of a shop window. Hooded, wearing a long winter coat that almost touches the ground, lit from behind, one hand suspended in a motionless wave.

'Hello,' she says.

I walk over and stop, an arm's length separating us. For a second, we just look. How strange is this, I think. Here is this woman. I know her. Clothed, unclothed. Wet, dry, hot, cold. Happy, sad, angry. I know her better than anyone else now. And yet, I'm not allowed any closer, in case someone sees us.

'Fucking rules,' I say, and she tilts her head, smiles.

'Can we get out of the rain?' she asks. 'Otherwise, my hair is going to frizz up.'

I nod. 'There?' I gesture towards the café next door to the shop.

'Bit open,' she says. 'I know another place, around the corner, tucked away.'

Five minutes later, we are sitting at a quiet table in a little coffee shop on a cobbled cul-de-sac. While Ali sorts herself out, muttering to herself about wet hair, I cast around at the old-fashioned furniture, the bowing walls, the flaking beams on the low ceiling above us.

'I didn't know this place existed,' I say. 'I wonder if Mum knows about it. I expect—'

'I love it,' she interjects, finally composed in her high-backed wooden chair. 'Especially their tea. It comes in proper china cups and saucers, with pots of hot water. Let's order.'

We chat about nothing much. But when tea and cake arrive and the waitress, dressed up in period apron and bonnet, has left us, the atmosphere changes. Ali reaches across the table, and I think she's going for the teapot, but she places her hand on my arm.

'I'm sorry if I was a bit short with you on the phone,' she begins. 'I know you had told me about next year, wanting to go sailing with your uncle. And the thing in South America.'

'Volunteering in Chile. Operation Raleigh. Good for my Spanish,' I say.

'Right, yes, that. It's just—'

'It wouldn't be forever, Ali.' I put my free hand over hers, trying to reassure her, although it looks a bit odd. I remove it and pour myself some tea, not that I'm going to drink it. I should have asked for hot chocolate.

'No, I know, it wouldn't seem like forever to you,' she continues, while I pour her a cup. 'But it would to me. That's why I wanted to come down and see you today. To tell you something.'

'Oh, okay.' Sensing this needs my full attention, I replace the pot on the table.

'The thing is, I know it hasn't always been easy, but we've been seeing each other now for months.' A strand of her hair falls forward, which she retrieves, loops it behind her ear and continues. 'The thing is, I love you, and I think you love me.'

'Oh my God – yes, Ali,' I say, my words stumbling in relief more than anything. I thought she had come to say she was cross with me. I feel my legs shaking under the table, my eyes stinging wet. 'I love you too,' I say, wishing this table wasn't in the way so I could throw my arms around her. I start to rise out of my chair.

'Wait, Joe,' she says, her eyes shining too, 'I haven't finished what I wanted to say. I need to ask you something.'

'Yes, what? Anything!' I'm leaning right over the table now, squeezing both of her hands in mine.

'Well, what if we were to take things further, what would you say?'

'I'd say yes!' I'm almost bouncing in my chair, carried away, but also immensely relieved that Ali's in such a good mood and definitely not cross, after all.

'Really?' she beams.

'Really,' I say, adding, 'I mean, by "take things further", what does that mean? What do we do?'

She releases her hands, leans forward and cups my face briefly, then folds her elbows on the table, her head nestling between her hunched shoulders.

'Well, let me just say, there's another reason why I love this street,' she whispers, and the corners of her mouth turn up slightly as she inclines her head to look out of the window. Gripped by this new twist, I follow her gaze, but all I can see through the rain are the misted sash windows of a shop opposite. I look back at Ali, her eyes darting from me to the shop.

'That shop is the other thing you love?' I ask, hesitantly.

'Look up,' she motions, and peering up I read the sign above the windows, yellow writing on a dark blue board spanning the width of the wall.

Silver and Stone. It's a jeweller's.

'What do you think?' she asks, her mouth twisting to one side.

'Ali, are you being serious?'

She nods, slowly, and I can see she is deadly serious. She turns again to face the jewellery shop and I swallow hard, trying to get my head around what is happening here. This train is moving faster than I can keep up, but after everything that's happened this term, that even after the abortion, Ali wants to be with me. And she is so happy, here, in this moment. How can I let her down? I can't. I can't refuse her.

'I'm quite ...' I start, but struggle to form the words, 'young, Ali, to get married.'

'Oh, we wouldn't have to get married, not yet anyway,' she laughs. 'This would be us, you and me, making a statement that we love each other. A commitment.'

'Yes,' I say, though I do feel a little puzzled. 'And we do that with a—' I nod my head at the shop.

'A ring, yes, of course.' She says the words with effortless ease.

'A ring. Wow. That is serious,' I say, blowing air through my cheeks.

'Exactly. That's what I'm trying to tell you.' She takes my hands again, lowering her voice. 'I'm serious about you. About us. Our future.'

Afterwards, standing side by side on the pavement outside the jeweller's, she points like an excited child in a sweet shop at all the different rings. I've never done anything like this before, but I make the sort of mmm–ing noises I think I'm supposed to, and she grabs my arm in hers.

'We must do this properly,' she says, like it's something we signed up to together, a long time ago. 'We must make it special.'

I'm not sure I have the words for this, so I simply say, 'It will be special.'

She squeezes my arm tighter, emits some high-pitched squeak.

'You know what would make it really special. Unique, like us?' she says.

'No.'

'If we got them to make a ring to our design,' she breathes. 'They do that here.'

'Our design?'

'Yes, of course. This should be something we do together.'

'And pay for together?' I'm guessing.

'Well, it is tradition for the man to pay,' she says, making a handprint on the glass window.

And that's when I stop breathing. It's only a moment. A fraction of a moment, I suppose. A handprint-shaped moment. Enough for me to feel my heart thump to a halt in my chest, miss its beat.

That afternoon, I'm relieved to find Mum is still out at one of her lunch parties and Gran and Grandpa snoozing in the sitting room. I creep into Mum's bedroom, to her bureau. I'm looking for something I haven't seen for years. I go through the drawers, flick through old family documents, school certificates. I'm giving up hope when, under a stack of papers, I find a bundle of small blue pocketbooks, tied with an elastic band. Each one bears a name on the outside cover. My parents, my sister, mine. My Woolwich Building Society savings account, into which my parents and grandparents, aunts and uncles, have deposited occasional sums over the years; birthdays, Christmases, and a one-off dollop of £500 dated from when I was very young, for something I can't remember. I turn the pages, my pulse beginning to race again, to the most recent balance. Almost £800. All the money I have. Why shouldn't I have access to it?

That evening, over the washing-up after dinner, I put a carefully scripted argument to Mum about how I'm old enough to be taking responsibility for my own finances. Why I think it's important that I learn about money and bank accounts. And, to my astonishment, she agrees, on the condition that I don't go spending what has taken my whole life to grow.

'It's for your future,' she says.

Exactly, I think, smiling to myself, feeling very grown up.

50

DECEMBER 1992

Ali does not hang around. Instead of returning to her parents' for the rest of the Christmas break as planned, she heads back home so that she can get to the jeweller's more easily when it reopens on Monday. When we speak on the phone the following morning, she explains that she has already arranged to meet with the ring designer that afternoon, to show them a drawing of what she has in mind. Apparently, based on her description over the phone, they might have a ring in the shop that matches her criteria, seeing as she's looking for something quite traditional. When she uses the words 'diamond' and 'white gold', I have to sit down.

I ask whether she wants me to come with her, because I'd need to time it for when Mum is out. But she says no, she can manage this without me. She will update me on our evening call. A wave of relief runs through me, although it seems a bit strange not to be going with her after what she said about this being 'something we should do together'.

Later, I'm sure I can hear her jumping up and down in her flat when she tells me about the ring they showed her.

'It's perfect,' she sings. 'A single diamond set in a simple solitaire with a white gold band. Oh, it's gorgeous!'

'It does sound nice,' I say, frustrated with myself that I can't match her levels of enthusiasm. I realize I'm preoccupied because there's one thing I really need to know.

'Do you know the best thing about it?' she continues.

It's cheap? replies the voice in my head, which I immediately bat away.

'It's almost exactly the right size,' she says, triumphantly. 'They just have to make a small adjustment, which will only take a couple of days, and then you can collect it.'

And then you can collect it. The words spin round my head, faster and faster. I can't keep up. I thought I was keeping it together, but suddenly it's real. This is all happening at a crazy speed.

'Hello, are you still there?' she asks, when I don't respond. I cough, try to collect my thoughts, prepare to answer without choking on my words.

'I'm here. Gosh, you're . . .' I can't say, *I thought this was a sort of joke, but you're actually serious about this, aren't you?* though it's all I can think in the moment. What's wrong with me? Of course she's serious. She told me that: she's serious about me. And I was there, in the coffee shop, outside the jeweller's, standing beside her; that was me. I got my building society account book; that was me too. So why does it feel like every time she mentions the ring, it's the first I'm hearing about it? It might be freezing outside, but the air in the phone box is suffocatingly hot.

'You are happy as well, aren't you?' she asks.

'Oh God, yes. I am so happy, as well,' I splutter. 'It's very exciting. Um, can I ask . . . and I'm sorry to . . .'

'Are you worried about what it costs?' she says, reading (part of) my mind.

'Well, no, I mean, well, kind of. I've got my savings. I just don't know what a ring costs.'

'I understand,' she says, immediately lifting a huge weight off me. 'For an engagement ring, it really isn't expensive.'

'That's such a relief,' I say, wiping beads of sweat from my forehead.

'But it is tradition that the man pays for the engagement ring,' she says calmly, but with a hint of teacher.

'Is it? I mean, right, yes, of course, tradition, you did tell me.' That word again.

'Okay, so it's the 28th today,' she says, sounding organized. 'They said you could collect it on the 30th—'

'Does it have to be the 30th?' I interrupt. 'I mean, is there a hurry?'

'Well, the thing is ...' Her voice goes all soft. 'I was thinking, you could propose to me on New Year's Eve. With the ring.'

My stomach is full of butterflies as I walk back up the hill. I had planned to go out with Nick and Ant and everyone on New Year's, but that's okay, I'll see them every day when term starts. What's one night out with the lads compared to this?

Dammit, I think, slapping my forehead with the heel of my palm. She forgot to tell me how much the ring's going to cost.

51

DECEMBER 1992

On the morning of 30 December, I take control of my own money. I've never felt more adult than when I leave the house with my own building society savings book, on my way to buy an engagement ring for my teacher, on my own. I mean, come on, what's more adult than that? I've even dressed up for it: my navy-blue suit trousers and jacket over a newly ironed pale blue shirt – my special occasion outfit. I wear my black school shoes because I don't have any others, and they're a bit scuffed, even after a vigorous application of Kiwi shoe polish. Brown shoes would look better, but school doesn't permit them.

I have to get my timings right so as not to arouse any suspicion from Mum. I'm dressed and out of the house before she's up and about. It means I'll have to hang around in town for the shops to open, but I can probably grab a hot chocolate from McDonald's while I'm waiting. I leave my Walkman at home.

At 9 a.m., I visit the jeweller's to see the ring. It's not really to show me the ring, of course, it's to show me the final bill. There's a whiff of McDonald's I can't seem to shake, as I stand in the jeweller's reception. I wait nervously, my hands clammy. I'm really trusting Ali meant what she said about it not being expensive. I'm hoping not more than £200, but I guess it could be a bit more.

At 9.15 a.m., I'm back on the street. In a cold sweat. The jeweller didn't even flinch. Just presented the bill on headed invoice paper. At first, I saw £150 and breathed a huge sigh of relief. But that was the resizing cost. I even looked up at him with a grateful smile, until he coughed, pointed to the total at the bottom. My face actually froze, piercing my temples with icy needles, and it felt as though someone had kicked me behind the knees so that I might buckle and fall.

Seven. Hundred. And Seventy-Five. Pounds! I wanted to scream, *But that's ALL my savings.*

But all I said was: 'Thank you. I'll go and get a cheque from my building society.'

At 9.30 a.m., sitting in the Woolwich, waiting for my ticket number to be called, I pull myself together. It's only money, I try to persuade the pathetic voices in my head. The main thing is, you're making Ali, the love of your life, so happy. Another voice, though, suggests that no, the main thing is that Mum can never find out that you blew your entire life's savings.

By 10 a.m., I have returned to the jeweller's, handed over everything I have, and left with a tiny box. Thank God he doesn't charge extra for that. I don't have any money left.

52

DECEMBER 1992

Nick isn't impressed with what he says – and I have to agree – is a pathetic excuse for not going out: singing in one of Mum's friend's husband's local church choirs on New Year's Day. I can't afford to miss it or turn up hungover, I tell him. You're a teenager; it's New Year's Eve; what the fuck's wrong with you? he retorts. What's wrong with me is that I'm all out of credible lies, and I suspect Nick knows it. He's just too decent or doesn't want to believe that my affair with Miss P is still a thing. When he puts the phone down on me, I feel crap, but I'm also relieved he didn't bring her up. This day of all days, when we're about to go way beyond a fling.

Fortunately, it's much easier to sell Mum the story that I'm out with school friends on New Year's. Perhaps because it's sort of true. She tries to pin me down to a time when I'll be home. We've always done a New Year's Day walk and it would be nice to continue that tradition, with "Gordon". I mutter something non-committal as I leave the house for the train station.

It's still light when the train pulls in, but it's freezing. I am completely underdressed, no hat, scarf, gloves; I clearly wasn't thinking about the weather when I left home. I feel in my pocket and pull out some coins. I can't afford the extravagance of a taxi, but it's hardly a ring. And I am freezing. Standing under the station's entrance archway, listening to 'Poor Boy', waiting for a cab to show up, I check for the hundredth time that the ring is safely tucked inside the zip pocket of my anorak. I feel a bit like Bilbo or Frodo, or whichever hobbit it is that gets out of his depth with a ring and can't wait to get rid of it. Not that I'm comparing the prospect of proposing to Ali with the quest to cast the Ring into the fires of Mordor. I know it's not remotely the same deal. This is much harder.

Proposing. Getting engaged. Buying a ring with my life savings. What a way to see out 1992, I reflect, as the cab rolls up and the weak sun folds into the clouds above.

If I have any lingering questions, doubts, niggles, they vanish when I see the warm light behind the shutters of Ali's flat. I don't need to get smashed with the lads tonight. I certainly don't need to stay cooped up at home, either, like I have been all Christmas. This is where I should be. And when Ali opens the door, even the shivering feeling I've been getting every time I see the jeweller's bill in my mind evaporates.

'Wow!' I exclaim, my jaw dropping.

'Do you like it?' She's wearing a figure-hugging black woollen dress. I say dress, but it's more like a tube that starts off the shoulder and stops above her knees, where thin shiny tights take over. She twirls around on the spot, tossing her hair like a woman in a shampoo advert, and I feel a warm stirring sensation.

'You look amazing,' I say, holding her close, kissing her face.

'Careful,' she squeaks. 'Your buttons are catching on my dress.'

'Sorry, sorry,' I say, wishing I had removed my stupid anorak before ringing the bell.

'That's okay, fiancé-to-be.' She grins. 'Come in. I'm so glad you weren't late.'

We haven't used that word before – fiancé – and I play with the sound of it in my head as Ali sways away into the sitting room to the strains of 'The Best Is Yet to Come' on the record player. It feels very grown up. I feel very grown up. Well, I do when I've taken off my anorak. I'm glad I thought to wear my favourite blue shirt, which goes fine with my black jeans. Although I'm regretting wearing my DMs with Ali dressed so elegantly. I don't know, I think, studying myself in the hallway mirror; I look pretty sharp.

'Are you coming?' Ali calls, and I find her sitting on the sofa, two glasses of sparkling white wine on the little coffee table in front of her.

'This is nice,' I say, sitting down beside her. She looks at me with big eyes, the greenness of them accentuated by her dark eye shadow and dark dress. It's funny to see her wearing make-up; she hardly ever does. Or perhaps I just haven't noticed. Mouthing along to Frank Sinatra, she hands me a glass and raises hers, suddenly breaking into song.

'I'm gonna teach you to fly, we've only tasted the wine, we're gonna drain the cup dry ...' Her smile widens, her cheeks lift, she blinks slowly. 'Cheers!'

'Cheers.' I smile back, uncertainly, wondering if she's going to pick up the next verse or expects me to. But that part of the scene is over, it seems; she's moved on.

'Anything else?' She blinks again, and her expression seems to form a question.

'Oh, yes. Happy New Year!' I say, leaning in to kiss her full on the mouth. She responds, but it's not a long kiss and she makes a delicate coughing sound as she draws back.

'Um, I meant, anything else as in . . . something to ask me?'

And I'm thrown. I don't know why because that's what this is all about, of course. But I've only just walked in.

'Right, of course!' I respond. 'You want me to . . . ask you now?'

'Yes! I mean, why not?' Then she laughs, quite loudly. 'Unless you've changed your mind!'

I laugh too, because I can't think of a reliable reply, and excuse myself, realizing the ring is still in my anorak pocket. When I return, a moment later, Ali is sitting in a more upright position on the edge of the sofa, and she's moved the coffee table to one side. Frank's disappeared.

'I'm not looking,' she says, her eyes closed. I'm not sure why, since she chose the ring, she knows exactly what's happening. But I play along, sitting again and taking another slug of the fizzy wine while she's not looking.

I hold the box in my hand, glance at the clock on the mantelpiece over the fire. It's not even six o'clock. I can't work out why she's in such a hurry for me to propose. I clear my throat in the empty silence.

'Ali,' I begin, cupping the box in both hands, holding it in the air between us.

Her lips fold into themselves. She opens one eye.

'Wait,' she whispers. 'You have to do it properly.'

'Isn't this properly?' I whisper back.

'On one knee. It's traditional.'

I can't help sniggering, saying under my breath, 'Traditional?'

'It's important. To me,' she says, a little less softly.

'Ali,' I say, again, now relocated to the floor, on one knee. Only it occurs to me, I haven't thought beyond this point. Why have I not scripted this bit? In a way, I'm surprised she hasn't; she's usually good at providing the right words for me. Words flap around, between my ears. Do I say 'please'? Is this an actual question, or an instruction? Do I need to use the word 'honour' here?

'Ali. Will yo—'

'Eeeeee,' comes a sound from her mouth, and her body tenses like an excited child on its birthday.

'Will you be my—' No, that's too grown up. I look down at the box, open the lid, away from me. 'Will you marry me?'

Ali's eyes pop open, she squeals, her hands shoot up to press flat against her cheeks, like this is a huge surprise, completely out of the blue.

'Yes! Yes! Yes! Ohhhh.' She makes a sound like an animal, almost a howl. It pushes me back on my heels, then I'm pulled into her body, her arms wrapped tight around my neck.

When at last she releases me, I'm surprised to find the ring already on her finger. Surprised, because I thought I was supposed to put it there. But who cares? The most important thing is Ali's truly happy, at last.

53

DECEMBER 1992

We're still on the sofa when the doorbell rings. In all the times I've been here, this is the first time anyone's come to the door. I throw myself on the floor.

'Shit. What do we do?' I ask, flattening myself, forgetting the shutters are closed, nobody can see in. It's just instinct.

'It's fine,' says Ali, getting to her feet, deftly changing the record and setting the stylus. 'I've invited some friends over.'

'You've what? Who?'

'Calm down, it's fine, I promise. Look, they're my friends Trace and Nigel and they know about us, remember?' says Ali calmly, effortlessly. I sit up and climb back onto the sofa. 'I had to tell someone, after ... what happened,' she adds quietly.

The doorbell sounds again.

'You'd better let them in, then,' I say, wishing she wouldn't, wishing they'd just go away. I can't believe she's invited people here, now, in this moment.

'You'll love them. They'll love you! They're really lovely. And I can't wait to show them this.' She waves her fingers, the ring catching the light, as she skips to the door.

'They sound . . . lovely,' I say to myself, standing up, feeling the earth move under my feet. Stand or sit?

A man and a woman step into the room. I'm halfway to sitting again, change direction, but it's clumsy so I push my knees straight with a move forwards, my hand outstretched.

'Oh, hello!' says the woman, in a tone that suggests this isn't our first meeting. The man smiles quizzically. They do seem familiar, or at least, she does. A tall woman with dyed blonde hair, not a natural colour like Ali's, lots of makeup. She's wearing a short black leather skirt and a tight-fitting leopard-print top. She has massive breasts. They fill my field of vision as she lurches towards me, ignores my hand, and seizes me in a suffocating hug, her breasts like detonated airbags, crushing my lungs. 'Congratulations!'

I utter a muffled thank you as she disengages. Ali must have told them already. I'm catching my breath when the man takes my hand for a firm shake.

'Hello there,' his eyebrows say. 'Wonderful news, delighted for you both. Ali . . .' He's still got my hand but is already turning to offer congratulations to Ali. He clearly doesn't want to look me in the eye.

Ali introduces them as Trace and Nigel Deakin, from down the road. Am I supposed to give them my surname? She hands them two glasses of sparkling wine from the dining table, which I hadn't noticed before. I also hadn't noticed that the table is laid for four people. It might be the alcohol, into which I dive headfirst when a second bottle is opened, or it's due to the come-all-ye engagement party I appear to have stumbled into, but I'm giddy at the edges.

It's not that I'm unhappy about the introduction of new

faces, and they do seem very nice, if a bit over the top, but I'm caught off guard. If I'm honest, I had imagined we'd start the evening in the bedroom. A chance to regroup, find each other again. Have some drinks. Then do the whole ring thing later, perhaps even at midnight. I hadn't anticipated Ali would be inviting an audience to witness the biggest night of my life. Or perhaps she thought I wouldn't go through with it. Were they drafted in as a sort of fall-back support act? Did I imagine it, or was that a collective sigh of relief that blew in with the cold night air when Ali opened the front door? It might explain the bear hug from Trace, the cautious greeting from Nigel, and Ali's near-constant hysterical laughter.

Trace and Nigel are drinkers. Or they're not, but tonight they're making one hell of an exception. In fact, when Ali asks me to fetch another bottle from the kitchen, Trace corrects her: 'Bring two!' As the chocolate pudding drifts into coffees, the booze starts to properly kick in, with Nigel lazily sprawled across the sofa and eyeing me across the room.

'So, how's school?'

54

JANUARY 1993

As the spring term gets underway, we reprise our roles, maintain a vigilant distance. Like hitting the reset button, except now we're carrying an even bigger secret around with us. The story is, she had a whirlwind reunion with her Spanish boyfriend, Carlos, over the Christmas break and – *ta-da!* – he proposed. This irrefutable news gives Ali every excuse to show off her ring and flash photos of her and the Spanish waiter getting cosy in the restaurant last summer.

Well, almost nobody knows. To pre-empt any awkwardness between me and Nick, I seek him out on the first day of term and explain what's happening. I wish I wasn't in this position, but the prospect of the girls in our Spanish class whooping over Miss P when they spot the ring is not worth the risk of not telling Nick. I choose not to tell him that it all went down on New Year's Eve. That would really piss him off, and I desperately need him on my side.

He's the one looking sheepish, though, when we squeeze into my study in the house. And something seems amiss when his reaction to my confession is perfectly calm.

'Aren't you cross, mate?' I have to dip my head to catch

Nick's eye. He doesn't answer immediately, standing against the door, shoulders drooping and hands deep in his trouser pockets. He blows air through his cheeks, then coughs.

'It's not me who's going to be cross,' he says.

'Eh? What does that mean?' I ask.

'In my defence, it was New Year's, and I was monumentally wasted.'

'What are you talking about, Nick?'

'I'm really sorry,' he says, running both hands through his thick curls. 'Ant knows.'

'What does Ant—' But I don't need to finish my question. It's obvious from the way his head drops to his chest. 'I see. Shit.'

The thing is, I don't go batshit crazy on him. I don't yell in his face. I don't even feel crushed, as I thought I might if it got out. Perhaps I always knew it would leak through the cracks of any friendship, no matter how strong. I know it was Nick who sussed out what was going on between me and Ali originally, but would I have kept it to myself this long if he hadn't found out? So, Ant knowing is a kind of release, another burst of steam from this pressure cooker. There's only one problem. Ant isn't Nick. He's nothing like as reliable. And that thought rinses through my veins like ice.

'I need to speak to him, then. Urgently.'

'Leave it to me, mate,' says Nick. 'Come over to mine after school.'

It might turn out to be for the best, that Nick spilt the beans. It's like he's become the protector of my secret. When I meet them in his bedroom later, it's Nick who swears Ant to secrecy, on pain of a lifetime of dead arms and wedgies. Ant makes a show of promising, but he has a facial tic that sends the edges of his mouth into a curl, which is both unfortunate and unnerving.

'Ant, seriously.' I step in. 'This isn't a piss-take. You cannot tell a soul.'

'Yeah, all right, vicar. I won't tell a soul,' he retorts, the curl breaking into a smile. 'It's okay. Don't worry. Your secret is safe with me.'

There's a few seconds' silence in the room, which I want to believe is the two of them contemplating the gravity of what we now share, until Ant says, 'So, Miss P. Come on, what's she like in the sack?'

Nick and I hurl ourselves at Ant, fists pummelling in all directions, all three of us ending in a heap on the floor.

'Okay, okay. Joke!' howls Ant from one of Nick's signature headlocks.

On the train home that evening, the pitch-black January night feels like it's hemming me in, that the train's progress is being hampered by an unseen force. Everything is too close for comfort. All I can do is put my trust in friendship.

55

JANUARY 1993

No matter how cool I try to play it, like not acknowledging her when we pass in the cloisters or in the dining hall queue, I'm dying to see Ali alone. As I see it, workwise, the pressure's off. I'm not going to Oxford, despite my housemaster and Mum keeping the flame alive; he wants to appeal their decision, convinced they've made a mistake, while Mum is simply in denial, probably because she's told all her friends I got a scholarship and doesn't know how to face them. Even the Head of Modern Languages is scraping the barrel, ambushing me after assembly one morning: 'You could reapply post A-level to read Oriental Studies, or Persian Studies?' What a joke, like anyone's going to need Chinese or Arabic.

No, I've put that 'city of dreaming spires' dream behind me, for practical reasons too. As Ali said, what would happen to her if I went to study in another city for three or four years? We're engaged now; it wouldn't be fair. It's going to be hard enough getting her to accept me doing Operation Raleigh and my sailing trip with Uncle Jack, about which he reminded me in a letter at Christmas. I think she'll be okay though, since she's not pushing actual marriage. For now, I'm keeping everything crossed for an offer from the local uni, which I should hear about soon – they said early in the New Year. And since there's nothing I can do to influence that outcome and my mocks are over, I've got some breathing space. The only hitch is Mum, who's made it clear she still expects me home on time and at weekends, insisting my grades are more important than ever, that this is no time for slacking off.

As the bell rings at the end of the first Spanish lesson of the new term, I hang back.

'Do you want me to return the Márquez book, Miss?' I say, as the others file out of the classroom.

'Ah, yes, but shut the door, would you? It's blowing in the cold,' she says, turning to wipe the whiteboard. 'I need a word anyway, about your mock results.'

I shut us in then perch on the edge of a desk near the door, so as not to arouse suspicion if someone enters without knocking. I watch her from behind, the arc of her arm as she swipes a cloth to erase her outline of the coming term's topics and homework plans. There, fanning through the air, is the symbol of our love. The ring. A tiny, discreet presence, but one which carries the weight of all our secrecy, whose exposure could destroy us in an instant.

'I hope you wrote all this down,' she says.

'Yes, Miss,' I say earnestly. 'I think I got most of it, Ali.'

'Shh!' she hisses, throwing me a glance over her shoulder. 'We have to—'

'Be careful, yeah yeah, I know,' I cut her off. 'Hey, that was a smooth line – about needing a word about my mock results. Nicely done.'

She finishes wiping, then starts sorting the exercise books on her desk.

'Have they been marked, then?' I add, hitching myself further up the desk, allowing my legs to dangle just off the floor.

'Yes, and I was in fact being serious,' she says, looking directly at me. 'I do need to talk to you about them.' She sifts through a pile on the side of her desk. I crane my neck and recognize last term's exam paper.

'That sounds ominous.' I grimace, squeeze my eyes shut. It can't be as bad as all that.

'Well,' she sighs, drawing out my papers – the essays, the reading and listening comprehensions, the grammar exam – holding them up to show me the marks. 'It's not what we were expecting.'

'Oh shhhhit,' I exclaim. *How the fuck did that happen?* I'm about to add, when I stop myself. I know why, and the expression on her face is warning me not to go there. But it vanishes in a heartbeat, and she brightens.

'Listen, I've had an idea,' she says, her voice animated. 'I've got the perfect solution to kill two birds with one stone.'

'What do you mean?'

She explains quickly, as a low hum of voices and hurrying feet builds in the corridor outside. The two birds are my grades and our lack of time together. Her idea, for which she's very pleased with herself, is risky. In fact, it sounds like complete madness.

'Okay, so I'm going to write to your mother, or maybe I'll phone her,' she begins.

'Whoa! You're gonna call my mum?'

'Don't interrupt. I'm going to propose giving you some private tutorials to get your grades back on track.'

'Wait a minute,' I say. 'You're suggesting extra lessons – private lessons? Ali, you've only met her briefly, so you don't really know her. There's no chance she's going to pay for private lessons on top of my school fees.'

'Aha! That's where you're wrong.' She claps her hands. 'I do know all that, which is why she's going to love Miss P – because I won't be charging.'

'What? Why wouldn't you charge?'

'Because I'm "very generous",' she says, pinching the air, 'and anyway, I'll make it seem like it's her idea – build on the Spanish study trip last summer. She'll feel as though she's enlisting my help.'

'Hang on, hang on, how—' I run a hand over my hair and down my neck, trying to keep up. I can't see how this is Mum's idea.

'I haven't got to the best bit. The other bird!' She drums on her desk. 'Where do you think these tutorials are going to take place?' She grins.

'At . . . your place?'

'Wrong! At yours!' She laughs, and my jaw drops open.

'Are you kidding me? That will blow our cover.'

'Not with this, it won't.' She holds up her ring finger, wiggling it with the pad of her thumb so that the diamond catches the light. 'Won't she be delighted for me, when I tell her the happy news about me and Carlos?'

I'm about to answer, when the door swings wide open and an unstoppable herd of uniforms and bags piles in.

'Right, thank you. Hand it in by next lesson,' I hear Ali call, as I'm spun out of the room by the twist of bodies.

56

JANUARY 1993

Ali must be pretty convincing on the phone, because not only does Mum agree to the idea of extra tutoring, but she invites Ali over for lunch to discuss the details. I'm still in awe of Ali's daring plan when I open the door to her the following Sunday.

'Hi, Miss, please, come in,' I say, and in she walks, as though she's been here a hundred times before. Like it's her second home. Not the home of the pupil with whom she's having an illicit and increasingly risky affair. In a mock servile voice, I ask, 'Shall I take your coat, Miss?'

'Thanks,' she says, all professional and teachery, but with a glint in her eye. 'I've brought your mum these.' She hands me a bouquet of flowers, while she takes off her coat. I notice they're not the kind I buy *her* from the corner shop. This is a proper bunch from a florist, with a fresh garden smell that mixes in the air around me with the sweet, heady scent of Ali's perfume, enveloping my senses. I'm standing there, staring at this woman in my house, and everything swims surreally before me. I want to throw myself at her. But my legs feel like they'll buckle under me if I make a move.

'Hey,' Ali whispers, 'keep it together.' Then louder, 'So, is your mum through here? Are you going to lead the way?'

Just then, Mum bustles into the hall from the kitchen, looking every bit at home in a full-length, flour-specked apron; a look I've never seen in my life. Seems like we're all role-playing today.

'Hello, Ali,' she trills, with first-name confidence. 'I'm so glad you could join us for Sunday luncheon.'

Ali steps forward with her flowers, and I can't help smirking behind her. Mum's acting as if this is some kind of family tradition, when in reality Sunday lunch is no different to every other day here, which is usually soup. And where did 'luncheon' come from?

We file into the kitchen, where Mum places the flowers on the counter, reaches for a tall vase from the wall cupboard then moves to the sink to run the cold tap. You'd think she'd been given a gold bar, or at least a gold star, with the fuss she's making of Ali's gift. Turning from the sink, she moves in to embrace Ali, pulling back just in time, remembering her apron.

'Oh, Ali!' squeals Mum, stepping back. I jump. What's Ali done, pulled a knife? But I follow Mum's gaze, which is fixed laser-like on the finger of Ali's left hand.

'Yes,' says Ali, smiling coyly, holding out her hand for Mum to inspect the ring. 'His name's Carlos,' Ali continues, as Mum grabs her hand. 'We met in Spain, last summer. He made a surprise visit just after the end of term and, well, this was my Christmas present.'

'Gosh,' coos Mum, not letting go. 'How wonderful! How exciting! Congratulations!'

'Thank you,' beams Ali, glancing across at me, the picture of innocence, then back to Mum, preening as if she were a member of the family, Mum's daughter, coming home with an A* report card. 'I feel so lucky. I've met my Mr Right.'

I watch, impressed, as Ali performs her part, delivering the lines I've already heard in rehearsal with word-perfect ease.

Lunch is something fishy in pastry of which Mum takes ownership, making a show of garnishing, while instructing me to open a bottle of wine. I could have sworn I'd caught sight of the something-en-croûte in the fridge, in Waitrose packaging. I tuck in, while Ali answers a barrage of engagement questions effortlessly. Throughout, I am silent, until the conversation changes to the topic of my extra tutoring. Ordinarily, the prospect of my teacher and mother discussing my academic failings in front of me would be cause to run away, but I'm sick of hearing about Carlos – even if he is made up – so it's a welcome relief.

Ali launches into Act Two of her pre-scripted routine, while Mum offers seconds, nods her head, tuts in my direction, rolls her eyes. All the reactions I'd hoped for when Ali walked me through her plan. Such is Ali's poise that, while she speaks, under the table she kicks off her shoe and begins to slide her foot up my leg. I'm already shoeless, and in return I mirror her movements, hidden by the long tablecloth. With my longer legs, I can reach further, run my foot along the inside of her bare thighs, which she obligingly separates, allowing me to press my toes into the soft fabric folds of her knickers.

When Mum gets up to fetch dessert, thanking Ali (again) for her generous offer to help me return my grades to where they should be, Ali shoots me a triumphant grin. Then, not even checking that Mum has her back to us, she grabs my big toe, rubs it up and down against her pubic bone and mimes an orgasm, before saying:

'Don't worry, I'm confident he'll be back on top before you know it.'

The private tutoring starts soon after, with Ali making fort-nightly visits. Mum and I both want her to come weekly, though for completely different reasons, but Ali explains that, regrettably, the spring term is too busy for more. Behind the scenes, Ali tells me it would be too risky to come that often and we should play it carefully so as not to attract unwanted attention from the school or give my mum any cause for suspicion.

'Don't you see?' she says, one evening in late January as I walk her to where she's parked her car further down the road. 'I'm deliberately not making myself too available to your mum.'

'Yeah, but she wants me to have as much tutoring as pos-sible,' I say.

'I realize that,' says Ali, 'but I'm being professional. Or at least, making sure I appear that way. It will serve us well in the end that I'm not here every week. And we don't want you to hit top marks too soon.'

'I'm not that bad, am I? I used to be right up there.'

'Of course you're not bad. Actually, you need to hold back a bit. Make more mistakes.'

'I can do that.' I grin. 'But how do you mean – it will serve us well?'

'Well, it gives us room for manoeuvre,' she says, with a wink. 'Means we can hike it up to weekly sessions at some point, perhaps nearer the end of term, the closer we get to the critical Easter revision period and the actual exams in the summer.'

'Right, I guess,' I reply, still not convinced. 'I'm not sure I follow.'

'Really? Can't you see that the more "help" your mum thinks you need, the more of my time she's going to want? And that's what I'm counting on.'

'Eh?'

'You really do need extra lessons!' She laughs. 'She will, effectively, be throwing us together. So, when eventually we come out, we can say it was partly down to her.'

Ali opens the car door and throws her bag on the passenger seat, while I lean against the Fiesta's boot and try to put the pieces of Ali's puzzle together. It sounds complicated to me, but I'm not about to question her tactics. She's brilliant at this psychological stuff.

'You look confused,' she says, straightening up.

'No, I get it. It's very clever. It's just, has it occurred to you that all we're doing in these sessions is, well, teaching, learning? With the occasional bout of footsie when Mum's out of the room?'

'Homework for next time.' She smiles mischievously. 'Find a way to get her out of the house.'

57

FEBRUARY 1993

February breezes in, no warmer than January, but with hope and promise in the form of brave white snowdrops, delicate-scented cyclamen and the first hints of life in the trees. I shelve my Nick Drake tapes, find myself playing UB40's '(I Can't Help) Falling in Love With You' on loop, before retreating to the more middle maudlin ground of Crowded House.

But there's still no news from the local university; no letter, no offer. The uncertainty bugs me a bit, but Ali's much more agitated. At one of our after-school tutoring sessions, she's even more fidgety than me. At first, I get the wrong end of the stick, mistaking her restlessness for nerves or excitement. In school, earlier that same day, I got a message to her that Mum would be out of the house later. Alone at last. I'm bouncing when I tell her because it's been impossible to find any privacy this term.

'You should have heard by now,' Ali says. We're sitting at the kitchen table, where I've laid out textbooks, notepad and pens, to make it look like a real tutoring session is underway in case Mum returns early.

'Yeah, I know, it's annoying,' I say, brushing it off and

glancing at the clock on the wall. It's still early, but I don't want to waste time on chat.

'Annoying? This is your future. This is about us. We need to know you've got a place.'

'I know we do,' I say, my voice sounding defensive for some reason. 'But what can I do?'

'Call them.'

'Oh right, can I do that?' I ask, surprised, since it's never occurred to me that you can speak to universities on the phone.

'Well, we can try.' Ali checks her watch. 'The admissions department will have gone home for the day, but the faculty staff often stay longer.'

We search my room for the original interview letter, which I remember had the telephone number.

'Hey, Ali. You're in my bedroom,' I say cheerily and point-edly, as we sift through paper on my desk.

'I know, and the sooner we find this number, call them, get an answer, the sooner we can do other things.' She speaks quickly. 'Is this it?' She holds up a piece of paper with the university's letterhead, scanning it and deciding it is. 'Where's the phone?'

Ali stands over me as I make the call from Mum's bureau in the sitting room. I'm amazed that someone answers, and it throws me. I stammer out my words, give my name and reason for calling. With a sigh from the other end of the phone, I'm told to wait. In the ensuing silence, Ali folds her arms over her chest and appears to close her eyes. Unconsciously, I start humming and doo-dooing a Soup Dragons' song.

'Don't,' says Ali, eyes still closed, her fingers tapping arrhythmically against her sleeve.

I'm about to counter the unsteady beat with my own fingers on Mum's blotting pad when there's a muffled cough at the other end of the phone.

'Right, thank you for waiting, although you shouldn't really be contacting us direct,' says the departmental voice, going on to express surprise that I hadn't received a letter yet.

'Okay, well, at least I don't have to give you bad news,' says the voice, sounding lighter. 'You have a place with us for this October, provided you get two B grades at A-level.'

A wave of relief rushes through me and Ali's fists are already pumping. I thank the person profusely and hang up. The phone is still in my hand when Ali throws her arms around my neck. We jump around the room together, swearing and whooping, then collapse on the sofa.

Half an hour later, we're still on the sofa, but down to our underwear and going at it like just-released prisoners. After, we wash each other in the shower in the downstairs bathroom, then lie in my single bed, under the duvet, our bodies pressed tight in the cramped space. It's a cold February evening outside and there's no light in the room, so it feels like night-time, like she's sleeping over at mine. Her breathing is slow. We don't speak for ages. I stare at the ceiling, into the darkness, and wonder whether my university offer can be deferred for a year. I don't say this out loud.

58

MARCH 1993

The spring term is curiously short. It races by, despite everyone saying how late Easter is this year. I have no idea what
they're talking about. For me, the weeks in February and early
March blur into one long routine of school business as usual:
endless revision, music lessons and grade exams, Chapel Choir
on Sundays, prefect duties. There are unremitting attempts to
get us outside playing games in the mud. It's like a punishment, and one which I battle to avoid with ever more elaborate
excuses. Even so, once a week I'm forced into shorts and vest
to at least give my housemaster the impression I'm doing my
bit. A couple of desultory lopes around the perimeter of the
hockey pitches before hiding for the rest of the afternoon in
the sports centre weights room. I'm safe here; no one wants
to be seen doing multi-gym.

Home tutoring, meanwhile, has increased to weekly visits, as
Ali planned. It's great, especially when Mum disappears, though
I have mixed feelings when I watch Mum and Ali chatting
away like friends over coffee. There's routine here as well, as
Mum plies Ali with an update on whatever they talked about
the previous week. It's usually all about Mum's work or her

role as a city councillor. Ali asks the right questions, nods and murmurs, with the occasional knowing wink in my direction when Mum isn't looking. Then it's usually Ali's turn to update 'us' on the latest with her fiancé. I don't know where Ali finds the energy – or memory – to keep the story rolling. Routine again, I suppose. I don't know what I think about it, I've lost count of the number of lies we've told, so I can't tell whether it's bad or harmless that we've pulled Mum into our web.

What I am sure of is that I have split myself in two. I've carved out two distinct versions of me. A double life. Old me, who goes to school, sits in lessons, does homework, sings in chapel, chats to the lads about nothing important. Other me, who exists in a parallel universe of secrecy orbiting Ali, lying on demand, pretending I'm not a teenager but a real grown-up man.

Then, the worst happens. We are exposed. It's a couple of weeks before school breaks up for Easter. I'm in the library, working on a German essay about Schubert, which I intend to regurgitate in the A-level written exam next term. From the other end of the long room, I hear the door open and close emphatically, then feet walking hurriedly, start-stopping, coming down the aisle, clearly looking for something, or someone. With a loud, deliberate tread, they approach. I look up.

'Oh, thank God, you're here.' It's Ali. I'm not overly surprised to see her. She has a copy of my timetable, so that she always knows where I am, if she needs me. In a study period, like today, the library is a good bet. This room has seen several exciting, illicit fumbles over the course of our relationship, but this doesn't look like a social visit. Her face is white, and she's lost her composure somewhere. Furtively glancing around, checking the other bays beyond mine to make sure we're alone, finally she sinks into a chair on the opposite side of the table, head in her hands.

'What the hell's wrong?' I ask, making to stand, to comfort her. She straightens up, pushes the air at me with her hand to prevent me from getting close. I perch on the desk instead. 'What's going on?'

'I have just been spoken to,' she begins, hands still fluttering in the air, her breath catching in her throat as she tries to gather herself, 'at break, in the staffroom. A warning. Jesus!' She throws her head back, lips pursed tightly, eyes wet at their rims, wide as though she's fighting the impulse to blink.

'A warning – about what?' I say, frowning, then peering out of my bay to double-check there's no one else here. 'Who spoke to you?'

'David.'

'Who's David?'

'David, er, Mr Roberts. You wouldn't have much to do with him. He's science. But we've always got on well. He's one of the good ones.'

'Really? So, what's he doing making you upset?' I ask, trying but failing to picture Mr Roberts. 'What's he warning you about?'

'Us,' she says, breathing heavily, staring at me, before wiping her eyes with her hand.

Someone, she explains, Roberts wouldn't say who, told him that someone else had told *him* that they'd heard Ali had been seen with a pupil. I ask where we'd been seen, by whom, and who are all these teachers spreading this shit? I can hear myself getting worked up.

'It's a rumour mill,' she says wearily, like it's not her first time, 'and, evidently, it's on the move, if that many people are talking.'

For a minute, we stop, take it all in. The air in the room seems thinner now. I take some breaths, run my fingers across my scalp, stealing a glance at my blazer for any signs of dandruff, instinctively brushing a hand across my shoulder.

'Shit, shit, shit,' is all I can say.

'Yes, exactly, shit,' she adds.

'But how?' I bring my palms flat to the table, my fingers spread, rigid. 'This is mad. I mean, why now? We haven't been meeting at the flat. I haven't been to yours for, God knows how long. We're so much less . . . visible than all those times before, like, last term, God . . .' I run out of words.

Ali doesn't answer for a while. She dips her head to her chest, one hand rubs the other in her lap, her right thumb and forefinger pulling at the fingers of her left hand, same on the other side, back and forth.

'I have to root this out before it takes hold. Find the source, and squash this fucking rumour,' she says, her voice harder.

'What should I do?' I ask.

'Nothing. Do nothing. Don't speak to anyone. Don't—' She cuts off, lifts her head and glances up at me. 'You haven't said anything to anyone, have you? You promised you—'

'No, no, of course not,' I lie automatically.

'Thank God it's almost the end of term,' she goes on. 'But I'm going to find out who started this vicious gossip.' Standing to leave, she adds, 'Obviously, we can't see each other, not for a while, not until this blows over. Tell your mother I'm too busy now – end of term, whatever.' She waves a hand, then hurries off.

I begin scrolling through every memory of when Ali and I were together this term, but they're few and far between. We really have changed tack this year. All the time since Christmas, New Year's, we've basically only met at my mum's house. It doesn't make sense that someone could have spotted us together recently. Unless they followed Ali. No, that's mad. So who?

I sit in silence for a few minutes, gazing out of the window. The bell rings for the change of lesson. Outside, the quad fills with a chorus of voices as pupils mingle and mill about between class. Mill. Rumours. Shit. Spreading. I don't move. I don't need to be anywhere.

The noise fades, stutters, falls to a whisper, dies. And in the void, a cold damp sensation creeps up my neck and across my face, finds its way into my hair. A knot forms and tightens in the pit of my stomach. I freeze. The face of Mr Roberts appears to me. I see him now, and instantly, I know who's talked.

Ant.

With school life having been much more normal this term, and me keeping a low profile, not disappearing at odd times, being careful not to behave secretively, my life hasn't been the subject of fascination that it was. I haven't really thought about it, assuming that everyone's either forgotten or figured it's over between Ali and me. Perhaps, they might have thought, I'd made it all up. They? Nick and Ant. What's more, they've been preoccupied enough with their own love lives recently, at long last. Nothing serious, but still a distraction. I'd hoped my situation would stay under the radar just long enough to get us to the end of the year.

But it has to be Ant. Because I've remembered who Mr Roberts is: he's Ant's landlord. In addition to being a science teacher, Mr Roberts and his wife run a sort of mini boarding house on the school campus. They have a few rooms, so there's only ever a handful of boys living there. Another weird anomaly of this place. I haven't been there, which is why Mr Roberts wasn't a face I could immediately place. But now I have, it's horribly obvious. Ant's blabbed.

But what if it isn't Ant? What if Nick has told someone else by now? Surely I would know. I want to find the lads, have it out with them. That way, maybe I can shut this down before it leaks any further, before Ali finds out they've known about us for months. No. There's no point bringing it up, throwing a grenade into the pit, forcing my carefully packed and stored secrets to the surface. I'd lose everything in the explosion. I'll have to wait for Ali to investigate further, hope for the best, then make a move if necessary.

Over the following days, paranoia grows inside me. In every lesson, every assembly, at lunch in the dining hall, in the library, I see faces staring at me, eyeing me with suspicion, and I'm convinced they all know, the whole school. Any minute, there will be a summons to the headmaster's office and that will be that. I'll be out. And shit, what about Ali – will she lose her job? Or worse, face the police? Ali said once that our relationship isn't illegal, so they can't lock her up or anything.

On the Thursday, with just a weekend and a few days before

the end of term, she places a note in my exercise book, bravely giving me the signal, two taps on the cover as she sets it down on my desk. She wants me to phone her that evening.

I call from the phone box, not risking prying ears at home. I'm shaking as I feed the green plastic card into the slot and dial her number. Has she found out that it's Ant? That I told our secret? Is this the moment when it all comes crumbling down? I hold my breath, waiting for her to pick up.

She gets straight to the point. She's tracked down the person spreading the rumour: some random history teacher – Mr Harris, someone I barely know. I lean back against the glass, the relief washing over me as Ali explains how she made Mr Roberts confess all he knew.

'He was reluctant at first,' she says. 'But I convinced him it's all complete nonsense. Reminded him I'm engaged, for God's sake, and why the hell would I be interested in a pupil?'

'Right, yes, good point,' I say, a little taken aback at the ease with which she dissed me to Roberts.

'Apparently, Simon Harris told someone, might even have been a matron, or perhaps a tutor in one of the boarding houses, can't remember, that he'd seen you getting out of my car in one of those streets near my building. And another time, saw you walking up my road as he was driving home. I told you to be vigilant.'

'Wait, hang on, Ali,' I interrupt her. 'That's got to be months ago. Way back at the beginning of last term, surely?'

'Yes.'

'So, how's it taken him this long to say something?' I ask. 'Or did he in fact tell early on and the rumour's been spreading ever since without us knowing?'

'I don't know. But I'll find out.'

'How?' I ask.

'I'm going to confront him. I'll catch him in his classroom after school, before he disappears for the weekend, and set him right. And I'll find out who else knows, and deal with each in turn. Then hopefully it will blow over during the Easter holiday.'

I listen in awe at how confident she sounds. I wouldn't want to be Mr Harris right now.

59

MARCH 1993

The next evening, we're back on the phone. She confronted Harris, she says, in a flat voice with a hint of triumph. She didn't wait to hear his side first, just stormed into his classroom after lessons, on the offensive, berating him for spreading vile rumours, not letting him get a word in.

'He clearly wasn't expecting petite Miss P to confront him with anything more challenging than a detention rota form or sponsorship request,' she laughs. 'So, I certainly had his attention.'

She went on to tell him she'd taken pity on me way back last year when she'd stumbled upon me in a state. Found out I'd been having a hard time, displaced at a new school, parents divorcing, mother's cancer, clearly fragile. And, from that point onwards, I'd formed a bit of an attachment to her.

'Hmm,' I interject. 'That's not quite right, though, is it?'

'What? You expected me to tell him the truth?'

'No, of course not, but it would have been good to agree a line first, wouldn't it?'

She doesn't come back at me straight away, leaving me to listen to a static hush. After a while, it's clear this is her answer.

'Yeah, you're right,' I say, to break the silence. 'Sorry, you know best.'

'We have to be believable,' she says slowly, enunciating her words as though talking to a child. 'I picked my truths carefully. Defensible facts, like that time I discovered you in that wine bar, remember?'

I don't disagree again, even if it does make me out to be the needy one. She goes on, saying that Mr Harris's manner turned to one of pastoral concern, especially when Miss P revealed how my mother had approached Ali, asking for her help when my academic grades were suffering in the autumn. That this had led to some extra tuition, always with my mother in the vicinity.

'What about what he says he saw?' I ask, fumbling my question, trying to keep up.

'I said you broke down in my classroom one day and I gave you a lift, said I couldn't go into details, as it was a delicate matter.'

'And he bought that?'

'Has to. Confidentiality.'

I don't really understand how that works, but I have more questions.

'Who else has he told?'

'Well, if he's telling the truth, he only told one other person – a matron in one of the boarding houses.'

'And she told ... Mr Roberts?' I cut in.

'No,' says Ali. 'Julie – Mrs Roberts, David's wife. Fortunately, the web doesn't seem too tangled,' she adds, evidently not seeing the tangled mess of who said what to whom and when in my head.

'How did it end, with Harris?'

299

'He apologized, unreservedly, realizes his mistake. I made him feel pretty shit about what he'd done, but I thought I'd better lay it on hard, in case he was tempted to tell anyone else. I don't think he has, but we can't be seen together, just to be on the safe side.'

I keep my head down for the next few days. Even outside the chapel waiting for end-of-term assembly, I'm able to hide in the sea of uniforms. But just as the doors open and the noisy crowd presses forward, I feel a tap on the shoulder. When I turn to see Mr Harris, my stomach churns. He asks me for a word and draws me to the steps that lead down from the quad to the playing fields. He's awkward, barely looking at me, but he's still a teacher, so there's an inbuilt superiority that makes me nervous.

'I wanted to speak with you, Gibson,' he begins, glancing around to make sure we're not being overheard.

'Sir?' My cheeks start to burn.

'It appears I owe you an apology,' he stutters, and I realize, raising my head to meet his eyes, that this is genuine. He means it. 'I allowed my mind to play tricks with unfortunate consequences, for which I am sorry.'

I have absolutely no idea how to reply to this. I can't bring myself to take the upper hand, to act like the wronged party in all this. It's easy for Ali; she's a teacher, an adult. But this doesn't feel right. Especially because the rumours are true.

'It's okay, sir,' is the best I can do.

'We should probably get to assembly,' he says, looking over my shoulder at the dwindling mob. I make to go, but he touches my arm. 'Thank you,' he says, and all the air in my lungs seems to escape.

60

April 1993

I feel like I'm barely surviving the last few days before the end-of-term bell rings, hiding in my study after assembly, and only leaving for the train station once I'm certain everyone else has gone home. Mr Harris may have apologized, but despite what Ali said on the phone, I'm going to assume the rumours have spread through the whole staffroom and anyone catching sight of me acting remotely suspiciously is going to report me.

When the doors slam shut and the train grinds its way out of the station, I allow myself to exhale. The Easter break can't come soon enough. All I want is the peaceful haven of my bedroom at home, away from the tight coils of suffocation that school has wound around me these past few weeks. And for once, someone is smiling down at me, because when I turn the corner into our road, my grandparents' car is parked outside. If they've come all this way, it can only mean one thing.

Mum is disappearing for a 'much needed holiday' in a place called Menton, in the south of France. She doesn't mention whether "Gordon" is going with her. Come to think of it, he hasn't been mentioned for a while. But clearly, the weighing scales of opportunity dipped heavily in favour of orange blossom, sun-dappled verandas and evening promenades along the Mediterranean coastline, and not in favour of supervising my revision for three weeks. Instead, she's installing Gran and Grandpa to babysit. I couldn't be happier. Not least since my weary walk up the hill from the station was punctuated with moments of panic as the proximity of my exams hit me full pelt in the chest. Their calming presence is exactly what I need as I attempt to scale the cliff face of my revision timetable. First task: write revision timetable.

All is quiet on the Miss P front as well. Partly her insistence that we keep a discreet distance, but also because she's spending most of the Easter holiday at her parents', as usual. I don't mind too much, seeing as our relationship has caused so much grief recently, but I do miss her. And I could murder a shag.

Easter weekend comes and goes. Mum is nowhere to be seen and Gran and Grandpa are taking longer naps and not much notice of me. After two solid weeks thrashing through two terms' worth of Spanish, German, English and French, the prospect of passing my exams is looking brighter. There are only a few more days left of the holiday and then the summer term; my final two months of school, ever. If Ali and I are going to see each other at all, it has to be now. I haven't heard from her for a couple of days, since receiving a postcard in an envelope, saying how much she misses me and pledging her undying love in left-handed writing. She adds that she'll be coming home shortly dot dot dot question mark, which I assume is a signal, though since she used an envelope and knows my mum isn't around, she could have been more explicit. I phone her that evening at her flat and the second I hear her voice, light, relaxed and purring, I'm under her spell all over again.

We plot a secret rendezvous. We meet in a side street and she drives us on winding roads, takes crazy turns down narrow lanes, pretending we're being followed, like spies. She giggles and sings and repeats again and again, 'Soon, we'll be free, we'll be together!'

We park, inevitably, at The Plough. The memories come flooding back. We even order the same food and drink as before. Flushed and tipsy, we trip down the hill to the brook and the trees. It's April, though, and there's a chill. We stand under the weeping willow, its trailing branches still waiting for their leaves that in a month would hide us. We kiss, but that's all. I make a half-hearted play to unclasp her bra, but I have to rummage under a couple of layers, and she jolts at the touch of my cold hands. We walk a bit, kiss a bit more, and by the little bridge that crosses the brook, where I would have fought that twat Graham for her honour, even though he'd have floored me, Ali unbuttons my jeans.

'If only this were May,' I sigh, apologetically, as she holds my cock in one hand, blows warm air onto her other hand. 'Sorry, Ali, it's too cold out here.'

'Damn. I really wanted to as well. It's been ages,' she says.

'I know, me too. I'm desperate. Perhaps we'll find some time soon, do you think?'

'God, I hope so,' she says. 'The summer term is an odd one. Everyone's preoccupied with exams and willing the weeks away. Then your year and Fifth Form go on study leave.' Her voice takes on a positive note. She lifts her head and kisses me, full and deep, for ages. 'I think our brush with disaster is over. I mean, fingers crossed, but we saw off Mr Harris and the others. And Mr Batsford will be on your side, if it comes to anything, won't he?'

'Hmm, I suspect a bit over the side,' I say, darkly.

'Ah, really?' She grins mischievously. 'Well, I'm not suggesting you let hi—'

'Ali!'

'Joke! Just, you know, don't rub him up the wrong way.'

'I'm going to be sick.'

'I think we're going to be all right,' she says, when we stop laughing. 'Then we can start planning our summer, and beyond.'

61

MAY 1993

The sun comes out, blossoms billow, showering the pavements with petals. The warmer air fills with a long-awaited fragrance. Although, on the downside, it's playing havoc with people's hay fever. Not for me, though. I sprint into my final term of school, revitalized and revised.

Some of the boys have bleached their hair blond, the girls are wearing flowery scrunchies in theirs, and there's a fresh energy running through the corridors. There's also abject fear at the imminent wave of exams rolling in on the all-too-near horizon. Term has hardly begun when the signs go up around campus: QUIET. EXAM IN PROGRESS. The languages timetable, with separate exams in listening, reading, writing and speaking, is the first out of the blocks and extends well beyond the mid-term break, into June, after most subjects are done. But I think I'm ready. The adrenalin kicks in and I strap myself in for the ride. Nothing is going to derail me.

Except, I'm wrong.

Two things happen. One that involves me; the other, Ali.

*

It turns out Ali's efforts to stamp out the rumours haven't worked. At least, not for me. It starts almost imperceptibly, I don't know precisely when, but one day it hits me; the teachers are ignoring me. They don't return my greetings in the corridor. When I have my hand up in class, I'm overlooked. Then Mr Grice makes a snide comment when addressing the German set about final preparations for the written exams.

'Everyone needs to pull out all the stops to score highly in these papers. There are no short cuts – at least not if you're studying German.' He pauses, shuffles something around on his desk, then adds, not looking up. 'Perhaps it's different if you're taking another language and getting special attention.'

None of the others appear to register the comment, but he may as well have walked over and landed a massive fist in my gut. It doesn't stop there. Messages about un-timetabled revision classes don't reach me, which puts me in trouble and results in two unnecessary detentions. Next, my other German teacher, Mr Siddel, someone who, Ali tells me, has always had a thing for her, starts picking on me. He takes any opportunity to single me out with particularly difficult questions, usually around grammar. There's no support from my classmates, but they're obviously taken aback. This isn't his usual banter. Gulika comes up to me after one humiliating lesson to see if I'm okay, but what can I say? By now, I've worked out that a campaign is being waged against me. I don't want to go running to Ali; she has enough to deal with, and it would just be a further distraction when what I really need now, in these final days before the exams, is a free mind and total concentration.

Despite my attempts to ignore the cold shoulders and

under-the-breath comments, it comes to a head in one of Siddel's classes. To illustrate how to use the German language's four grammatical cases, he's showing us a music video of Die Toten Hosen. We all see through it – any excuse to lure us to the dark side of German rock music – and the opening verse draws theatrical groans from everyone in the room. It's our usual reaction, but this time he doesn't play along. Instead, leaning back on his swivel chair in the middle of the room, centre stage, he presses pause on the remote. We're all sniggering at the screen, but this sudden halt catches us out. We look towards Siddel. Slowly, he rotates his chair to face me. I stare back, but something in the squinting of his eyes, the slight flare of his nostrils, brings a clammy sensation to my forehead. I look down. I feel his eyes boring through me. My scalp prickles and a speck of white on my sleeve draws my hand up to brush it off.

'Got a bit of a dandruff problem, haven't you, Gibson?' he says, and twelve red faces around twelve open mouths turn in my direction. My fingers, caught in the act, still touching my upper arm, seem to swell.

'You want to get that treated,' he persists, as several bottoms shift uneasily in their seats. 'Then again, it's all part of being an adolescent, isn't it?'

The silence that follows seems to stretch on and on. I try to breathe, calm and steady, hold my nerve. But I fail. I snap.

'I might be an adolescent, but at least I'm not a . . . cunt.'

The air evaporates. A chasm opens. Stunned expressions greet my outburst and a thin smile slithers across Siddel's weasel features. Now I see what's happened. I've been set up. Since the beginning of term. It's a contest and he's won. Whether he was the instigator, the ringleader, it doesn't matter. His face reflects their victory. They've all won.

'Showing your true colours, Gibson. Not really a surprise,' he says, a hint of teeth appearing through sneering lips. 'Though you're good at disguise.'

'Fuck you!' I yell in an explosion of spit and broken vocal cords. I don't know where he's going with this, but I sense I'm about to be exposed and I have to stop him. He opens his mouth, but he's speechless as I jump to my feet, step forward one pace. A hand grips my blazer from behind, holds me back. I don't know what I plan to do, don't know what I'm capable of. Am I stronger than him? Hard to tell. Am I really going to go for him?

'I think you'd better go, Gibson, don't you?' he says, not moving from his chair.

With my shirt clinging to the sweat on my back and my heaving chest sending ripples of damp up and down my spine, I grab my things and leave the room, slamming the door behind me. By the time I reach my study, my face is soaked in tears. I slump across my desk, bury my head in my arms, as yet oblivious to what this means, what I've lost, and the price I will have to pay.

I say nothing to Mum that evening; I can't have her worrying and shouting. I say nothing to Ali, either, though it surely won't be long before she hears. The next morning, after house assembly, when all the boys have dispersed to their lessons, Batsford calls me into his office. I sit, numb, in the chair on the other side of his desk, awaiting the inevitable bollocking.

But it doesn't come. Instead, he considers me through steepled fingers pressed to his mouth.

'I don't know what's going on, and in many ways, I don't want to know. What I do know is that you can't call a teacher a – that word. Even if we've all been close, on occasion,' he adds in muffled tones to the carpet beneath his desk.

'Am I going to be expelled, sir?'

'What? Lord no. You're going to stay, sit your exams, do your best, and keep your head down.' After another weary pause, he continues. 'I've heard what people, my colleagues, have been muttering, and I have to tell you, I don't like mutterings, gossip, tittle-tattle,' he says, with feeling. 'However, they've been hard to ignore, these things that are being talked about … about … you and Miss … So, I decided to speak to her myself.' At this, he hoists himself upright, while I sink lower. My brain was racing, but now it feels suspended in zero gravity. I'm floating in a state of bewilderment.

'I am content with what she told me. The extra tuition was requested, I understand, by your mother. I respect why Miss P decided to keep this arrangement under her proverbial hat. She also explained the reason you've been seen with her off campus.' His tone changes, softens, and as he speaks, he gets up, moves to sit on the edge of the desk. In this small room, he's very close. 'I just wish you'd come to me first, Joseph, when you were experiencing these difficulties at home. I had no idea how your parents' divorce was affecting you.'

My instinct is to look up at him, ask where he's getting this information, but the second I raise my eyes, I'm staring unavoidably at his groin, just inches from my face. I look down again, think, and the penny drops. Ali must have heard about the outburst in Siddel's lesson, realized what would happen next, and made a direct line for the one person who could fight my corner. And clearly, he has.

'Thank you, sir. I really appreciate you supporting me,' I say, eyes still down. I'm aware of him shifting his weight. I assume he's returning to his chair, but next I see his hand reach towards me, past my shoulder, my arm, my hand, to my thigh.

'That's quite all right,' he says, his voice thicker, deeper now. 'I only want what's best for you, dear boy.'

Whether it's because he can feel the tautness in my leg, the freeze of my shoulders, the quickening of my breath, he lifts off and finally returns to his side of the room. I take my cue and stand.

'One thing,' he says breezily, like that never happened. 'You can't go to any more German lessons, with either Mr Siddel or Mr Grice.'

'What? How am I supposed to keep on top? I mean, there are still lessons remaining before the exams, sir.'

'You'll just have to do your best. Check with your classmates what's being covered in lessons.'

I'm dismissed. Shaking my head, I trudge down the corridor to my study. In the quiet of my matchbox-sized room, I reflect on where I am. On the one hand, I've been spared the ultimate punishment, thanks to Ali, no doubt. With any luck, the school is going to turn a blind eye. I can only pray that Batsford's wandering hand isn't a signal and that his backing doesn't come with its own set of conditions. All the lads have speculated about his preferences, but I really don't want to be the one to find out the truth. On the other hand, I'm being denied vital revision lessons at the most important stage of the year because of what? Their fucking jealousies. Either way, when I get home that evening, I still don't tell Mum what's happened. Instead, I get my German books out and read.

When we speak on the phone the following evening, Ali is in a furious mood, and I assume there's been another round of muck-spreading in the staffroom. But it's not that. In fact, that's all gone quiet, apparently, gone away like it never happened. No one's talking, not even whispering, about us. That's weird, I think, that the school isn't hauling us over the coals, expelling me and reporting Ali to whatever authority it is teachers get reported to. The police? The government? I don't have time to dwell because Ali is in full flow.

The evening before, she went for dinner with some friends. People I know as well, as it turns out: Celia and Ned's eldest daughter, Fiona, and her husband, Carl. He's an occasional piano teacher at the school and she teaches primary school kids somewhere nearby.

'It was a really nice evening. Things were all jolly and relaxed. After the meal, we were sitting around, chatting. I sat next to Carl, who was friendly, but he was acting a bit odd as well, sort of uncomfortable. Then he said he'd heard the rumours. At which point, Fiona came over, started asking me questions. About you, as well. I felt awkward, so,' she takes a breath, 'I'm afraid I told them. Not everything, obviously, just the basic facts. They listened, didn't appear shocked. I told them it's a secret, that they mustn't tell anyone.'

'So, why are you so angry?'

She sighs. 'Because later, when I was saying goodbye, Fiona suddenly said, "I won't tell anyone about your affair, but if I'm asked, I won't lie for you either." I mean, can you believe she said that? The sanctimonious bitch! Some friend she turned out to be.'

'Oh, shit. Do you think she will keep quiet?'

'Christ, I don't know,' Ali practically yells. 'What I do know is that she's betrayed any trust I had in her. You see, you can't trust anyone.'

62

MAY 1993

Somehow, despite these obstacles, I get through the remaining weeks of the first half of term unscathed. Ali was right; everyone's too distracted in their own little worlds to keep the wheels of the rumour mill turning. I'm pretty much left alone to wade through weeks of exams. I even manage to join the others in the Sixth Form common room at the end of each week for some ceremonial textbook binning. It almost feels normal.

As the summer term bank holiday approaches at the end of May, with study leave and the big exam push around the corner, attention at school turns to Speech Day and the much-anticipated Prom. I haven't given it any thought, or maybe I've been blocking it out deliberately, until Ali brings it up one evening on the phone.

'Are you going to invite me to the Prom, then?' she asks, with no trace of how impossible this would be.

'Good one,' I say.

'I'm serious. It's on the eve of the mid-term break, then it's study leave. Unless you're in one of the school cricket teams . . .' – she coughs – 'you'll only have to be in school for exams. Or at least, you won't have any lessons.'

I try to explain that I do still have music commitments –
concerts and Chapel Choir – and with four subjects, a lot of
exams which require me to come to school.

'Fine, well, of course, if you don't want to take me to
the Prom.'

'Of course I do, but how?' I ask.

The truth is, I'd rather not go to the Prom at all. I can't
avoid Speech Day because it's obligatory, but I'm not even
telling Mum about that – too embarrassing, and it's not as
if I'm winning any prizes. As for the evening Prom, on the
one hand, it could be a real laugh, chance to go nuts, smoke
something questionable with Nick beforehand, generally piss
about. There's even been some chat about an all-nighter, carrying on the party by the river, walking the streets at dawn,
back to Nick's for bacon rolls.

On the other hand, everyone at this school goes to the
Prom, not just the pupils. Teachers, school governors, quite
a few parents. It would be really special to arrive with Ali,
and hilarious. It would be like a little victory, a stick in the
eye for the gossips. We could eat, drink and dance together
all evening. I'd love to see the look on some of their faces –
Siddel, Grice, Harris. Though I'd feel bad about Batsford, and
it would be awkward for Ali, around Mr and Mrs Roberts.
And then there's the headmaster; what would he make of
it? Did the rumours ever reach him? But then who gives a
shit? We would be gliding round the dance floor, Ali looking stunning. What's the worst they could do now? They've
effectively turned a blind eye as it is. And yet, the picture in
my head jars when I try to imagine the scene playing out: Ali
and I dancing in the middle of the huge marquee, surrounded

by a circle of everyone from school. Everyone, including my friends, classmates, the whole year group. That's the picture I'm struggling to see.

I don't share half of this with Ali, but I do get carried away on the phone about how cool it would be to waltz in, the two of us, spin round and round, see if we can remember some of our dance moves from the revue, hold each other in a sexy embrace for the slow numbers. This is exactly what she was thinking as well, she says, with 'slightly less of the sexy. I don't want to lose my job, but we danced together at the revue, so what's the difference?' We try to form a plan.

'In an ideal world, you'd come with your parents – well, your mum. She knows me, after all. You'd be on a table, and I'd make sure I was on the same one. I can't imagine she'd have a problem with us being there together, you asking me for a dance, as a thank you for all the help and support this year.'

'Not going to happen,' I say firmly. 'I can't stand being with Mum in social situations, around others. She'd embarrass me. And she'd probably end up dancing with Batsford. Ugh, no.'

'Also, there's another reason to keep her away,' adds Ali. 'Can't risk someone having a word in her ear about us. It's not worth the hassle, even if I am supposed to be engaged. We're not ready to cross that bridge with your mum. Know any other tame adults you could rope in as camouflage?'

Actually, I might. It would be a bit of a long shot, but there's a couple – Don and Judy – old friends of my parents from London. We used to go and stay with them, and my sister and I would play with their kids while our parents reminisced about university days. They've always been kind to me, sending me presents and cards. Since Mum and Dad's divorce,

Don has made a point of keeping in touch with me, writing every so often with bits of news from their life in London, the occasional life tip. I don't share the letters with Mum. Not for any other reason than trying to be sensitive to her feelings; bringing up names from our old life – before my parents' divorce – anything about people our family socialized with, sends her into a spiral of woe. What's more, Don and Judy made a point of not taking sides after the separation, trying to be neutral, and that really pissed Mum off. I know she's not in touch with them and hasn't been for ages.

For a couple of days, I let the idea of inviting Don and Judy to act as surrogate parents take shape. Ali's all for it.

'They're your parents' age and have no connections here? Perfect. Let's use them.'

To my astonishment, they reply immediately to my invitation. They'd love to come, saying they'll make a weekend of it.

School hums with anticipation over the next two weeks, as temporary metal structures begin appearing on the sports field just beyond the chapel. Wet weather slows progress at first, but when the white canvas is spread out on the grass then hoisted into place to cover the framework, the sun comes out. It's like something from a fairy tale with its gleaming canopies and dramatic sloping roofs. There's a main tent, presumably for Speech Day and the Prom. Then a slightly smaller, but still huge, tent behind that.

'That's where the real party will be, in there,' says Nick, one sunny morning, pointing to the smaller one. We're sitting on the parapet, after an exam, our backs leaning against a statue. I've tilted my face to the sun's warmth, while Nick babbles on about the Prom, who's taking who and what he's going to take – *know what I mean?*

He's asked me who I'm taking, but I keep dodging the question. It's been made considerably easier that not a single girl in our year has hinted at wanting to be asked by me. I should be insulted, I suppose, but it's a relief. Sitting in the sun, he asks again. This time I tell him about Don and Judy.

'Most of us have got our parents coming for a bit of it,' he yawns at me. 'That's not what I mean, and you know it. Who are you taking?'

'No one, really,' I answer.

'Come on. There must be a girl you want to ask.'

I lower my face and look at him for a few seconds. He reads my expression.

'Oh. Mate, no,' he says, bringing his palm to his forehead and holding it there. 'Please don't tell me you're bringing her.' I don't say anything, but look away, across the cricket pitch. 'Jesus, Joe. I thought, I assumed that was all over. Are you fucking insane?'

He sounds genuinely angry. Angrier than I imagined, so, even though I haven't specifically said anything, I back-paddle.

'As I said, I'm not going with anyone, in that way,' I tell him.

He doesn't look convinced, but he doesn't push it either. Instead, he turns away, lifts his head to catch the sun, like me.

'You're weird,' he says flatly.

63

May 1993

Nick might be right. My whole life is weird and Prom night only makes it more so.

Entering the main tent with Don and Judy gives me a semblance of normality. The middle-aged murmurs of parents and teachers, punctuated by the pizzicato squeals of excitable pupils, settles into a relaxed thrum as the evening gets underway. There's an air of buoyant chatter as drinks are poured and plates of food appear. Everything seems to be in order.

Then Ali walks in. She is late. It's unlike her and I'm surprised when I see her. She's not usually someone given to making an entrance, but this evening, picking her way through the forest of tables, she is anything but invisible. I am not the only one with my jaw hanging open.

It's impossible not to take her in. I can feel the men in the room, probably some of the women too, appraising her. She is dressed in a proper ball gown, unlike the more fitted outfits the other women and girls are wearing. Ali's looks like something I saw my sister wear for a party in the eighties, with puffy shoulders and a ballooning skirt. Except, unlike with my sister, Ali is rocking this look, and not just because her bust is pushed right up to bursting. The dress is dark green, although this colour probably has a special name, like deep sea or forest, emphasizing her eyes. She moves in slow motion and the dress shines when it catches the light. To top it off, her hair is piled high on her head in full Bond-girl-bombshell display. It must have taken her hours; no wonder she's late.

It's suddenly very stuffy. Men and boys are pulling at their collars. With the vases of flowers on the tables and enormous pot plants placed around the room, it's a hothouse in here, and the temperature rises the closer Ali gets to the one empty seat in the room, at my table. When she sits down, it's as if the whole tent sinks a foot into the playing field below.

Fortunately, there is one person apparently oblivious to Ali's entrance, and that's Don. While everyone's attention was elsewhere, Don has been arranging his place setting, happily nibbling at his canapés and drinking his wine. So, when Ali sits down, it's as if she has merely returned from a brief visit to the ladies. He launches into a conversation with her that helps to revive and resuscitate the tent around our table. Once the congregation has resumed dining, I dare to lift my gaze. Glowering back at me from the far side of the room is Nick.

When the meal is over, everyone my age bolts. They leave as one and I watch them go with envy. My friends don't even glance in my direction. Nobody comes to scoop me up. It's fine, I guess, but I can't help feeling a bit disappointed. Nick is nowhere to be seen.

I'm trapped in a room full of grown-ups doing that thing grown-ups do to fill time: mingling until the bar opens. A huge curtain at one end of the room is drawn back to reveal the dance floor and coloured spotlights, wandering robotically around the empty space, searching for a purpose. Like caged animals released, a pack of hollering mums rush the floor, throw down their handbags and start the dancing.

At our table, Don is still gabbling, entertaining us with jokes and anecdotes, as if he's preparing a set for this evening. Ali catches my eye, nods her head to the dance floor and mouths, 'now'. This is it. The moment we've been planning has arrived and there are no excuses I can make. Time to go over the top. It seemed a lot easier when we were just talking about it from the safety of the telephone box. My hands are damp as I rub them on my trousers. Ali gathers the folds of material and begins to stand. But before I can rise to the occasion, Don is on his feet.

'May I have this dance?' he booms. Ali is caught off guard and can only smile back. She can hardly say no. A reprieve for me, perhaps. I suspect the convention is that I should ask Judy if she'd like to dance, but I remain glued to my chair. They return after only one song, Don perspiring heavily, Ali a little less serene. Another man at the table stirs, looks emboldened, like he's about to whisk Ali away again, regardless of his glaring wife. Ali darts at me, gives no opportunity for someone else to step in, clutches my shoulder and practically hauls me out of my chair and onto the dance floor. By now, the whole room is jumping to the sound of eighties classics and discarded inhibitions. As we begin our best revue moves, I feel as if we're an island of curiosity, at odds with everyone else's jiggling, bouncing, air-guitaring. One song blends into another and we just keep dancing. I lose track of time, until I'm seized by the need to pee.

'This is fun!' shouts Ali, flopping into her chair, reaching for a tumbler of water. 'Don't be long,' she calls over her shoulder.

'It's fucking insane,' I say to the tiled wall in the toilets. 'God, she's gorgeous, she's gorgeous, you're so lucky,' I mutter randomly, my eyes closed. I was bursting for a piss but now it won't come. I've just danced ten songs straight, half an hour twirling around a dance floor with my Spanish teacher in front of everyone. 'What are you doing? God, what the fuck is going on?' I press my forehead to the wall. 'What are *you* doing – what is *she* doing, more like? Couldn't be more blatant if we stripped off and started going at it in the middle of the room.'

I'm still rambling to myself when a splintering crash snatches my head back.

'Come on, come on,' I whisper urgently, willing myself on. I've never been good at pissing in front of others. I seize up. I don't turn my head, but from the corner of my eye a tall, gangly form approaches to take up a swaying residence at the urinal beside me.

'Oh, sweet release!' My neighbour moans, leaning right over the bowl, one hand flat against the tiles for support. 'So, here you are,' he says. It takes a moment before I realize he's addressing me.

'Here I am. How are you, Nick?' I answer coyly. 'Can you stop staring at me, please? You know I find it difficult enough when anyone else is around.'

'God, you're so uptight, mate.'

'We're still mates, then?' I force myself to look up at him. Under his mop of curly damp hair, he's grinning at me.

'Of course we are, you dick,' and he throws open his arms.

'Nick, no!' But I am powerless to stop him hugging me into his chest, our bodies contorted, top halves turned inwards, bottom halves (mine at least) straining to maintain respectability.

'So, where did you get to? Where is everyone?' I ask as we head back across the quad in the direction of the music.

'Where? In there, obviously.' He points to the other tent behind the main marquee. I squint and listen. He's right; there are more flashing lights and a drumbeat I hadn't heard before.

'Oh, of course,' I remember. 'There's another tent for dancing!'

'Even slower than usual,' he says, placing a sympathetic hand on the top of my head. 'Come on, I'll show you.'

We reach the steps down to the playing field. To the right is a mown path that leads back to the main tent. I hesitate. I should take it, or Ali will wonder where I am.

'Unless you need to hurry back for anything,' says Nick, going in the other direction. 'Have they started playing bingo yet?'

I let Nick lead me round the back to the other tent. Opening the flaps, he marches in. I stand rooted in the doorway, stunned at the sight and sound. The beat barrels into me, more sonic boom than song. Bodies fuse, spring apart, spark like atoms, rebound, repeat. Nick tugs my arm, but I don't move, and he disappears, swallowed up by the mass.

The blurred faces begin to take recognizable forms and features as I tune in. The noise builds, flailing limbs edge closer until I'm in their orbit. A small figure flies out of the twisting shoal, clasps my wrists roughly and drags me in. I don't resist. I can't resist.

Rotating, I fix my eyes on the small hands around my wrists to keep my balance. I find the rhythm, sharpen my focus, trace a line up thin forearms, bare upper arms, glistening neck, and reach the grinning, unspectacled face of Lika.

'Wow!' I shout, taking her all in. Not that there's a lot of her, but with her unpinned black hair, short dress hugging her tiny frame and this unfamiliar confidence, she is transformed. 'You look amazing, Lika!' I yell over the music, but my words are drowned out. I can't tell if she registers my attempts to speak, so I just grin at her. Her eyes are wide, unblinking, shining, like she's here but not here. The music drops to a low pound of arrhythmic chords, and in the lull I open my mouth to try to speak again. Lika's hair is all over her face, her head down, shoulders swaying, her body limp though somehow managing to stay upright. Her hands are still attached, vice-like, on my wrists, but it's like dancing with a ragdoll.

The pulsing chords build; a slow, rising progression. My ears can't help but analyze them. Harmonics now, signalling a shift, putting the room on notice. The wooden floor lifts and falls under the impatient stomp of feet. Like the sound when a guitar jack is pulled out of an amp, a split second of silence, then a single high note pierces the air, hangs. The bodies around me stir, feet pound louder now, voices respond in a tribal howl.

Lika's limbs solidify, and she begins to turn. By the time the wall of chords has climbed up to meet the high note, we're spinning, arms straight out. Lika throws her head back. I steady us with my hands mirroring hers on me, shocked at the narrowness of her forearms. Another split second and Lika is off the ground, in the air, throwing herself forward, so fast

I have to release a hand to catch her. Her legs are around my waist now, her arms around my neck, head buried in my neck, and we're still spinning. Or at least, I am, but somehow she's driving me in circles.

The music races, thunders to its climax and the chords beat a retreat in rhythmic echoes. The lights cut. The room plunges into a moment of total darkness and recovery. I'm drenched, panting on the spot. Lika, still clinging to me, breathing heavily, prises her head off my shoulder. I'm very aware of my arms around this girl's waist and loosen my grip to release her. But she's not going anywhere. Her thighs tighten, her hands grab the back of my head. In the pitch dark, all I can see are her still-shining eyes. Then I feel her lips on mine, her tongue, a new taste in my mouth.

When the lights come back on and the next song begins, Lika slides off me. Without a word, she walks away. Dazed and feeling guilty as hell, I steer a clumsy path out of the tent.

'Bingo?' calls a chirpy voice in the shadows outside.

'Not now, Nick, I have to go.'

I don't hear his reply. My ears are ringing.

'Where have you been?' asks Ali, in a tone that suggests she's forgotten where we are.

'Yes, master Gibson, where have you been?' says Don, mimicking Ali in a teacherly voice, taking a gulp from his wine. It hasn't occurred to me, until then, that he and Judy might have sussed what's going on, but his intervention pops the bubble of tension and I'm grateful.

I drain a full glass of water and reach for another. 'I

bumped into Nick,' I say, trying to compose myself and sound convincing.

If Ali is offended by Don, she manages not to show it. Rolling the stem of a wine glass between her fingers, she sits back in her chair.

'You're quite right, Don. I'll put my cane down,' and they laugh, but when Don turns away to speak to his neighbour, Ali peers at me through side eyes.

Rehydrated and with my breath back, I ask Ali to dance, to make it up to her. Make up for my absence, not for anything else; I'm not about to confess what just happened in the other tent. For another hour we dance, drink, sit, chat, and I'm pretty sure Ali's forgiven me. Then the DJ changes pace and the opening bars of 'Have I Told You Lately' sees a surge of mums forcing less-enthusiastic dads onto the dance floor. I catch Ali's eye across the table, shrug and do a pretend sad face. We might have got away with our rock 'n' roll dancing, but I don't think anyone is going to accept us smooching around to Rod Stewart.

When the inevitable 'Lady in Red' makes an appearance, I push back my chair.

'No,' I say, 'not this.'

'I agree,' says Ali. 'Where school prom meets cheesy wedding reception, it's time to go.'

A shared loathing for Chris de Burgh scatters the dance floor and people start to drift away. The evening is ending. Overall, I'd say it had been a success, except for the blip. I mean, that wasn't my fault, was it? Everything happened so fast. How could I have stopped her – dropped her? It was Lika, for God's sake. How was I supposed to know she would jump me and go in for the full snog?

As agreed, and meticulously planned, Ali leaves the marquee first, making a point of saying goodbye to random colleagues and parents *on her own*. Ten minutes later, accompanied by Don and Judy, I leave too. We say our goodbyes and they head off to their hotel, while I make my way along the tree-lined perimeter of the school grounds. Skirting the playing fields, the flashing lights and beats make the second tent look like a spaceship. It sounds like fun. Now they're playing 'Jump Around'. I want to be in there with everyone. No fucking Chris de Burgh for them. I slow down, come to a halt, consider my options. But really, there's no choice. It's not worth the hassle, and anyway, this will be the first night in ages that I've stayed at Ali's. With teachers, governors and parents swarming around the campus and the surrounding roads now, it's an unbelievably stupid time to go wandering the streets to her flat.

'If I can't have House of Pain,' I mutter to myself, 'I'm not being denied Flat of Sex. Or something. Stop talking to yourself. Nutter.'

I end up staying with Ali for two nights, and with each hour the mist of guilt recedes. I find every creative way possible to make it up to her. It's just like the early days, this time last year.

Somehow, without the structure of a lesson timetable, everything seems to go much faster in the second half of term. Exams come and go. Go okay, I think. Most of my time is spent at home on study leave, ticking off the days. When I'm at school, I don't see any of the usual faces, just those of the people sitting the same exams.

Quite early on in June, there's a German written paper and

SEVENTEEN

I can't help but come face to face with Lika outside the exam room. In uniform, hair plaited, reading from a textbook with her glasses perched halfway down her nose, it's the Gulika I know. She looks up, smiles, and says 'hi' without the slightest flicker of recollection.

64

JUNE 1993

'Beer?' asks Nick.

'Yes,' I say.

'Wine?'

'Yes, yes.'

'Beer, wine and . . . vodka?'

'Yes, all of them – all in one glass if necessary.' I'm exasperated. 'Just, come on.'

I'm impatient, standing by the door of Nick's bedroom, watching him change out of his school clothes. Although most of us finish our exams on different days, by pure luck Nick and I finish on the same day and we are going to celebrate, hard. We have nowhere else to be. He doesn't need to clear it with anyone, of course, and I have a free pass.

'Your mum know you're staying the night at mine?'

'Yep.'

'And Miss P. Cleared it with her?'

He's got his back to me as he drags a T-shirt over his head, so I can't see the expression on his face, but I can hear it in his voice. I growl my reply.

'Well,' he says, 'you and I are due a chat about that.' He puts a brotherly arm around my shoulders, runs his knuckles across the side of my head. 'But first, we're going to get shitfaced.'

It's a warm evening. The sun is still high, giving some light to the sheltered courtyard of The Crown. The Spin Doctors' 'Two Princes' pounds from the sound system inside, giving way to something mellow from Lenny Kravitz's *Mama Said.* We are two bottles of beer in before we really come up for air. For Nick, I think it's more of a stalling technique than any urge to slake his thirst. I know he wants to say something, ask about Ali probably, but I don't offer him any prompts.

'Um . . .' He plays with the empty bottle in his hand.

'Yes, Nick?'

He's prevaricating, which is unlike him.

'Yeah, so, it's Glastonbury soon. Don't know if, I mean, you can still get tickets if you, you know, maybe, do you want to come?'

'I can't, mate. Sorry.'

I do want to. I would love to go, having missed last year, but I know I can't. Not for any reason to do with Ali this time; it's my sister's birthday and she's making a rare appearance. Before I can tell Nick this, he's off.

'Of course you can't. You can never come out. You never do. Have you got any idea how much you've missed? I can't remember the last time we hung out properly. What's happening, mate? What's going on?'

'I know I've been crap, but it's complicated.'

'Yeah, it's always fucking complicated with you. I don't understand.'

I probably wouldn't either. I don't retaliate or try to defend myself. It's not his fault he's angry. Perhaps I should confide, tell him something of what's been going on. I inhale deeply and exhale as steadily as I can.

'Listen, I don't know if I can explain my behaviour. It's a bit of a fog, to be honest. But I'll try, if you'll let me speak.'

He nods.

I tell him what happened at the end of the spring term: the rumours, Ali being alerted by Mr Roberts, how she tracked the trail back to Mr Harris and confronted him for spreading malicious gossip. Nick is about to protest, understandably, but I hold up a hand and say, 'I know, I know, but we couldn't exactly come clean.' He throws his hands in the air when I tell him how Harris apologized to me on the last day of term. I tell him how we thought we'd got away with it, until the beginning of the new term and all the shit I went through; teachers ignoring me, picking on me, and how it all came to a head in Siddel's class.

'Oh yeah, when you went mental and called him a cunt.'

'With good reason,' I say. 'It was all over the staffroom. Siddel was calling for me to be suspended or worse, but Ali came up with a plan to get me off the hook. That came with some of its own consequences, but she got Batsford on my side. That seemed to do the trick and it only cost me a thigh rub in his office.'

'He what?' splutters Nick. 'That's gross. You should report him.'

I stare at Nick. 'Really, you think?' I frown. 'Who am I reporting him to? Don't you see? School's not interested in anything like this. It wants to bury this kind of thing. With the stink that was brewing up around me and Ali, they had their opportunity to kick me out, but it went dead. Mate, they've turned a blind eye all year.'

I reach into my pocket for a pack of cigarettes, take one, light up and lean back against the wall of the courtyard. Nick is quiet.

'You know, there's one thing about all this that still nags me.' I blow an untidy ring of smoke into the still air. 'There's a missing link I can't figure out.'

'How do you mean?' says Nick.

'Why did the rumour travel in that round-the-houses way to Roberts? Apparently, it was Mrs Roberts who told him, but a matron who told her . . . from a house tutor who told the matron? I'm struggling with that chain; it's messy.'

'I'm struggling without beer.' Nick gets to his feet, disappears inside.

When he returns, he looks shifty.

'Nick, is what I just said, about who told who, a surprise?'

'Yes, of course.' He clears his throat. 'And no.'

And in that moment, I know my hunch was right. It must have come from Ant, after all. Yes, Harris had seen me getting out of Ali's car, but the rumour only escalated when Ant blurted it all out to his landlady, Mrs Roberts. All the pieces fall into place.

'Ant, you shit,' I spit. 'Everyone's known about us? The teachers, tutors, housemasters? The headmaster? Is that what we're saying?'

He shrugs, shakes his head. 'Looking that way. Sorry.'

'Well, what did I say about blind eyes?'

*

We drink in silence for a few minutes.

'Can I ask you something else? Just one more thing,' he says, 'then I promise we'll change the subject.'

'Yes, for fuck's sake, please let's change the record. I just want a normal conversation, a night off from all the heavy stuff.'

'Well, in a way that's my point. That's what I want to ask you. I mean, it's hard enough coping with all this now, but what about when you go to university? I know you're going to uni here so you won't be far from Miss ... her ... but uni, it's about growing up, meeting new people, new girls. Aren't you bothered about missing out? Don't you want a bit more than one evening off the heavy stuff?'

'To be honest, Nick, I don't know what I want. There are some things I would like to do next year. I still want to take a year out. Maybe it looks a bit different to how I imagined, but I still really want to go sailing with my uncle, do some travelling before uni.'

'And is Miss ... has she accepted all that? Your plan for a year out?'

'We haven't talked about it for a while, but I don't see why not. She knows it's something I really want to do.'

'Well, I don't know her the way you know her, obviously, but I bet she kicks off when you tell her.'

'But that's a relationship, isn't it? Ups and downs ... and we do have lots of ups.'

As if to mark the end of this heavy session and the end of our school life, Nick raises his bottle.

'I feel like you'll leave us all behind,' he says, his mouth turning down slightly at the corners. He leans forward.

'Whatever happens in your mad world, Joe, I'll be here. I'm always your friend.'

'Jesus, mate, you make me want to cry.' I lift my bottle to ring loudly against his, and we down our beers.

A short burst of laughter escapes my lips.

'I'll be asking you to be my best man next.'

Nick snorts loudly.

'You had better fucking not. Give it a few years, you dick. We're still teenagers!'

PART THREE

SEVENTEEN
YEARS LATER

65

MAY 2010

I lean against the cupboards in the tiny galley kitchen of the canal boat, *Gypsy*, resting my hands on the countertop, filling the space. Bending slightly, my back to the towpath, I peer through the window at the waterscape. Nothing is still; nothing is solid. I am thirty-four, out of my depth and on my own for the first time in seventeen years.

Gypsy breathes, in and out, back and forth. Her lift and fall, barely perceptible to the people on the bank, feel like pitch and plunge to me.

It's been a week already, I berate myself. *It's only a canal boat. You should have found your sea legs, found a rhythm by now, surely.* But still the water beneath the boat moves, sways, rolls me up and runs me down.

A shift, underneath my feet. I spin round, eyes adjusting, fluid to solid. I push myself up the step, through the cabin door, forget to duck. Rubbing my head, I clamber up and leap onto the path. Whatever knot I tied to the mooring pole has come loose and sent the rear of the boat drifting across the canal. Shit. Another boat is bearing down, only fifty yards away. I run up the bank, but before I reach the pole the rope slides like a snake through the grass and disappears into the water. The other boat is getting nearer. I wave my arms wildly to attract its attention.

A cyclist appears, pedalling leisurely.

'Your front end's going,' she says flatly, not stopping.

I look to my left in horror and stare as the knot at the other end of the boat quietly unties itself. I put my hands to my head, scream inside.

'My home!' The words wrench out of me. I plant my foot and jump. I land: one foot makes the gunwale; the other doesn't. My knee smacks into the steel hull. I wince, scrabble my fingers to find purchase on the canvas cover of the fore-deck, dragging my leg up, heavy and burning, to the edge of the hull where it meets the cabin side. I feel my way gingerly along the gunwales. Sheer boat on one side, watery soup on the other. I glance up the canal and can see the people on the other boat more clearly.

It's a stag party. Of course.

Every Saturday the canal fills with groups of stags and hens, let loose on the water with sixty-foot canal boats, crates of beer and a twenty-minute *Canal Boating for Dummies* DVD. I have to get to the platform at the rear, and the rope. One trip and it's over. But, somehow, I cling on. I've made it.

Gypsy is almost ninety degrees to the bank, spanning the entire channel. Quickly, I gather in the wet rope. The cows in the field opposite have ambled down to loiter and gloat. So, it seems, has a crowd of people on the bank: joggers, cyclists, dog walkers, all pausing to watch. Lifting the soaking coils into my arms, I hold up a limp end, but no one moves to help.

Noise floods my ears. The stags are yelling at me. The group on the towpath, the sodding cows, even the water, all loud in my ears. I'm really very tired.

'Over here.' The voice is clear and calm. I search the bank but can't find it. 'Here,' the voice calls to me again. A man with long hair under a wide-brimmed hat, rough beard, paint-mottled work clothes, stands apart from the group, arm out, beckoning.

I throw the rope. He catches, pulls, arm over arm. Slowly, *Gypsy* responds. Before the fenders have touched land, the man is tying the knot I promise I will now learn to tie. I jump ashore.

'Thank you so much, I—' But he doesn't stop; he's run to the bow to repeat the process. Working quickly, he secures *Gypsy* to the bank with experienced hands. I watch him, busy with the rope, adjusting something, attending to detail. Meanwhile, the stags have powered onwards. The cows have lost interest and wandered off. The onlookers are dispersing. The suffocating noise has lifted, but my breath is shallow. I'm drained.

I look back at my boat. My uncle's boat, actually. He's letting me live on it for as long as I need, until things get a bit clearer, settled. I take in the scale of her. Made for outdoor living, all dark blues and greens. Inside, beautifully crafted wood-panelled compartments like scaled-down rooms in a normal house: study, bedroom, bathroom, sitting room, kitchen, all in a line and connected by a narrow corridor on one side. Everything neat and in its place. It has to be. Clutter is your enemy on a boat. At 6ft, I'm not the ideal height for living on a canal boat and I have the bruises to prove it, although it's surprising how your mind and body adjust to hobbit-like compactness.

Gypsy is my home, I suppose, though I don't want to use that word. Too strange, too soon. My temporary home? That doesn't sound right either. Unsettling; not very homely. Before today's drama, being here on the cut, moored up against the burgeoning banks of the canal, has felt more like an adventure. Easier to allow myself to think of it that way.

The grass verge between water and path is growing tall, brushing up high against the port side. The trees and hedges are in full leaf. The cow meadow shimmers in the breeze like a giant quilt, freshly thrown, settling at the top of the hill where it meets neat, expensive gardens. *What is real?* I wonder, as I stare into the middle distance of my new surroundings.

I sense a presence at my shoulder. I jump. A strong hand grabs my arm and pulls me back. I twist off balance, almost fall. Another hand darts out to steady me.

'Careful, friend,' he says kindly, concern in his tone, pointing down. 'You don't want to go swimming in there.'

I look down.

'Jesus!' I'm right on the edge of the bank. A cold wash runs through me, and I take a big step back from the brink.

'You okay?' he asks in an accent, something northern and reassuring. Newcastle, perhaps, or even further north.

'I'm fine,' I manage, attempting an easy smile. He doesn't look convinced.

'Well,' he nods at *Gypsy*. 'She's fine leastways, no damage. That lass isn't going anywhere in a hurry.' He smiles and holds out his hand. His skin feels like rope, rough and taut. A gardener, perhaps, or a builder.

'I'm Pete. My boat's a few hundred yards that way, at Wild Cat Field.' He points vaguely in the direction of the open country. The wilds.

'Oh, right. I'm Joe. Wild Cat Field sounds very . . .' – I think for a moment – '. . . different to this part of the canal.'

'Yep.' He turns slightly, facing the regimented line of pristine pleasure boats, snaking towards the town. Floating, gleaming retirement homes, bobbing up and down.

'You should come, bring *Gypsy* out to the wilderness. It's quieter, less traffic, less hassle.'

'Traffic?'

'Not so many cyclists and joggers and that. No tourists peering in at you, catching you in the nip.'

I know exactly what he means. I already feel like a goldfish in a bowl, a curiosity in a museum, and it's only been a few days. Pete retrieves his bike from the hedgerow. 'Come down sometime if you like,' he says over his shoulder.

66

June 2010

It takes me about a month to summon the courage to take *Gypsy* down the canal. It's a warm summer's day, the sun high overhead, its rays flickering on the surface of the water. I'm on my way to see Pete for what has become a regular get-together, usually at a waterside pub near his boat. We've been meeting up every weekend since I arrived on the cut, with me cycling along the canal to his mooring. It's not therapy, he says, he's just happy to listen. And he's heard it all. He's watched me fall and picked me up, got me back on a level, of sorts.

I'm going to be taking a couple of weeks' break. Pete has offered to keep an eye on *Gypsy* while I'm gone, provided I can take it down to his mooring and hitch alongside. He's moved on beyond the fields, deep into the wilds.

Of all the pubs today, he chooses one I used to go to with Ali, suspended high above rushing water below, the carved sweep of a painter's brush through the valley.

'Shall I park up here?' I call to Pete, who's emerging from the stern of his boat. He face-palms by way of reply, extends an arm and waves me alongside.

*

'I was thinking about you this morning, about everything you've told me,' he says, lighting up in the galley. After a quick drink in the pub's waterside garden, we've returned to his boat to eat. Wearing unfussy jeans and a faded brown festival T-shirt, he moves easily around his boat in time to tracks from *Protection*, a Massive Attack album I haven't heard in years. Unhurried but efficient, relaxed but purposeful. Pete's all the things I'd like to be.

'You realize, don't you,' he continues, not pausing to exhale, pointing a wooden salad server in my direction, 'that if what happened to you happened in a school today, there'd be police, lawyers, a court case. It's a criminal offence and there's good reason for that. Look at the toll it's taken on you. No wonder you're not over it. It's abuse, lad.'

'I suppose it's a fine line,' I mutter from my step in the open doorway at the back of the boat.

'What are you talking about? It's not a fine line at all. Call it what it is. Sexual abuse.'

'Oh, come on, Pete, I was party to it. I let it happen. It takes two—'

'Don't even finish that two-to-tango bollocks. It's not the point. She was thirty-five. You were seventeen, for Christ's sake. A kid.'

I strike a match to light an incense stick in a holder on Pete's ancient wood burner, still warm from the morning's fire; even in June, days start with a cold snap on the canal. I hope this diversion might signal a change of topic. But it seems Pete wants to get things off his chest.

'What I want to know is, what happened next? I mean, you were still with her when you left school. When did it end?'

343

I sip my beer and turn sideways so I can look out onto the bank and the bridge. I stroke my hand across my face and cup my chin.

'About four weeks ago.'

I run Pete through the main events of the intervening years since leaving school. How she convinced me not to take my gap year and go straight to university. How three years later, aged twenty-one, I stumbled out of there with a second-class degree, a ring on my finger, a sensible haircut, and a one-year-old in a buggy.

'Wait, what? You had a baby while you were still a student?'

'Yep.' I shake my head. 'Married at the end of my first year. Baby at the end of my second year.'

'Fuck!' Pete fills the cabin with noise, and I retreat to the deck outside where his scruffy lurcher, Molly, is lounging under a bench seat. She lifts her head sharply at the out-burst, then resettles, resting her long chin on my boot, eyes half-closed.

'I know,' I agree. 'That third year was surreal. Ali was still teaching and I would have to bring the baby into school at break times so Ali could feed him. In the staffroom, teachers coming and going.'

'You are actually shitting me.' Pete appears in the doorway, holding out another beer. 'What was that like?'

'Weird. Horrible. Excruciating,' I say, taking the bottle. 'I'd stand there, waiting for Ali to finish, a pariah, surrounded by my former teachers. I always expected someone to voice their disapproval, make a snide remark. But no, they never said anything. Just blanked me.'

'Wow. Do you think they were in denial?'

'Possibly. That is the default position of those types of schools.'

I explain how the need to find somewhere to accommodate a family with another baby on the way forced me into a world of work I neither understood nor gave a shit about. 'No one really likes their job,' she'd said, as I signed the mortgage papers. 'In any case, you're doing this for our children.'

Ali never went back to full-time work. She left teaching as soon as she got pregnant with our second. I think the school was only too glad to see the back of her. How they let her stay when our first was born, I still don't really know. Perhaps they were anxious about repercussions if they made her redundant, even despite the circumstances and who the father was. 'POSH SCHOOL SACKS PREGNANT TEACHER' wouldn't have been an attractive headline and would have only stirred up bad press for the school.

It was up to me to bring in a regular income, pay the bills. She stayed at home with the children while, increasingly, I had to stay away for work. I couldn't earn enough for us in the town where we lived. I changed jobs every couple of years, chasing the bigger salary to keep everyone happy – 'everyone' being Ali and her parents. I had little contact with mine. Ali's relationship with my mum had soured very quickly.

I did look for distractions from the boring slog of work – hobbies that might one day, somehow, become a career. I started a band, gigged a bit, dreamed of touring, until the demo we sent off got zero interest. I tried willow weaving, imagining a bucolic life deep in the countryside. I enrolled in a cheese-making course, dreamed of keeping my own goats.

I drafted a business plan for an organic café, before 'organic' was a thing. I made enquiries about taking over a surf shop on the coast. I bought a banjo, for some reason. But really, I was glued to a treadmill of convention and Ali had the controls; she was always in charge. 'Daddy's going through another phase,' she would sigh to the kids, rolling her eyes, just before I gave up whatever my latest pursuit was. Basically, she made the decisions. We were living according to her plan.

The sun drops in the west. Dusk comes to the canal, and in the darkening stillness, the aromas of Pete's cooking waft through the boat and out to where he joins me on deck. He likes to eat late and I'm in no hurry. He fishes in his pocket for tobacco and rolling papers, simultaneously hefting himself off the bench to sit confidently on the edge of the boat opposite me.

'How was it, being a dad so young?' Pete asks. 'I mean, it must have been strange, being out of step with everyone around you, your mates.'

I feel Molly sigh, perhaps in sympathy, at my feet. I lean down to scratch the wiry hair behind her ears and to deflect the sudden sting behind my eyes.

'Well, you're right,' I reply. 'But, I suppose I wasn't really aware of being out of step. I didn't see my friends that much. They were doing their thing, and I was on another track. But as for being a dad? I loved it. I might have looked stupidly young, and I did – Jesus, you should see some of the photos, I'm a child in them – but I wasn't thinking about that when I read their bedtime stories, taught them to ride bikes, dressed up as a dinosaur for their birthday parties . . .'

My voice chokes, stops and we sit quietly. Pete isn't a

hugger, but he does pass me a newly rolled cigarette. For a few hushed moments, smoke lifts in wisps, drifts across the surface of the still water.

'What about Nick? Did you keep in touch?'

'Yes,' I say, smiling at last. 'Nick was as good as his word. We've had on-and-off contact, but he's been a constant friend. He was even my best man. Took it really seriously, right up to ...' – I can't help laughing – 'his speech. It was a total shambles. Basically, he buckled the second he had to stand up and face a room full of, well, grown-ups.'

'Poor fella,' agrees Pete. 'So, how did it come to this – you living on a boat?'

I explain how, eventually, I burnt out. A midlife crisis, I suppose, except it was about fifteen or twenty years before most men. The doctor signed me off work with exhaustion. It was the beginning of the end, I realize now. I picked up pieces of work here and there, but it was clear my career, as I'd known it, was behind me. The strain chipped away. As much as I loved being a dad, I was failing as a husband. Failed as a son, too; all those lies. Poor Mum. Poor Dad. They deserved a better son, and I haven't been much of one all these years. Although, just recently, with all this going on, we've begun to repair our past.

I was numb inside. Bit by bit, the barrel of my life was emptying and then, something happened. I began to see a new path opening before me. Or, at least, a path that diverged from Ali's, since she didn't want any of the things we had talked about in the beginning. For years, I still believed a time would come for our adventures. That we would leave the cul-de-sac of our life and try something different with the kids – live somewhere new, another part of the country, another country entirely. But she had no intention of changing her life.

'But you did,' says Pete.

'Yes. I suppose.'

'And you're here now, aren't you? On your own adventure.'

'What if I'm stalled?'

'You just said your eyes had opened to the outside world, or something like that.'

'The thing is, I'm scared to move. I'm scared of losing my children. I'm scared of how I'll support myself, let alone them.'

We sit staring at the deck between us, both locked in our own thoughts. I glance back down the canal and rummage around in my head, bumping into memories, images, faces. I fix my gaze on the yellow tones of the bridge, fading in the half-light. Such a solid, stable thing.

'I have to ask,' says Pete, at last, lifting his head. 'While you're beating yourself up about the past, what's Ali doing? I mean, does she feel guilty about what she did?'

'Ha! Are you kidding?' I snort. 'Not for a second. No way. Lately, of course, she's just focused on her anger towards me for leaving her. I get that. But Ali feel guilty? Ali take responsibility for how this all started? Not a chance. As far as she's concerned, this is all on me.'

'Wow. Sounds like she's erased her part in it all,' says Pete, his tone a mix of incredulity and sympathy.

'Feels like that,' I reply, and lean over the side of the boat, dip and swirl my fingers in the cool water.

'You never did go sailing, then?' asks Pete, tapping another cigarette on the table.

'No, never.'

'No wonder you can't tie a knot.' He smiles. 'Maybe the ocean's not for you.'

'Hmm, maybe not.'

'In which case, perhaps a good walk is what you need. I think you could do with a long view, a horizon. A place of greater space, to put all this life of yours into perspective, to move on.'

'How? This will always be hanging over me.' I draw my hand out of the water and wipe it across my head, down my neck. 'Besides, no one will take me seriously. I'm the boy who slept with his teacher then married her.'

He shakes his head.

'Someday, things will have to change. Schools will have to stop turning a blind eye to the abuses happening under their noses, all the time.'

'People won't care, Pete. They won't understand that what happened to me at seventeen took another seventeen years to wear me down.'

'They will care because this is your story. And when they're ready to listen, you'll find the words to speak your truth.'

ENDNOTE:
FEMALE PERPETRATORS WHO
ABUSE IN ORGANIZATIONS

Following heightened awareness and interest in organizational child sexual abuse over recent years, in 2018 Dr Andrea Darling highlighted the need for the categorization of women who sexually abuse within organizational contexts to more fully understand the characteristics and nature of this particular type of abuse and subsequently developed an initial categorization. Five categories of abusers were identified:

- immature regressed
- sexual and risky
- saviour syndrome
- unrequited infatuated
- psychologically troubled

Immature regressed were young women in their twenties and new to their profession, who developed over-friendly relationships with children in their mid-teenage years for intimacy needs or sexual gratification. *Sexual and risky* were women in their thirties who were concurrently in adult relationships and engaged in highly risky behaviour with adolescents. *Saviour syndrome* were women in their mid-thirties to mid-forties who were experiencing problems and stressors in their adult relationships and became occupied helping the victim to fulfil their own emotional and intimacy needs. *Unrequited infatuated* were women in their thirties and forties who had mental health difficulties and were infatuated with males in their mid-teens, viewing them as potential romantic partners and professing their love for them. The final category, *psychologically troubled*, referred to those with long-standing mental health problems who displayed extremely immature cognitions.

DR ANDREA J. DARLING, MA (HONS), MSC, PHD, PGCE
Honorary Research Fellow, Department
of Sociology, Durham University

Darling, A. J., & Christensen, L. S. (2020). Female child sexual offenders. In I. Bryce & W. Petherick (Eds.), *Child Sexual Abuse: Forensic Issues in Evidence, Impact and Management* (pp. 119-136). Academic Press.

AFTERWORD

Stories of abuse against children emerge in the media with alarming and increasing frequency: every story is different, but each has its own individual horror, its own pain and distress, its own disastrous consequences. Just as shocking as the stories of neglect and cruelty to tiny children are the cases in which adults prey on teenage girls and boys using celebrity, authority or just sheer numbers, inflicting pain and damage of a different kind. When these stories emerge, some after many years, they are complicated, long-hidden secrets; they tell of manipulation and molestation, of mental and physical cruelty, of dishonesty and deceit. Common to almost all cases are people who have witnessed the abuse but said nothing; the bystanders who saw the signs but did nothing.

I was seventeen in 1992 and at that time my abuser could not have been prosecuted. It was not until the Sexual Offences (Amendment) Act 2000 (an Act of the Parliament of the United Kingdom) that it became illegal for a teacher to have sexual relations with any pupil under the age of eighteen, even if the relationship was consensual. The act introduced a new offence of 'having sexual intercourse or engaging in any other sexual activity with a person under eighteen if in a position of trust in relation to that person'.

The amended act showed that this behaviour is abusive and needs to be regarded as such. It is a form of sexual violence recognized in law, making it a criminal offence, and punishable by up to five years in prison.

Despite changes in law in the intervening years and efforts by some institutions to introduce safeguarding measures, abuse of children in schools persists. In 2022, a new report from the Independent Inquiry into Child Sexual Abuse highlighted shocking and horrific instances of child sexual abuse in schools, with some teachers exploiting their positions of trust to groom and abuse children. The report says schools are not as safe for children as they should be, and children's interests do not always come first when allegations of sexual abuse are made.

Despite numerous changes and improvements to safeguarding over the past two decades, the report says that some children continue to experience sexual abuse and sexual harassment in schools. Schools need to accept that 'it could happen here'.

Many of the schools examined by the inquiry responded inadequately to allegations against their staff and in some cases there was a culture which discouraged reporting. Too often, the inquiry saw examples of headteachers who found it inconceivable that staff might abuse their positions of authority to sexually abuse children, were unaware of current statutory guidance or did not understand their role in responding to allegations against staff. It was clear that some staff were more focused on protecting the reputation of the school than protecting the interests of the children.

The report highlights that for many victims and survivors, the impacts of abuse have been profound and lifelong. Many of those in positions of authority and responsibility have not been held to account for their failures of leadership and governance. Many perpetrators have not been brought to justice.

I began writing this memoir in 2011, but it has taken more than a decade to complete. Despite changes in the Sexual Offences Act, the climate for sharing such experiences has not, until recently, offered a receptive platform.

Encouraged by participating in The Truth Project, which ran for six years to 2021 as part of the Independent Inquiry into Child Sexual Abuse, I have been able to analyze the long-hidden secrets and accept the impact on my life of this abuse of authority. I have brought my experience to the page to help others, to help those whose stories have been buried. I have found a voice to tell my story, one that I hope will empower others to speak and be heard.

Seventeen is, however, written under a pseudonym and there is an important reason for this: when many survivors and victims of child sexual abuse share their experiences, they do so anonymously. I was only able to find my voice thanks to the safe environment of anonymity provided by The Truth Project. Certain details, such as names and places, have also been altered to protect the privacy and conceal the identities of individuals.

Acknowledgements

Writing *Seventeen* was like hiking a pilgrimage without a map, the long and winding road stretching out ahead of me, with no clear end in sight. That was until I stumbled upon a creative writing course, and everything changed. Signposts appeared and way-markers guided me in the form of my inspirational tutors, Cathy Rentzenbrink and Shannon Leone Fowler.

Shannon became my mentor and, with her encouragement, insight and sensitivity, I finally felt empowered to bring *Seventeen* into the light. I owe her so much for taking me forward, for believing in me and brightening my way.

The litmus test for any first-time writer is the submission process. The writing course had prepared me well: I kept to the appropriate font size and typeface, shed the waffle and polite padding, tightened my pitch, went for it. I released *Seventeen* and held my breath. To say we have been blessed, my memoir and I, with the agent who picked us up would be a massive understatement. I needed validation and the wonderful Donald Winchester from Watson, Little gave me just that. I can't thank him enough for taking me on, for being a true champion, for his limitless patience (believe me, I've tested it), and ultimately, for bringing us to the door of Simon & Schuster.

From the point at which Alison MacDonald commissioned *Seventeen* to this moment has been another journey entirely. It has not been straightforward, because this is not an easy subject to bring to the page. But with her wisdom, boundless enthusiasm, brilliant notes, and extraordinary reserves of calm and patience (yep, tested hers as well), Alison steered us through. I am indebted to her.

I also want to say a huge thank you to the wider team at Simon & Schuster. To Sabah Khan, Hannah Paget and their fantastic publicity and marketing colleagues. To Pip Watkins for grasping the brief so intuitively and encapsulating *Seventeen* in that single, powerful image. To the sales and distribution team, and Gill Richardson in particular, for her enthusiasm from the very beginning. And to everyone at Simon & Schuster for the invaluable work you do to bring books to bookshelves – thank you.

Finally, I want to thank my best friend and fellow traveller (she knows who she is), without whose unconditional love and support, I would not have been strong enough to write this book.